Fairey Swordfish
in British, Canadian and Netherlands service in World War Two

Compiled by Neil Robinson
Illustrated by Peter Scott

First published in the UK in 2014 by

AIRfile Publications Ltd
Hoyle Mill
Barnsley
South Yorkshire S71 1HN

Compiled by Neil Robinson
AIRgen Publications

Illustrations Copyright Peter Scott 2014

978-0-9575513-1-2

The rights of Neil Robinson and Peter Scott to be identified as author and illustrator of this work have been asserted by them in accordance with the Copyright Designs and patents Act 1988

All rights reserved. No part of this book may be reproduced or transmitted in any form or by any means, electronic or mechanical, including photocopying, recording or by any information storage and retrieval system without permission from the Publisher in writing.

Design: Mark Hutchinson

Printed in the UK by
PHP Litho Printers Ltd
Hoyle Mill
Barnsley
South Yorkshire S71 1HN

Dedicated to the memory of
Barry Ketley
1947 - 2014

AIRfile

to inform and inspire

A range of illustrated camouflage and markings guides, full of well-researched, clear and unambiguous full colour illustrations, with detailed informative captions, produced by a cooperative of well-known aviation enthusiasts, authors and illustrators, designed to provide comprehensive camouflage scheme and markings coverage, culled from a variety of areas including previously published material, official and private documents and photo collections, and primary sources.

Used either as a one-stop reference source, or as an integral part of your research in to the fascinating study of colour schemes and markings carried by combat aircraft from World War One to the present day, each AIRfile aims to show the chronology and development of the schemes and markings of the aircraft in question, including the many anomalies and inevitable misinterpretations and errors occasionally to be found on operational military aircraft.

Fairey Swordfish
in British, Canadian and Netherlands service in World War Two

By Neil Robinson
Illustrated by Peter Scott

The Fairey Swordfish is one of World War Two's most iconic and recognisable torpedo bombers. Designed by Marcel Lobelle for the Fairey Aviation Company, the TSR II as it was designated then, first flew on 17 April 1934. Introduced in to RAF and Royal Navy, Fleet Air Arm service in 1936, the aircraft was finally operationally retired in May 1945, and despite its obsolescent and antiquated looks, outlived several 'more modern' types intended to replace it, remaining in frontline service through to the end of the war in Europe.

Affectionately known as the 'Stringbag' by its crews, because of the seemingly endless variety of stores and equipment that the aircraft was cleared to carry, likening the aircraft to a housewife's string shopping bag which was common at the time, it was effectively outdated by the outbreak of war in September 1939, but achieved some spectacular successes during the conflict, notably the sinking of one and the damaging of two *Regia Marina* (Italian Navy) battleships in Taranto Harbour in November 1940 and the crippling of the *Kriegsmarine* battleship *'Bismarck'* in May 1941.

Initially operated as a Fleet Torpedo and Reconnaissance bomber from Fleet carriers and shore bases, during the second half of the war, it changed role and was successfully used as a convoy escort and anti-submarine bomber flying from smaller Escort carriers, as well as a shore-based training aircraft.

Swordfish also flew from Merchant Aircraft Carriers (MACs), civilian cargo ships or tankers modified to carry three or four aircraft each, on anti-submarine duties with convoys. Three of these ships were Dutch-manned, operating Swordfish from No 860 (Dutch) Naval Air Squadron (NAS). The rest were manned by pilots and aircrew from No 836 NAS, at one time the largest FAA squadron with some ninety-one aircraft on strength!

Of the 2,392 Swordfish built, 992 were Mk Is, 1,080 were Mk IIs, the most numerous version, and 320 were Mk IIIs. Of these, 692 were constructed by the parent company, Fairey Aviation Ltd at Hayes in Middlesex and 1,700 by Blackburn Aircraft Ltd, at Sherburn-in-Elmet, in the (then) East Riding of Yorkshire, which were sometimes dubbed the 'Blackfish'.

Neil Robinson
June 2014

Contents

Chapter 1:	Chapter 1: The colourful days of peace – 1936 to 1939	p4
Chapter 2:	The early war years – 1939 to 1940	p20
Chapter 3:	Taranto	p36
Chapter 4:	Sink the Bismarck!	p40
Chapter 5:	The Channel Dash and new markings 1942-43	p44
Chapter 6:	Change of role – 1943 to 1945	p54

On the front cover: One of the 400 Fairey Swordfish Mk IIs built in the HS serial range, by Blackburn Aircraft Ltd at their Sherburn-in-Elmet plant during 1942/43, powered by the 690hp Bristol Pegasus XXX engine. HS645, coded 'B', was serving with 816 NAS, aboard HMS Tracker, in late 1943 when this photograph was taken. Finished on the production line in the Temperate Sea Scheme with Sky under surfaces, HS645 was repainted in the white 'anti-submarine' scheme either at an MU or in-service. Note the weathering on the fuselage, fin and rudder, revealing the original camouflage underneath and the red individual aircraft letter 'B' on the removable inspection panel on the rear fuselage. The aircraft was fitted with ASV aerials on the leading outer wing struts and is carrying a small smoke marker bomb.

(M Derry Collection)

Chapter 1

The colourful days of peace
1936 to 1939

K5933, one of a batch of eighty-six Swordfish Mk Is delivered between January and August 1936, resplendent in the overall Aluminium (silver) scheme with Cerrux Grey painted metal panels. Red, White and Blue roundels were carried in all six positions. K5933 was allocated to 825 NAS but collided with another Swordfish, K5976, off Alexandria on 30 January 1939.
(All photos Barry Ketley Collection)

Design and development

The Swordfish was based on a Fairey Private Venture (PV) design to an Air Ministry requirement for a spotter-reconnaissance aircraft – 'spotter' referring to the observation of the fall of a warship's gunfire. A subsequent Air Ministry Specification S.15/33, added the torpedo-bomber role. The Torpedo-Spotter-Reconnaissance prototype, TSR.II, (the original PV design was the TSR.I), K4190, first flew on 17 April 1934, powered by a 635hp Bristol Pegasus IIM nine-cylinder air-cooled radial engine.

It was a medium-size, biplane configuration, with a metal frame mostly of tubular steel, covered in fabric, with folding mainplanes that pivoted back along the fuselage as a space-saving feature to allow storage on board a carrier or a cruiser. The Pegasus radial engine drove a Fairey-Reed three-blade, fixed-pitch, metal propeller and the aircraft had fixed landing gear, which could be exchanged for floats.

The Swordfish had accommodation for three crew members – pilot, observer and telegraphist/air gunner. It was armed with a single fixed Vickers 0.303 inch (7.7mm) machine gun on the starboard forward fuselage firing forward and a rear-mounted Vickers or Lewis 0.303 inch (7.7mm) machine gun handled by the telegraphist/air gunner.

The prototype was then fitted with an uprated Pegasus IIIM3 engine providing 690hp, and had a few aerodynamic changes to improve spin handling, a slightly longer fuselage and slightly swept back wings to compensate for the shift in the centre of gravity. Trials went well, and in November 1934 K4190 was fitted with floats for sea trials, which culminated in catapult launch and recovery by the battleship *HMS Repulse*. The floats were then replaced by wheels for final evaluation. The Air Ministry was suitably impressed and placed an order for three pre-production machines.

The first of the three pre-production aircraft, K5660, (the other two being K5661 and K5662), the type now officially named 'Swordfish', was flown on 31 December 1935. The last pre-production aircraft, K5662, was fitted with floats for service trials on water. The three prototypes were followed by a production order for eighty-six Swordfish Mk I aircraft placed in 1935, of which some 992 were eventually built, (692 by the parent company Fairey and 300 by Blackburn Aircraft Ltd), and the type entered service in 1936 with the Fleet Air Arm, then still part of the RAF, replacing the Short Seal in the torpedo bomber role.

By 1938, the Swordfish had replaced all other torpedo bombers in Fleet Air Arm service, and by the outbreak of World War Two in September 1939, thirteen squadrons had been equipped with the type, with twelve of the squadrons at sea on the aircraft carriers *HMS Ark Royal*, *HMS Courageous*, *HMS Eagle*, *HMS Furious* and *HMS Glorious*.

Early colour scheme and markings

From its introduction in to service, Fairey Swordfish were finished in an overall Aluminium (silver) paint scheme with Cerrux Grey painted metal panels. Red, White, Blue roundels, in the pre-war Bright shades, were carried above the top mainplane, below the lower mainplane and on the fuselage sides. The aircraft's serial number was applied to the rear fuselage in 8 inch high black characters and on the rudder, in 6 or 7 inch high black characters.

At the time the Swordfish entered Fleet Air Arm service, the Royal Navy was operating a unit identification system of coloured Aircraft Carrier Identification Bands, applied around the aircraft's mid-fuselage. Each colour, or bands of different colours, identified the parent 'carrier:

HMS Courageous – Blue
HMS Glorious – Yellow
HMS Furious – Red
HMS Eagle – Black
HMS Hermes – Green
HMS Ark Royal – Blue-Red-Blue

Two new aircraft carriers under construction at the time, HMS Illustrious (Black-Green-Black) and HMS Victorious (Red-Black-Red) were issued identification bands but the system had changed before they entered service.

Individual aircraft were identified by a three digit Fleet Number, invariably applied over the Carrier Identification Band, in white numerals on 'dark' colours and black on 'light' colours, and Squadron Commanders' and Flight Leaders' aircraft were further identified by colours on the fin, either covering the entire fin area or in bands or checks. Coloured spanwise bands or 'squares' of colour(s) were sometimes applied on the upper surface of the top mainplane, or in a 'square' on the top mainplane centre-section, and occasionally coloured bands were applied along the fuselage, either side of the Carrier Identification Band. The squadron's badge, invariably in a standard naval (battleship) frame, was often applied to the fin too.

4 AIRfile

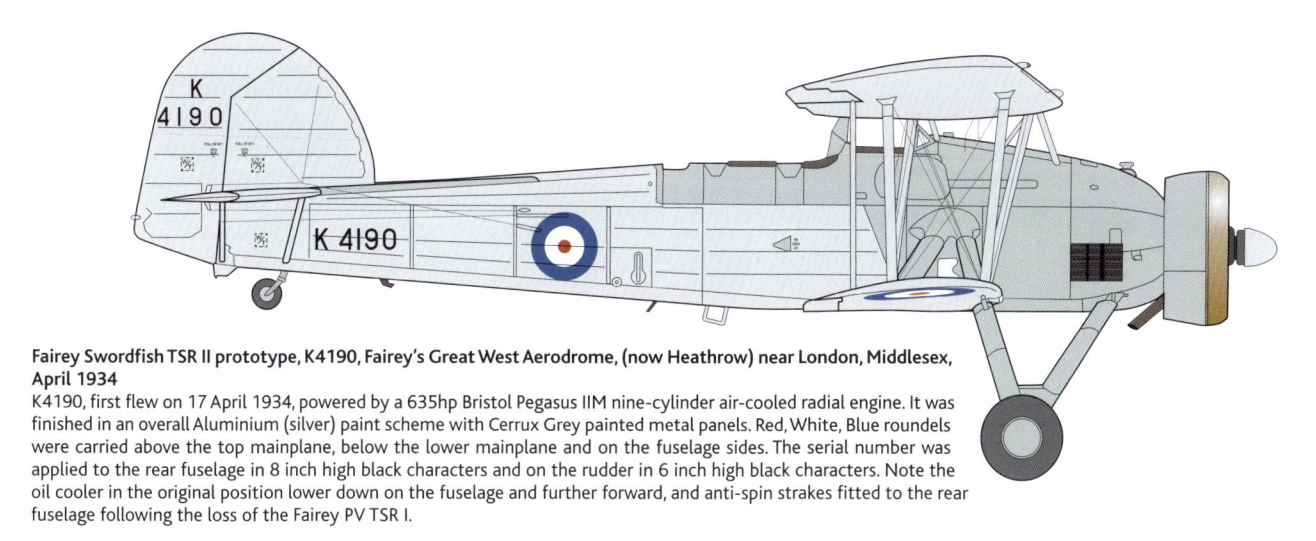

Fairey Swordfish TSR II prototype, K4190, Fairey's Great West Aerodrome, (now Heathrow) near London, Middlesex, April 1934
K4190, first flew on 17 April 1934, powered by a 635hp Bristol Pegasus IIM nine-cylinder air-cooled radial engine. It was finished in an overall Aluminium (silver) paint scheme with Cerrux Grey painted metal panels. Red, White, Blue roundels were carried above the top mainplane, below the lower mainplane and on the fuselage sides. The serial number was applied to the rear fuselage in 8 inch high black characters and on the rudder in 6 inch high black characters. Note the oil cooler in the original position lower down on the fuselage and further forward, and anti-spin strakes fitted to the rear fuselage following the loss of the Fairey PV TSR I.

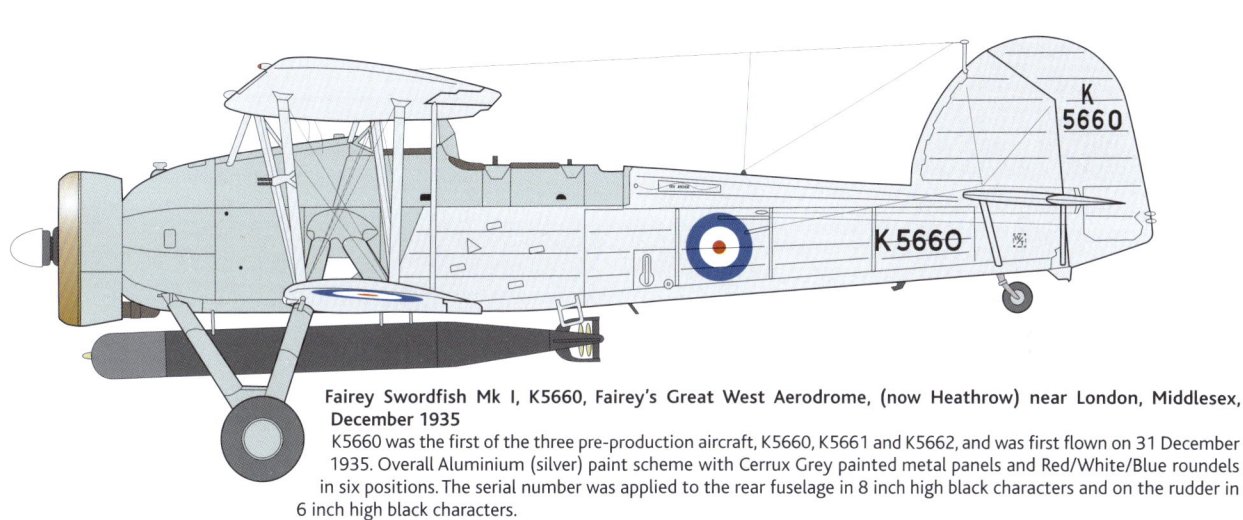

Fairey Swordfish Mk I, K5660, Fairey's Great West Aerodrome, (now Heathrow) near London, Middlesex, December 1935
K5660 was the first of the three pre-production aircraft, K5660, K5661 and K5662, and was first flown on 31 December 1935. Overall Aluminium (silver) paint scheme with Cerrux Grey painted metal panels and Red/White/Blue roundels in six positions. The serial number was applied to the rear fuselage in 8 inch high black characters and on the rudder in 6 inch high black characters.

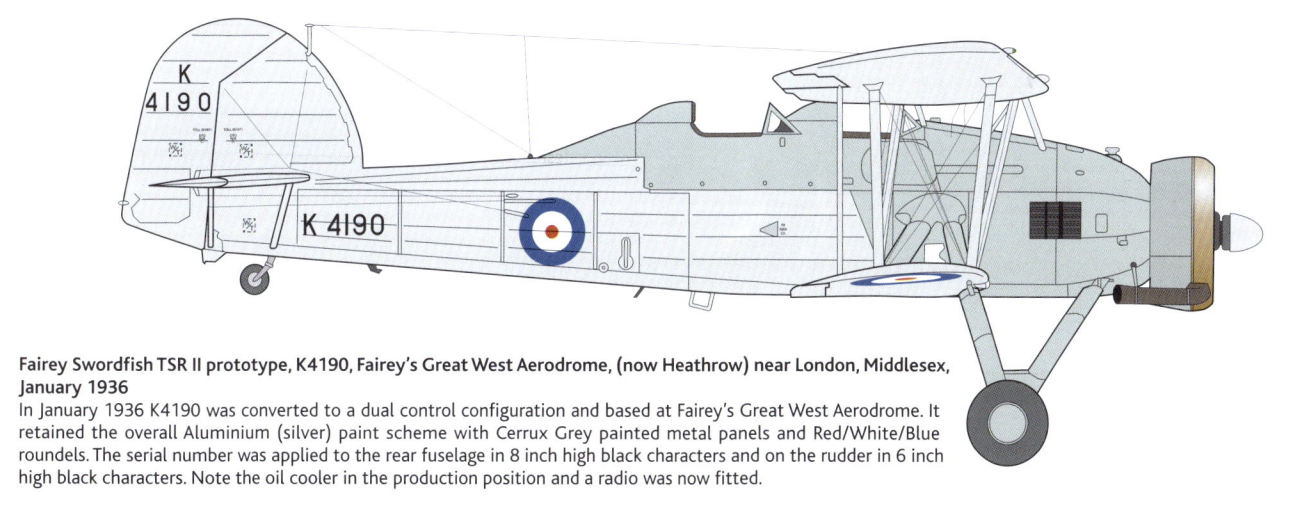

Fairey Swordfish TSR II prototype, K4190, Fairey's Great West Aerodrome, (now Heathrow) near London, Middlesex, January 1936
In January 1936 K4190 was converted to a dual control configuration and based at Fairey's Great West Aerodrome. It retained the overall Aluminium (silver) paint scheme with Cerrux Grey painted metal panels and Red/White/Blue roundels. The serial number was applied to the rear fuselage in 8 inch high black characters and on the rudder in 6 inch high black characters. Note the oil cooler in the production position and a radio was now fitted.

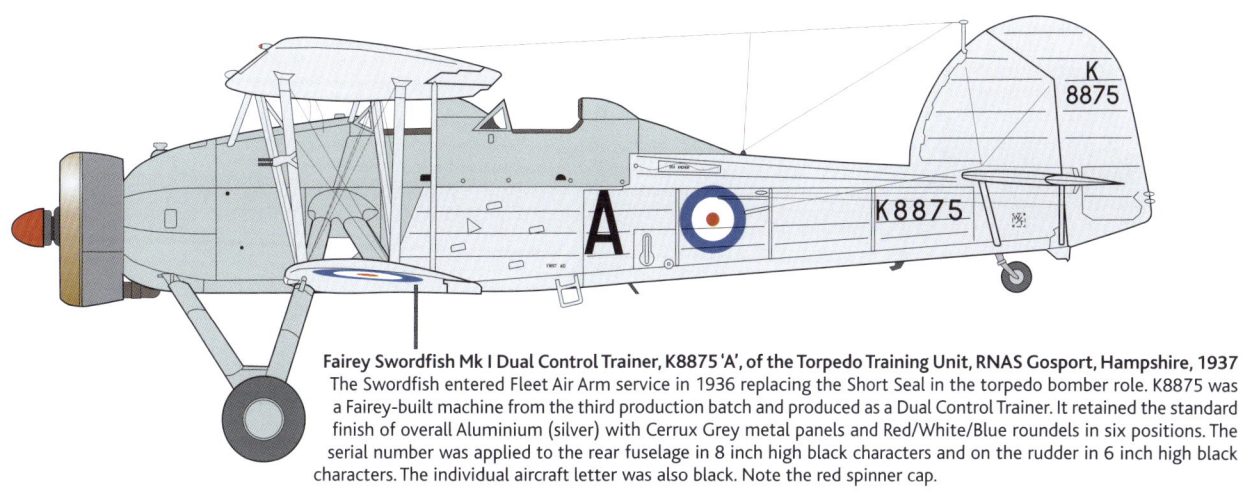

Fairey Swordfish Mk I Dual Control Trainer, K8875 'A', of the Torpedo Training Unit, RNAS Gosport, Hampshire, 1937
The Swordfish entered Fleet Air Arm service in 1936 replacing the Short Seal in the torpedo bomber role. K8875 was a Fairey-built machine from the third production batch and produced as a Dual Control Trainer. It retained the standard finish of overall Aluminium (silver) with Cerrux Grey metal panels and Red/White/Blue roundels in six positions. The serial number was applied to the rear fuselage in 8 inch high black characters and on the rudder in 6 inch high black characters. The individual aircraft letter was also black. Note the red spinner cap.

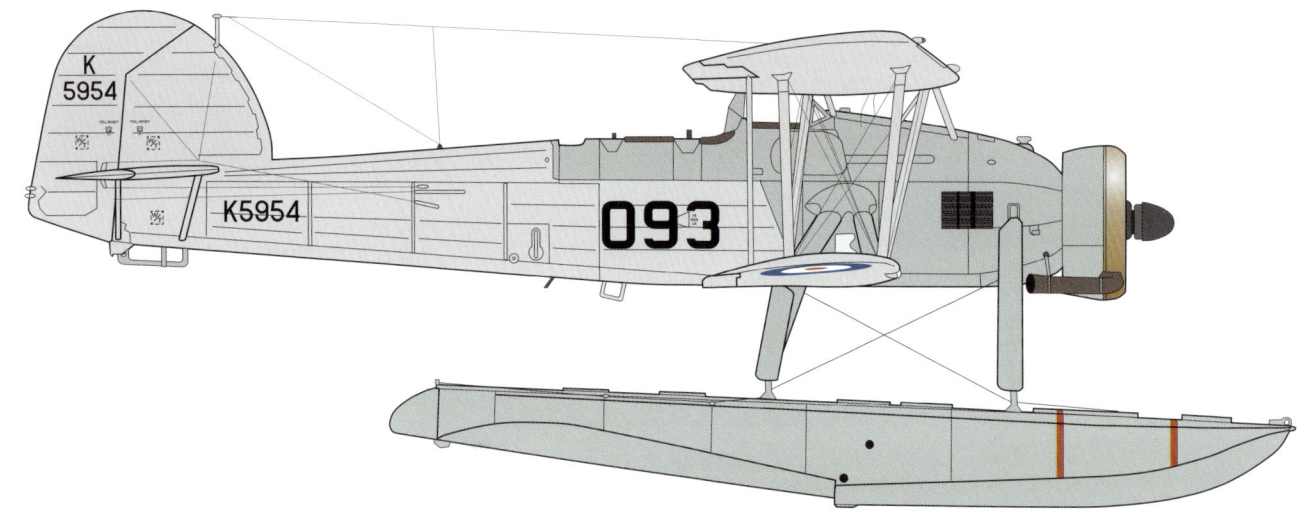

Fairey Swordfish Mk I, K5954, '093', of 705 NAS, Ship's Flight, operating from the battleship HMS Repulse, 1936
K5954 was from the first production batch and was amongst the first Swordfish to be allocated to a FAA unit. Built in floatplane configuration, it was finished in the standard overall Aluminium painted fabric with Cerrux Grey metal panels scheme with Red/White/Blue roundels in six positions. The serial number was applied to the rear fuselage in 8 inch high black characters and on the rudder, in 6 inch high black characters. The Fleet Number '093' was also in black on mid fuselage. Spinner cap appears to be dark grey or dark metal.

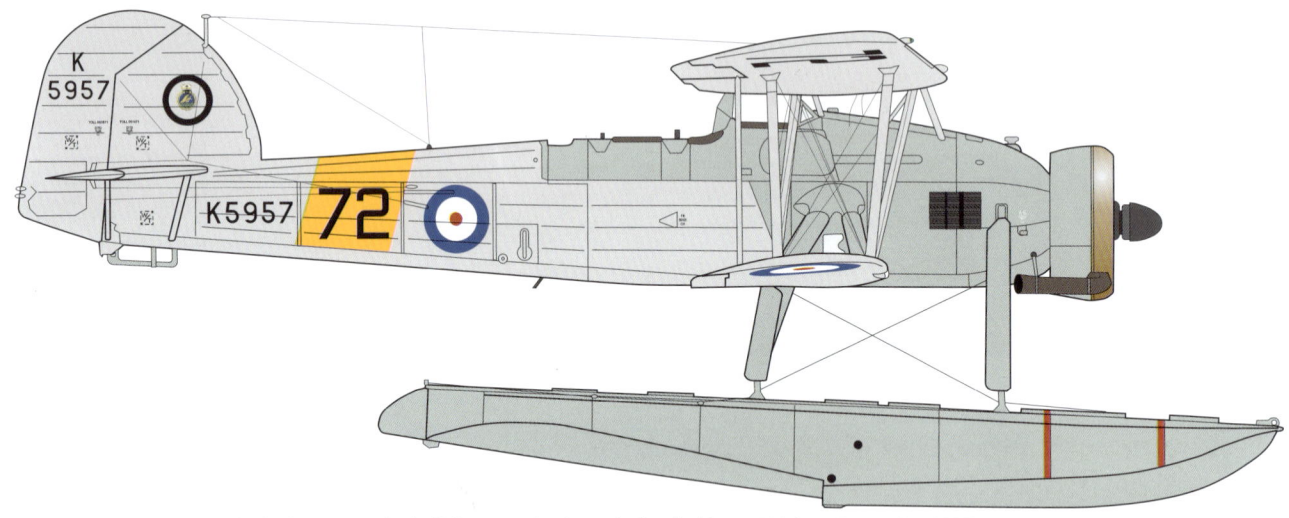

Fairey Swordfish Mk I, K5957, '72', of 701 NAS Ship's Flight, operating from the battleship HMS Malaya, September 1937
K5957 was from the first production batch and built in floatplane configuration from the outset. It was one of four Swordfish transferred from 812 NAS based aboard HMS Glorious over to HMS Malaya for anti-piracy patrols along the mouth of the Dardanelles. K5957 remained with HMS Malaya as part of 701 Ship's Flight and was recoded '075'. It was finished in the standard overall Aluminium painted fabric with Cerrux Grey metal panels scheme with Red/White/Blue roundels in six positions. The serial number was applied to the rear fuselage in 8 inch high black characters and on the rudder in 6 inch high black characters. Note how the Yellow Carrier Identification Band, (which identified HMS Glorious), was terminated along the fuselage lower longeron line. The Fleet Number, '72' was applied in black on the Carrier Identification Band and repeated under both top mainplane wing tips. The squadron badge was applied to the fin surrounded by a black circle. The floats were painted Cerrux Grey and the spinner cap was either black or dark grey. (See also profile on p16).

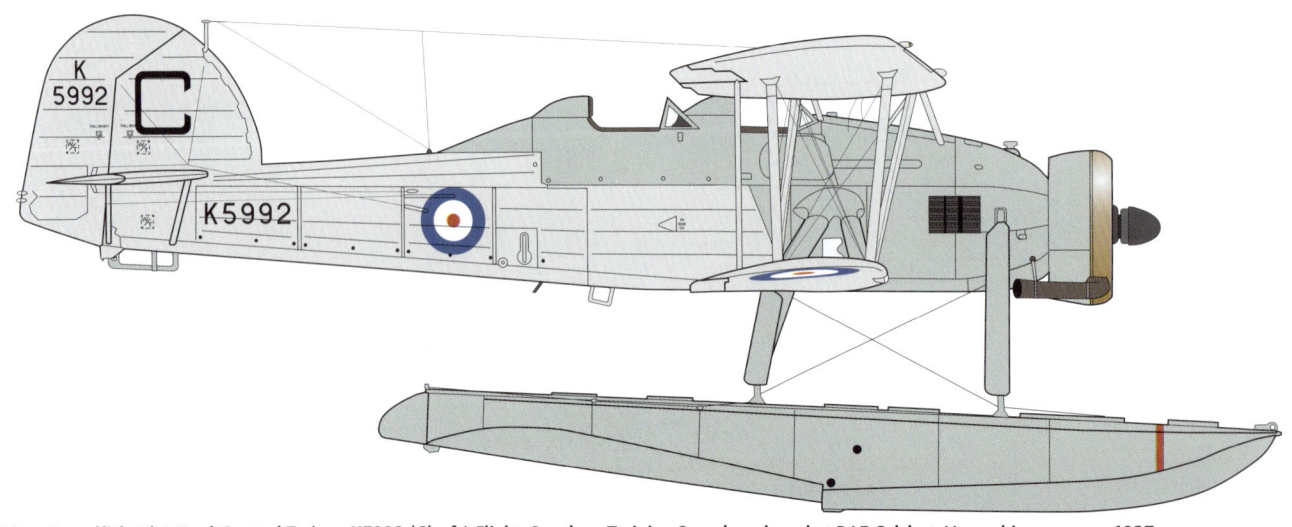

Fairey Swordfish Mk I, Dual Control Trainer, K5992, 'C', of A Flight, Seaplane Training Squadron, based at RAF Calshot, Hampshire, summer 1937
Also from the first production batch, K5992 was built in Dual Control Trainer configuration and finished in the standard overall Aluminium painted fabric with Cerrux Grey metal panels scheme with Red/White/Blue roundels in six positions. The serial number was applied to the rear fuselage in 8 inch high black characters and on the rudder in 6 inch high black characters. The individual aircraft letter 'C' was also in black on fin. Spinner cap appears to be dark grey or dark metal.

Swordfish Mk I, L2728, a Fairey-built machine from the fourth production batch, photographed flying low having just dropped an 18 inch torpedo. Finished in the Aluminium/Cerrux Grey scheme with roundels in the standard six positions and black serial numbers on the rear fuselage and rudder, the aircraft carried the identification number '8', whilst serving with the Torpedo Training Unit, at RAF Gosport in 1939. (see profile on p18)

Nos 823 and 825 Naval Air Squadron Swordfish Mk Is photographed flying over HMS Glorious circa 1937. All the aircraft are finished in the Aluminium/Cerrux Grey scheme with Red/White/Blue roundels in the standard six positions and black serial numbers on the rear fuselage and rudder. No 823 NAS's aircraft can be identified by the black fins favoured by the squadron. Most of the Swordfish seen here feature black fuselage top deckings. HMS Glorious could carry over forty aircraft after her refit in 1935.

Above:
K6000, in the markings of 821 NAS, circa 1938, with the white Fleet Number '678' applied over the Blue Carrier Identification Band for HMS Courageous. Note also the blue 'flash' along the fuselage and the blue mainwheel hubs.

Left:
Formation of Swordfish Mk Is from 814 NAS flying over HMS Ark Royal in early 1939, with L9777 '701' in the lead, possibly a Section Leader, flanked by L9779 '702' and L9733 '703'. The Carrier Identification Bands are Blue/Red/Blue chevrons, identifying HMS Ark Royal, with the Fleet Numbers in red on the rear fuselages.

Below:
Swordfish Mk I, L2742, '529', of 701 Ship's Flight, operating off the battleship HMS Hood, circa 1938. A Fairey-built machine from the fourth production batch, modified in to floatplane configuration for use aboard Royal Navy battleships, L2742 still carried the Blue Carrier Identification Band and white Fleet Number '529' from its previous service with 810 NAS aboard HMS Courageous – see profiles on pp12 and 19.

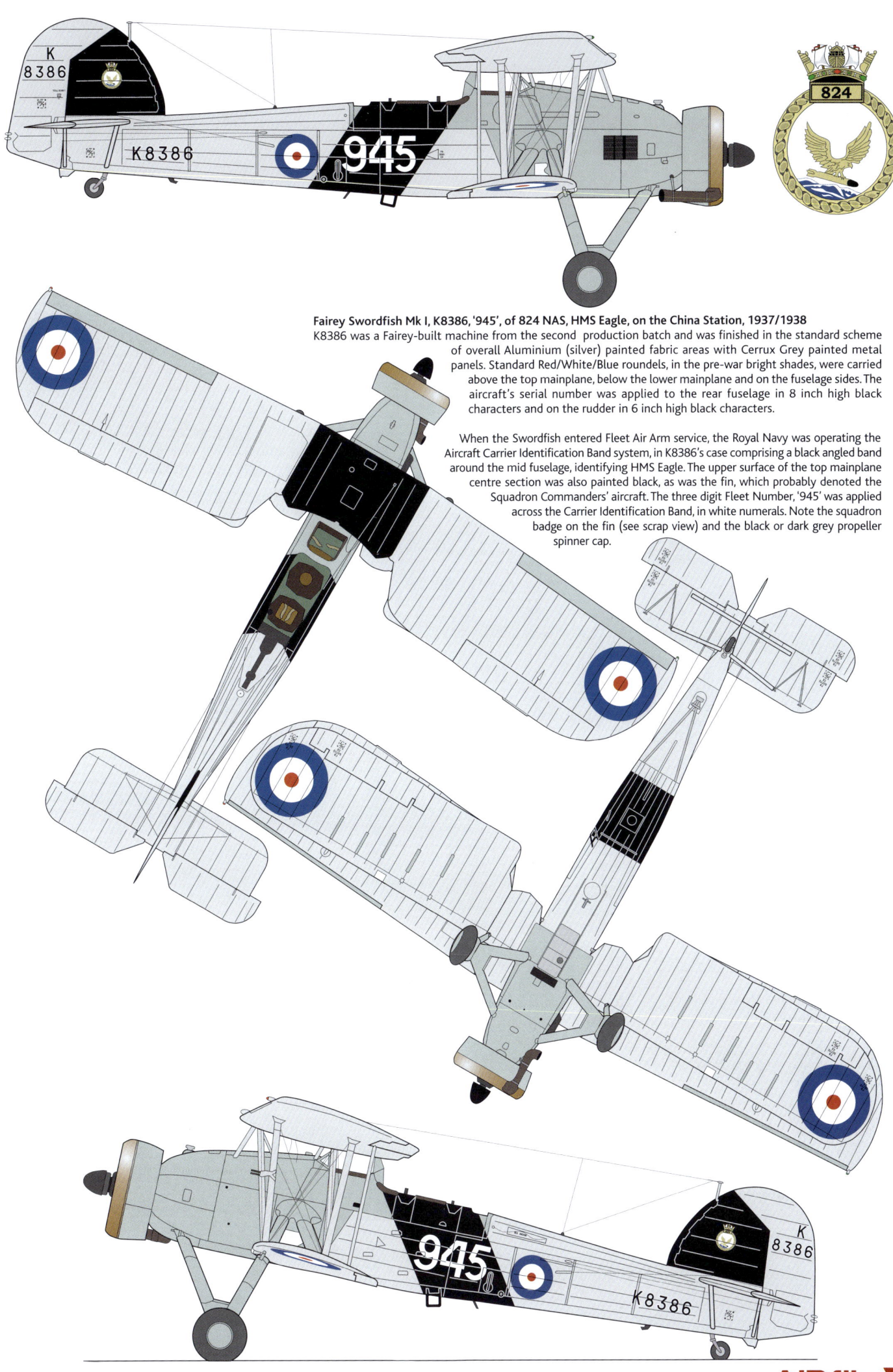

Fairey Swordfish Mk I, K8386, '945', of 824 NAS, HMS Eagle, on the China Station, 1937/1938

K8386 was a Fairey-built machine from the second production batch and was finished in the standard scheme of overall Aluminium (silver) painted fabric areas with Cerrux Grey painted metal panels. Standard Red/White/Blue roundels, in the pre-war bright shades, were carried above the top mainplane, below the lower mainplane and on the fuselage sides. The aircraft's serial number was applied to the rear fuselage in 8 inch high black characters and on the rudder in 6 inch high black characters.

When the Swordfish entered Fleet Air Arm service, the Royal Navy was operating the Aircraft Carrier Identification Band system, in K8386's case comprising a black angled band around the mid fuselage, identifying HMS Eagle. The upper surface of the top mainplane centre section was also painted black, as was the fin, which probably denoted the Squadron Commanders' aircraft. The three digit Fleet Number, '945' was applied across the Carrier Identification Band, in white numerals. Note the squadron badge on the fin (see scrap view) and the black or dark grey propeller spinner cap.

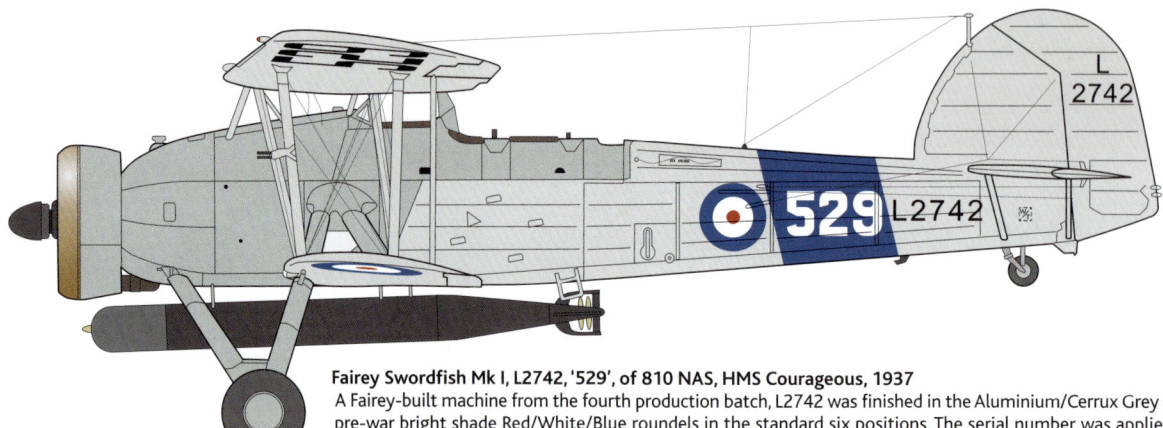

Fairey Swordfish Mk I, L2742, '529', of 810 NAS, HMS Courageous, 1937
A Fairey-built machine from the fourth production batch, L2742 was finished in the Aluminium/Cerrux Grey scheme with pre-war bright shade Red/White/Blue roundels in the standard six positions. The serial number was applied to the rear fuselage in 8 inch high black characters and on the rudder in 6 inch high black characters. Blue Carrier Identification Band, identifying HMS Courageous, with white Fleet Number, '529'. Note the Fleet Number repeated under both top mainplane wing tips. Spinner cap appears to be dark grey or black.

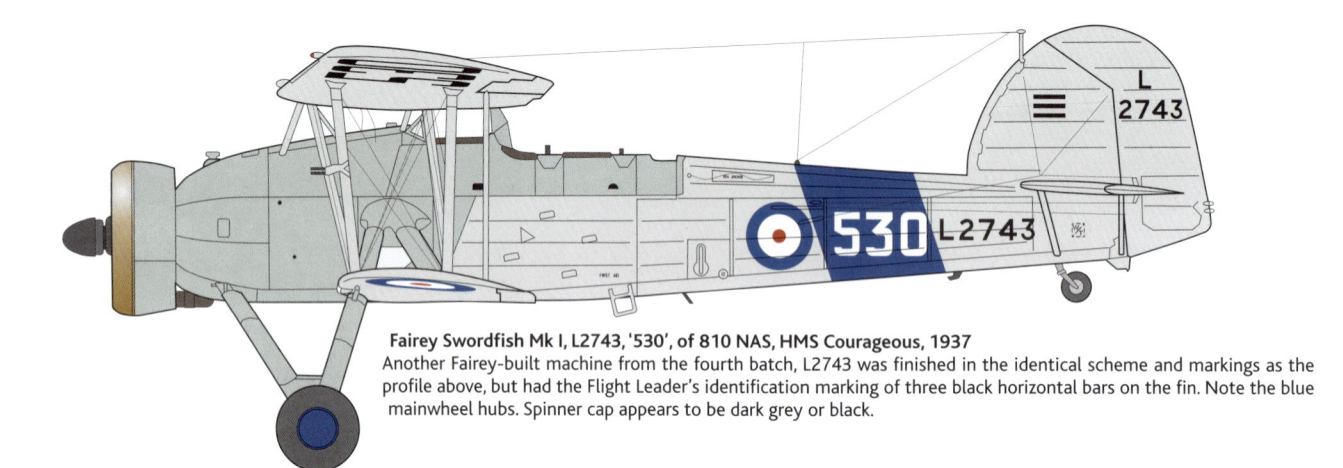

Fairey Swordfish Mk I, L2743, '530', of 810 NAS, HMS Courageous, 1937
Another Fairey-built machine from the fourth batch, L2743 was finished in the identical scheme and markings as the profile above, but had the Flight Leader's identification marking of three black horizontal bars on the fin. Note the blue mainwheel hubs. Spinner cap appears to be dark grey or black.

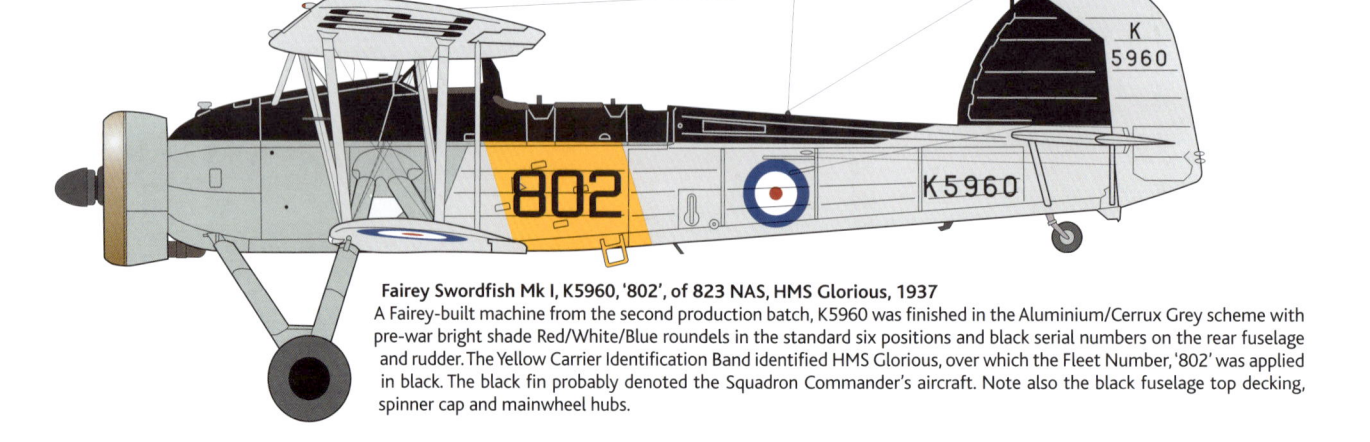

Fairey Swordfish Mk I, K5960, '802', of 823 NAS, HMS Glorious, 1937
A Fairey-built machine from the second production batch, K5960 was finished in the Aluminium/Cerrux Grey scheme with pre-war bright shade Red/White/Blue roundels in the standard six positions and black serial numbers on the rear fuselage and rudder. The Yellow Carrier Identification Band identified HMS Glorious, over which the Fleet Number, '802' was applied in black. The black fin probably denoted the Squadron Commander's aircraft. Note also the black fuselage top decking, spinner cap and mainwheel hubs.

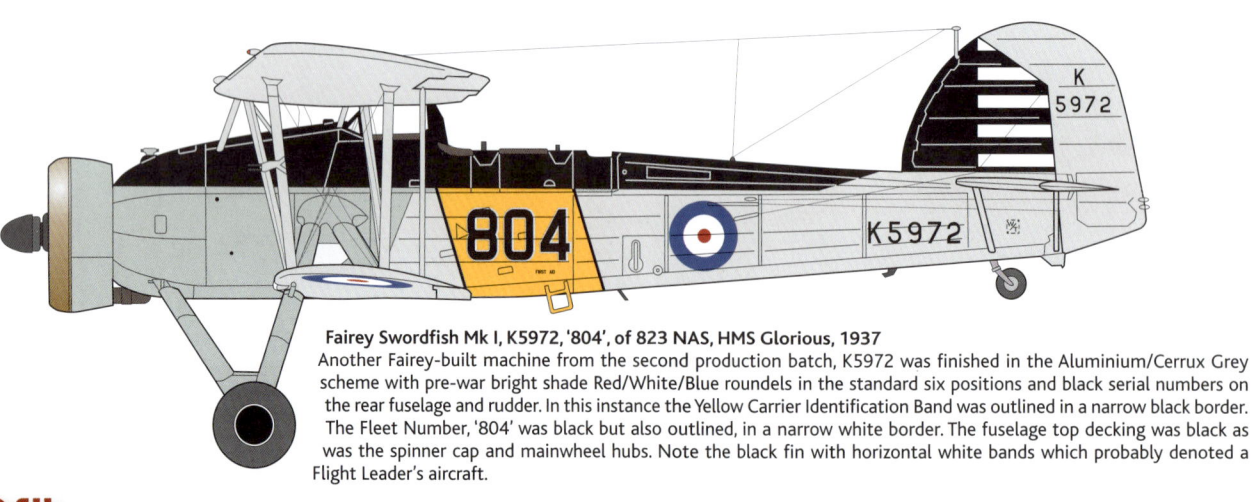

Fairey Swordfish Mk I, K5972, '804', of 823 NAS, HMS Glorious, 1937
Another Fairey-built machine from the second production batch, K5972 was finished in the Aluminium/Cerrux Grey scheme with pre-war bright shade Red/White/Blue roundels in the standard six positions and black serial numbers on the rear fuselage and rudder. In this instance the Yellow Carrier Identification Band was outlined in a narrow black border. The Fleet Number, '804' was black but also outlined, in a narrow white border. The fuselage top decking was black as was the spinner cap and mainwheel hubs. Note the black fin with horizontal white bands which probably denoted a Flight Leader's aircraft.

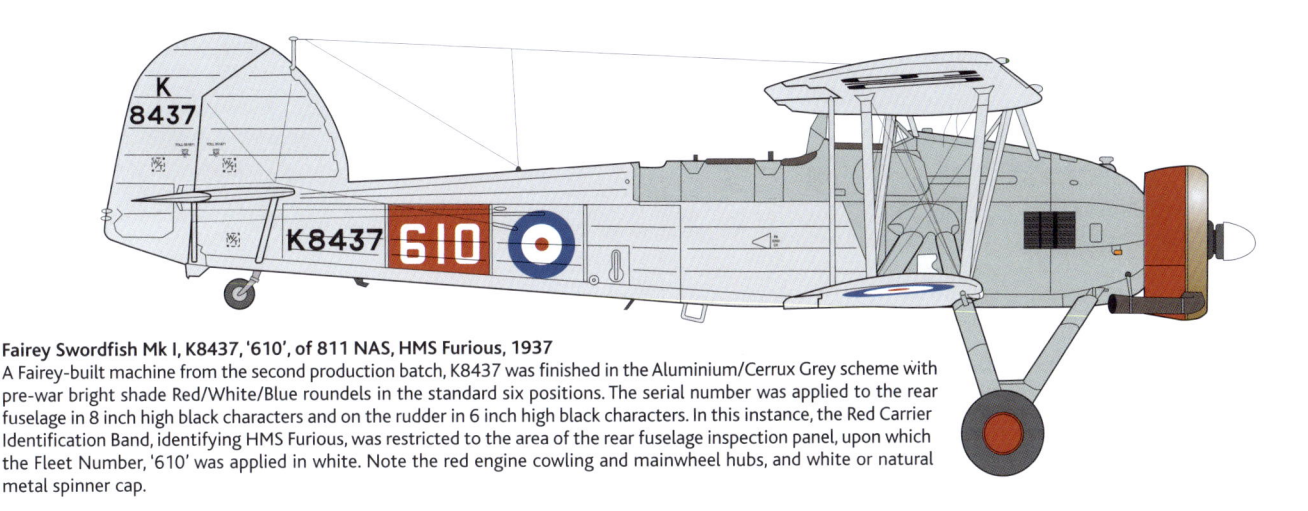

Fairey Swordfish Mk I, K8437, '610', of 811 NAS, HMS Furious, 1937
A Fairey-built machine from the second production batch, K8437 was finished in the Aluminium/Cerrux Grey scheme with pre-war bright shade Red/White/Blue roundels in the standard six positions. The serial number was applied to the rear fuselage in 8 inch high black characters and on the rudder in 6 inch high black characters. In this instance, the Red Carrier Identification Band, identifying HMS Furious, was restricted to the area of the rear fuselage inspection panel, upon which the Fleet Number, '610' was applied in white. Note the red engine cowling and mainwheel hubs, and white or natural metal spinner cap.

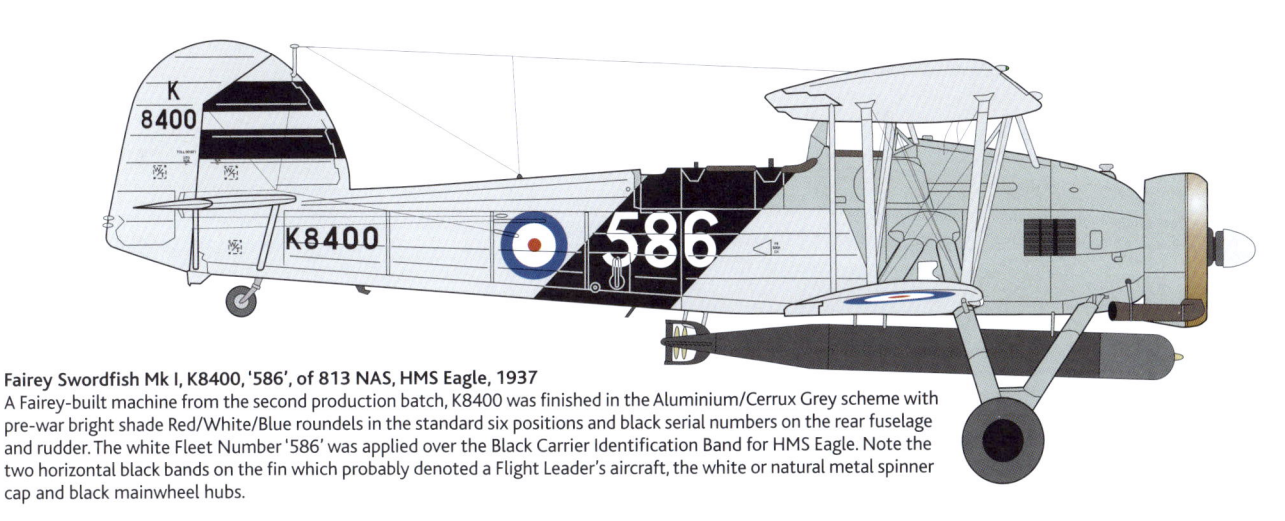

Fairey Swordfish Mk I, K8400, '586', of 813 NAS, HMS Eagle, 1937
A Fairey-built machine from the second production batch, K8400 was finished in the Aluminium/Cerrux Grey scheme with pre-war bright shade Red/White/Blue roundels in the standard six positions and black serial numbers on the rear fuselage and rudder. The white Fleet Number '586' was applied over the Black Carrier Identification Band for HMS Eagle. Note the two horizontal black bands on the fin which probably denoted a Flight Leader's aircraft, the white or natural metal spinner cap and black mainwheel hubs.

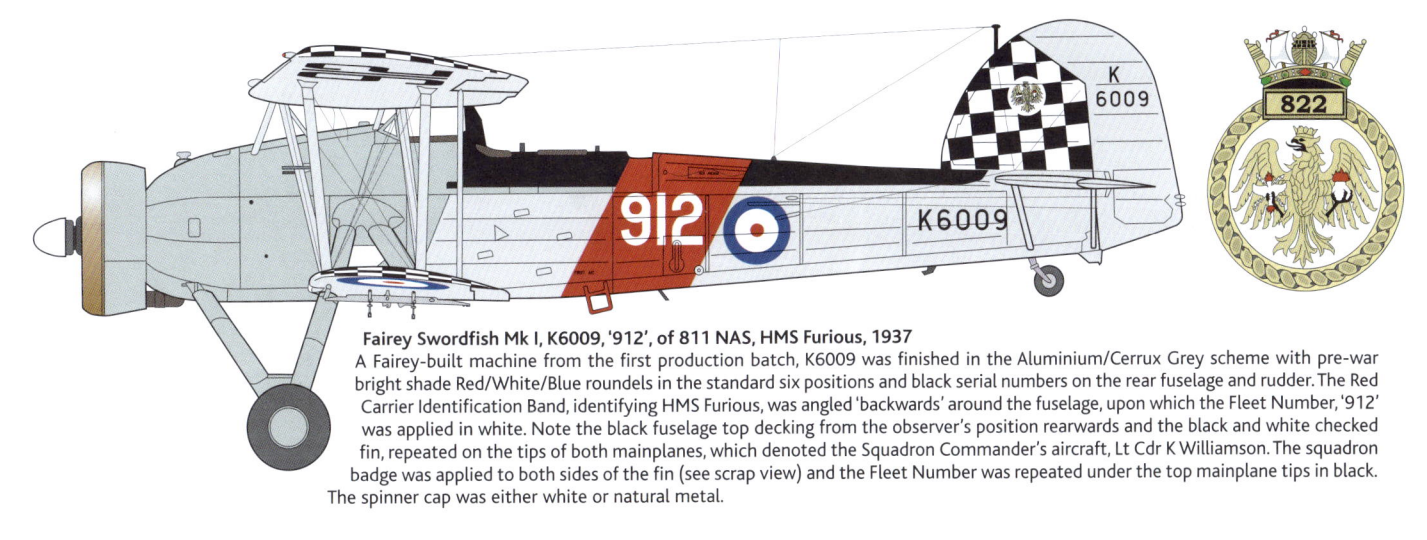

Fairey Swordfish Mk I, K6009, '912', of 811 NAS, HMS Furious, 1937
A Fairey-built machine from the first production batch, K6009 was finished in the Aluminium/Cerrux Grey scheme with pre-war bright shade Red/White/Blue roundels in the standard six positions and black serial numbers on the rear fuselage and rudder. The Red Carrier Identification Band, identifying HMS Furious, was angled 'backwards' around the fuselage, upon which the Fleet Number, '912' was applied in white. Note the black fuselage top decking from the observer's position rearwards and the black and white checked fin, repeated on the tips of both mainplanes, which denoted the Squadron Commander's aircraft, Lt Cdr K Williamson. The squadron badge was applied to both sides of the fin (see scrap view) and the Fleet Number was repeated under the top mainplane tips in black. The spinner cap was either white or natural metal.

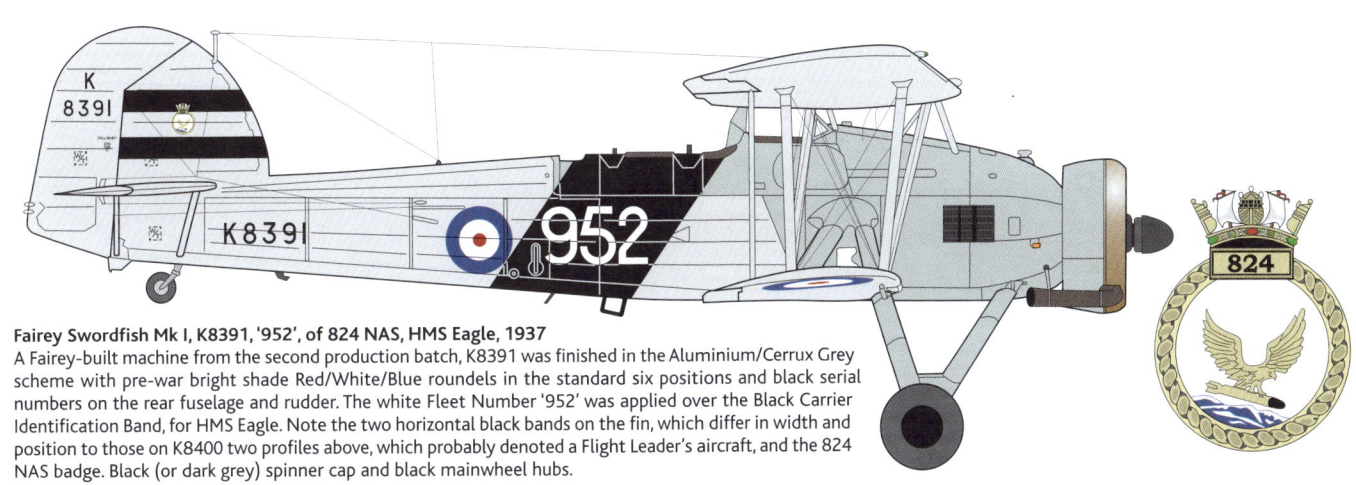

Fairey Swordfish Mk I, K8391, '952', of 824 NAS, HMS Eagle, 1937
A Fairey-built machine from the second production batch, K8391 was finished in the Aluminium/Cerrux Grey scheme with pre-war bright shade Red/White/Blue roundels in the standard six positions and black serial numbers on the rear fuselage and rudder. The white Fleet Number '952' was applied over the Black Carrier Identification Band, for HMS Eagle. Note the two horizontal black bands on the fin, which differ in width and position to those on K8400 two profiles above, which probably denoted a Flight Leader's aircraft, and the 824 NAS badge. Black (or dark grey) spinner cap and black mainwheel hubs.

AIRfile

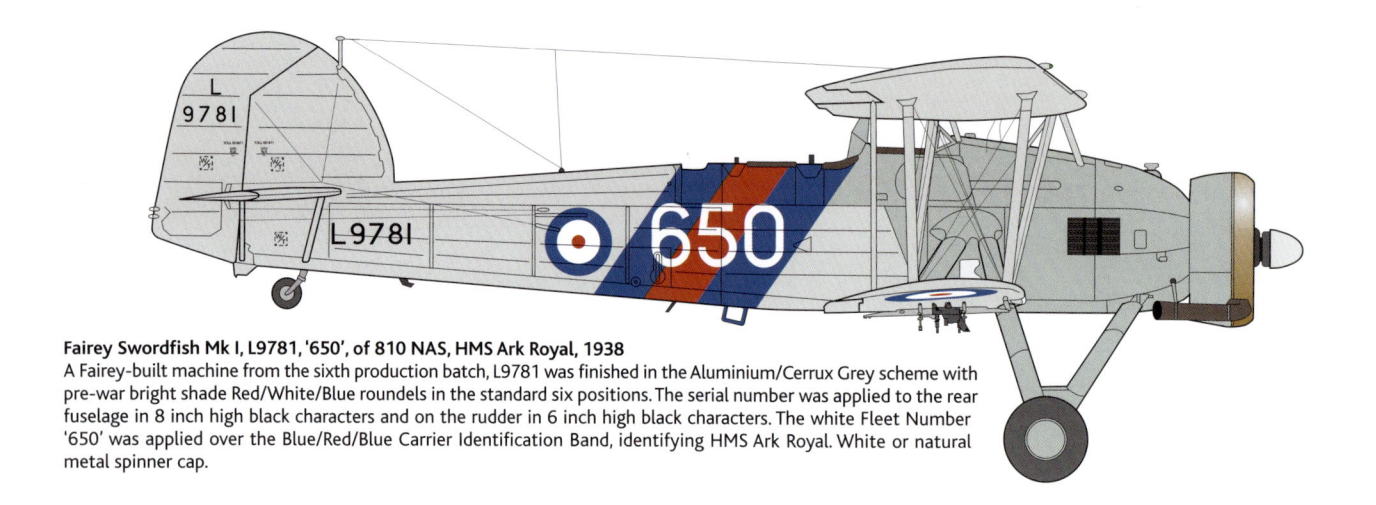

Fairey Swordfish Mk I, L9781, '650', of 810 NAS, HMS Ark Royal, 1938
A Fairey-built machine from the sixth production batch, L9781 was finished in the Aluminium/Cerrux Grey scheme with pre-war bright shade Red/White/Blue roundels in the standard six positions. The serial number was applied to the rear fuselage in 8 inch high black characters and on the rudder in 6 inch high black characters. The white Fleet Number '650' was applied over the Blue/Red/Blue Carrier Identification Band, identifying HMS Ark Royal. White or natural metal spinner cap.

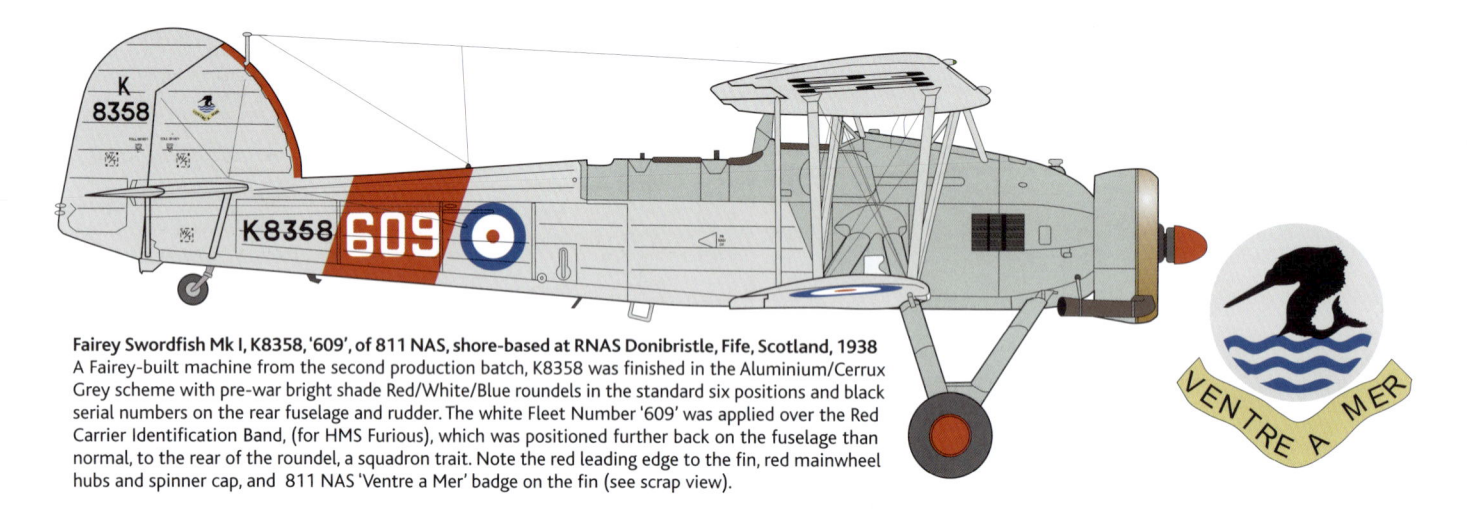

Fairey Swordfish Mk I, K8358, '609', of 811 NAS, shore-based at RNAS Donibristle, Fife, Scotland, 1938
A Fairey-built machine from the second production batch, K8358 was finished in the Aluminium/Cerrux Grey scheme with pre-war bright shade Red/White/Blue roundels in the standard six positions and black serial numbers on the rear fuselage and rudder. The white Fleet Number '609' was applied over the Red Carrier Identification Band, (for HMS Furious), which was positioned further back on the fuselage than normal, to the rear of the roundel, a squadron trait. Note the red leading edge to the fin, red mainwheel hubs and spinner cap, and 811 NAS 'Ventre a Mer' badge on the fin (see scrap view).

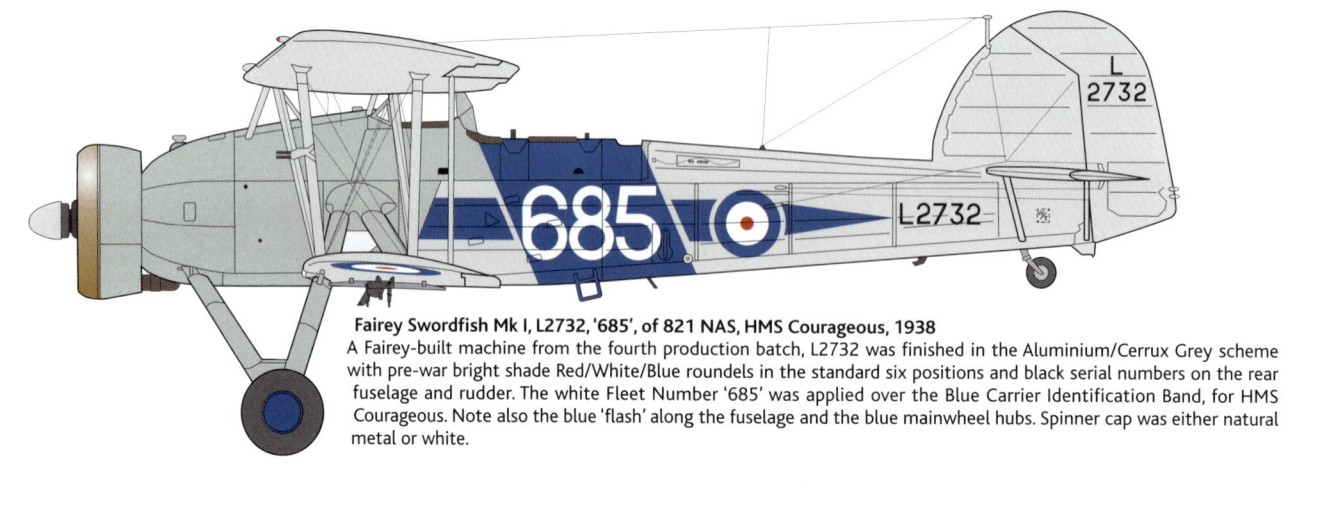

Fairey Swordfish Mk I, L2732, '685', of 821 NAS, HMS Courageous, 1938
A Fairey-built machine from the fourth production batch, L2732 was finished in the Aluminium/Cerrux Grey scheme with pre-war bright shade Red/White/Blue roundels in the standard six positions and black serial numbers on the rear fuselage and rudder. The white Fleet Number '685' was applied over the Blue Carrier Identification Band, for HMS Courageous. Note also the blue 'flash' along the fuselage and the blue mainwheel hubs. Spinner cap was either natural metal or white.

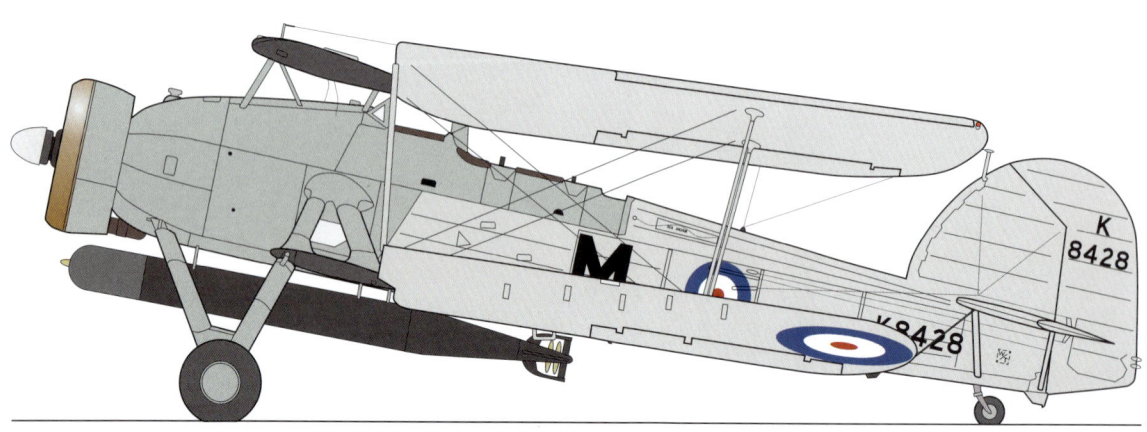

Fairey Swordfish Mk I, K8428, 'M', of the Torpedo Trials Unit, RAF Gosport, Hampshire, October 1938
A Fairey-built machine from the second production batch, K8428 was finished in the Aluminium/Cerrux Grey scheme with pre-war bright shade Red/White/Blue roundels in the standard six positions and black serial numbers on the rear fuselage and rudder. The individual aircraft letter 'M' was black and the spinner cap was either natural metal or white.

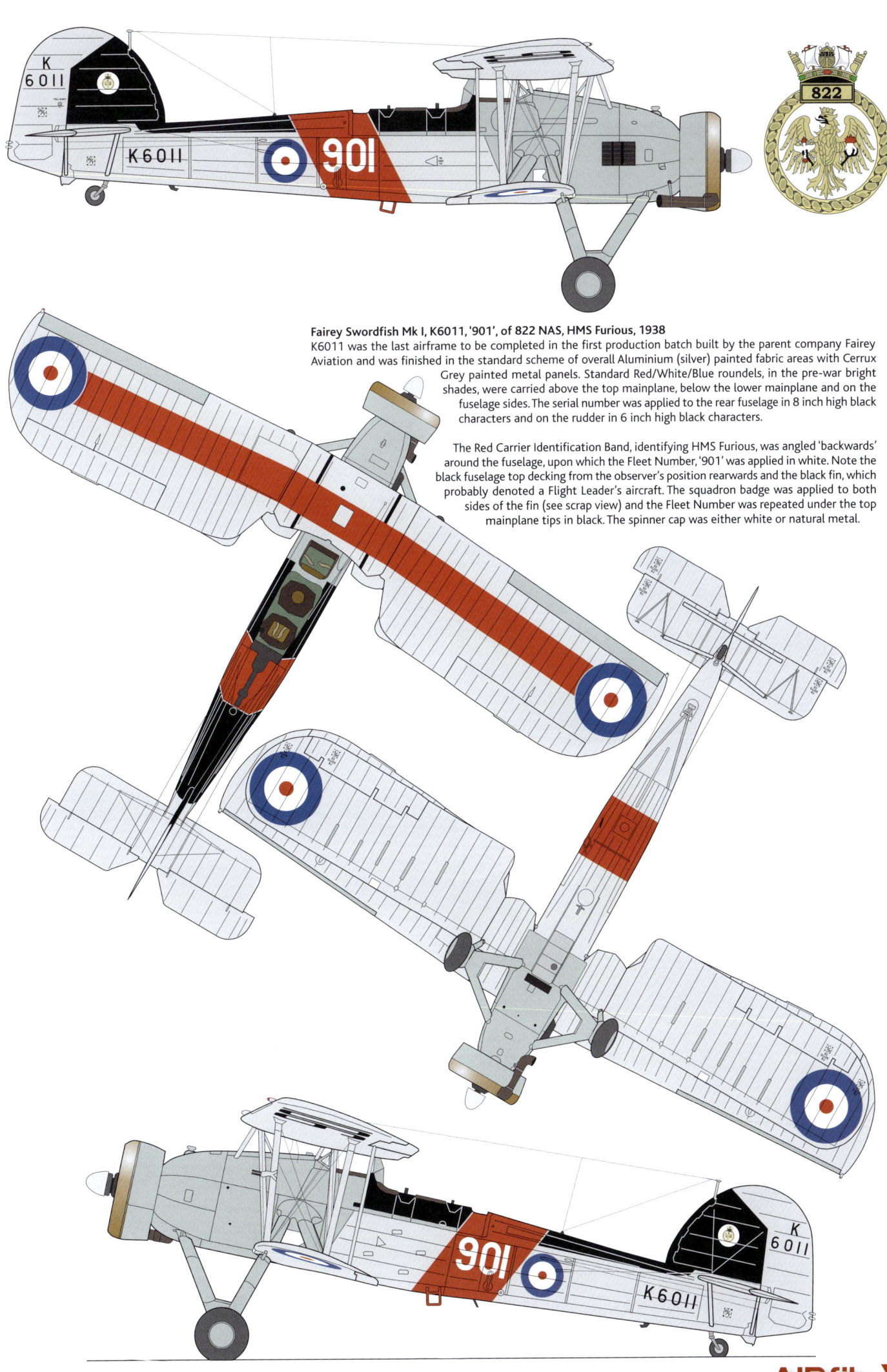

Fairey Swordfish Mk I, K6011, '901', of 822 NAS, HMS Furious, 1938

K6011 was the last airframe to be completed in the first production batch built by the parent company Fairey Aviation and was finished in the standard scheme of overall Aluminium (silver) painted fabric areas with Cerrux Grey painted metal panels. Standard Red/White/Blue roundels, in the pre-war bright shades, were carried above the top mainplane, below the lower mainplane and on the fuselage sides. The serial number was applied to the rear fuselage in 8 inch high black characters and on the rudder in 6 inch high black characters.

The Red Carrier Identification Band, identifying HMS Furious, was angled 'backwards' around the fuselage, upon which the Fleet Number, '901' was applied in white. Note the black fuselage top decking from the observer's position rearwards and the black fin, which probably denoted a Flight Leader's aircraft. The squadron badge was applied to both sides of the fin (see scrap view) and the Fleet Number was repeated under the top mainplane tips in black. The spinner cap was either white or natural metal.

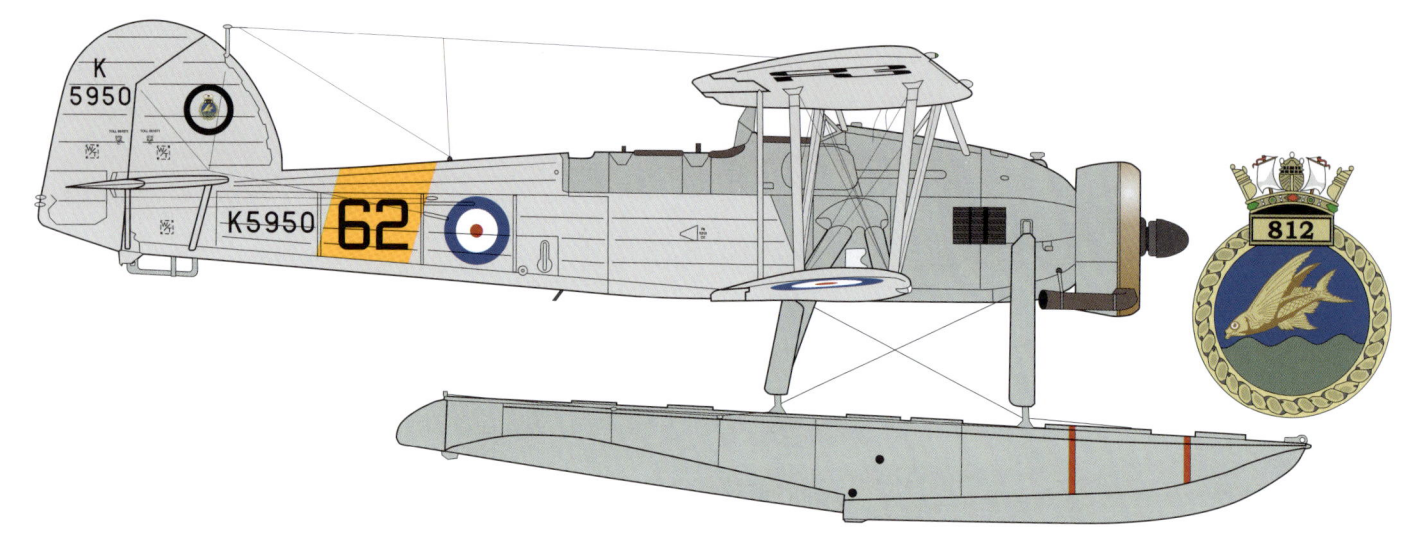

Fairey Swordfish Mk I, K5950, '62', of 812 NAS, HMS Glorious, 1937
A Fairey-built floatplane from the first production batch, K5950 was finished in the Aluminium/Cerrux Grey scheme with pre-war bright shade Red/White/Blue roundels in the standard six positions and black 8 inch and 6 inch high serial numbers on the rear fuselage and rudder. Note how the Yellow Carrier Identification Band, which identified HMS Glorious, was terminated along the fuselage lower longeron line. The Fleet Number, '62' was applied in black on the Carrier Identification Band and repeated under both top mainplane wing tips. The squadron badge (see scrap view) was applied to the fin surrounded by a black circle. The floats were painted Cerrux Grey and the spinner cap was either black or dark grey.

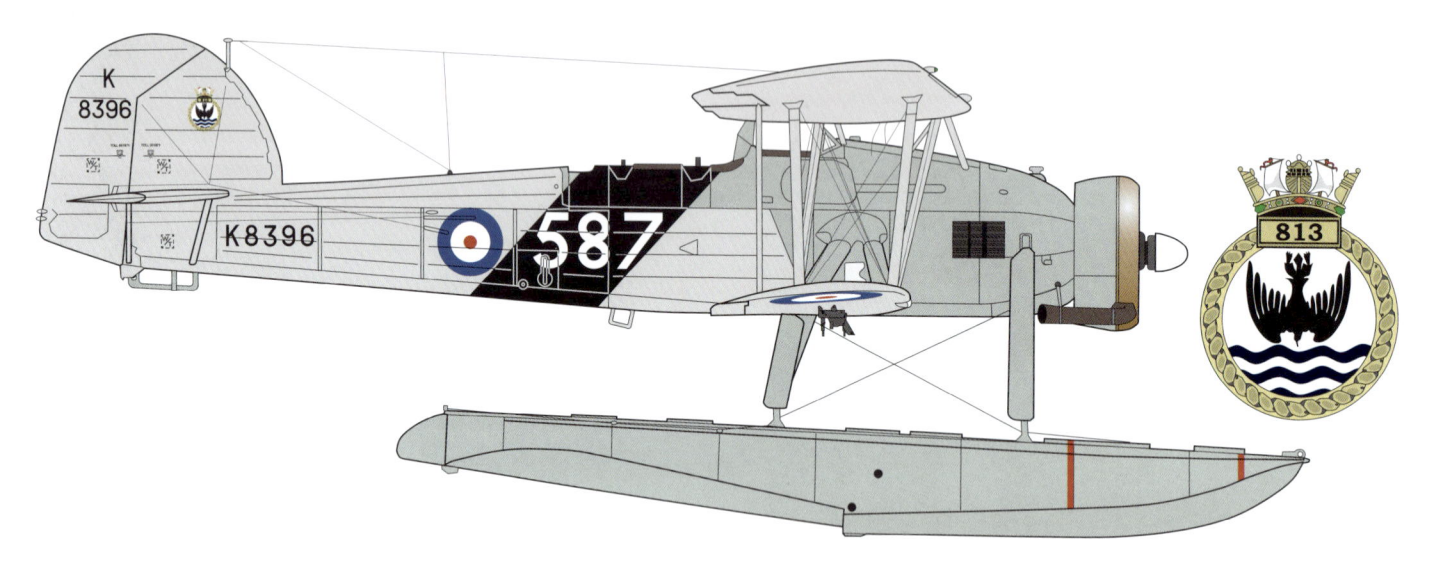

Fairey Swordfish Mk I, K8396, '587', of 813 NAS, HMS Eagle, 1938
A Fairey-built floatplane from the second production batch, K8396 was finished in the Aluminium/Cerrux Grey scheme with pre-war bright shade Red/White/Blue roundels in the standard six positions and black serial numbers on the rear fuselage and rudder. The Black Carrier Identification Band, which identified HMS Eagle, had the Fleet Number, '587' applied over it in white. The squadron badge (see scrap view) was applied to the fin in the so called 'battleship frame'. The floats were painted Cerrux Grey and the spinner cap was either white or natural metal.

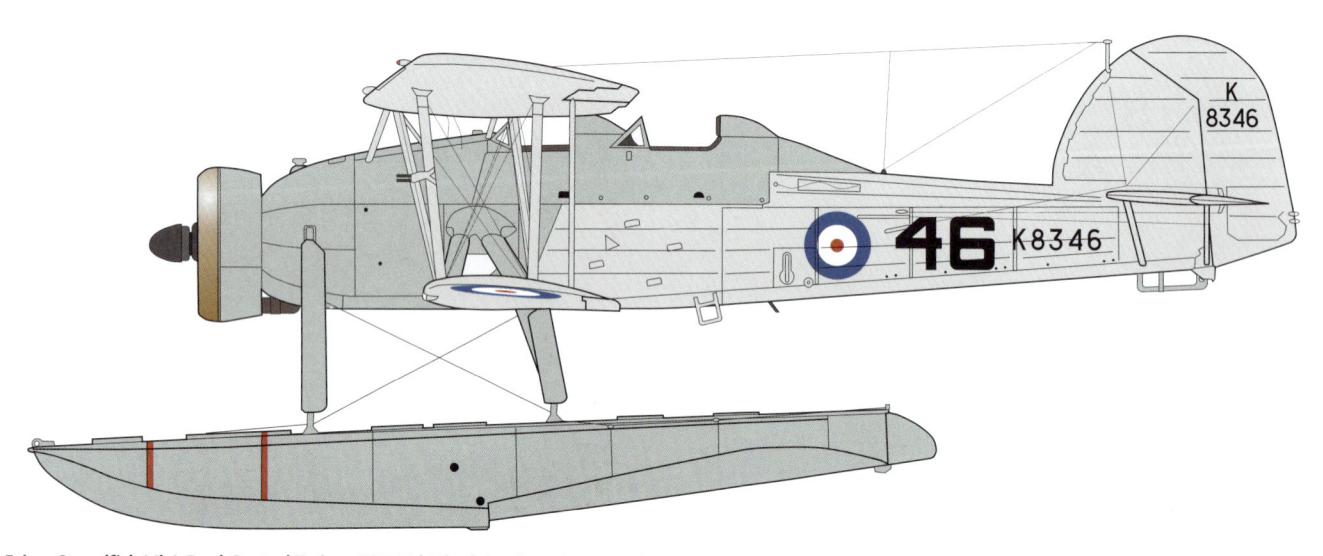

Fairey Swordfish Mk I, Dual Control Trainer, K8346, '46', of the Floatplane Training Unit, RNAS lee-on-Solent, Hampshire 1938
A Fairey-built, dual control floatplane trainer conversion from the first production batch, K8346 was finished in the Aluminium/Cerrux Grey scheme with pre-war bright shade Red/White/Blue roundels in the standard six positions and black serial numbers on the rear fuselage and rudder. It would appear the the 'last two' of the serial have been used for the aircraft's individual aircraft letter. The floats were painted Cerrux Grey, and the spinner cap was either black or dark grey.

Fairey Swordfish Mk I, K8449, '649', of 820 NAS, HMS Courageous, March 1938

K8449 was the last airframe to be completed in the second production batch built by the parent company Fairey Aviation and was finished in the standard scheme of overall Aluminium (silver) painted fabric areas with Cerrux Grey painted metal panels. Standard Red/White/Blue roundels, in the pre-war bright shades, were carried above the top mainplane, below the lower mainplane and on the fuselage sides. The serial number was applied to the rear fuselage in 8 inch high black characters and on the rudder in 6 inch high black characters.

The white Fleet Number '649 was applied over the Blue Carrier Identification Band, identifying HMS Courageous, and a white 'square' with a blue cross was painted over the upper surface of the top mainplane centre section. The squadron badge was applied to both sides of the fin (see scrap view) and the Fleet Number was repeated under the top mainplane tips in black. The spinner cap was either white or natural metal.

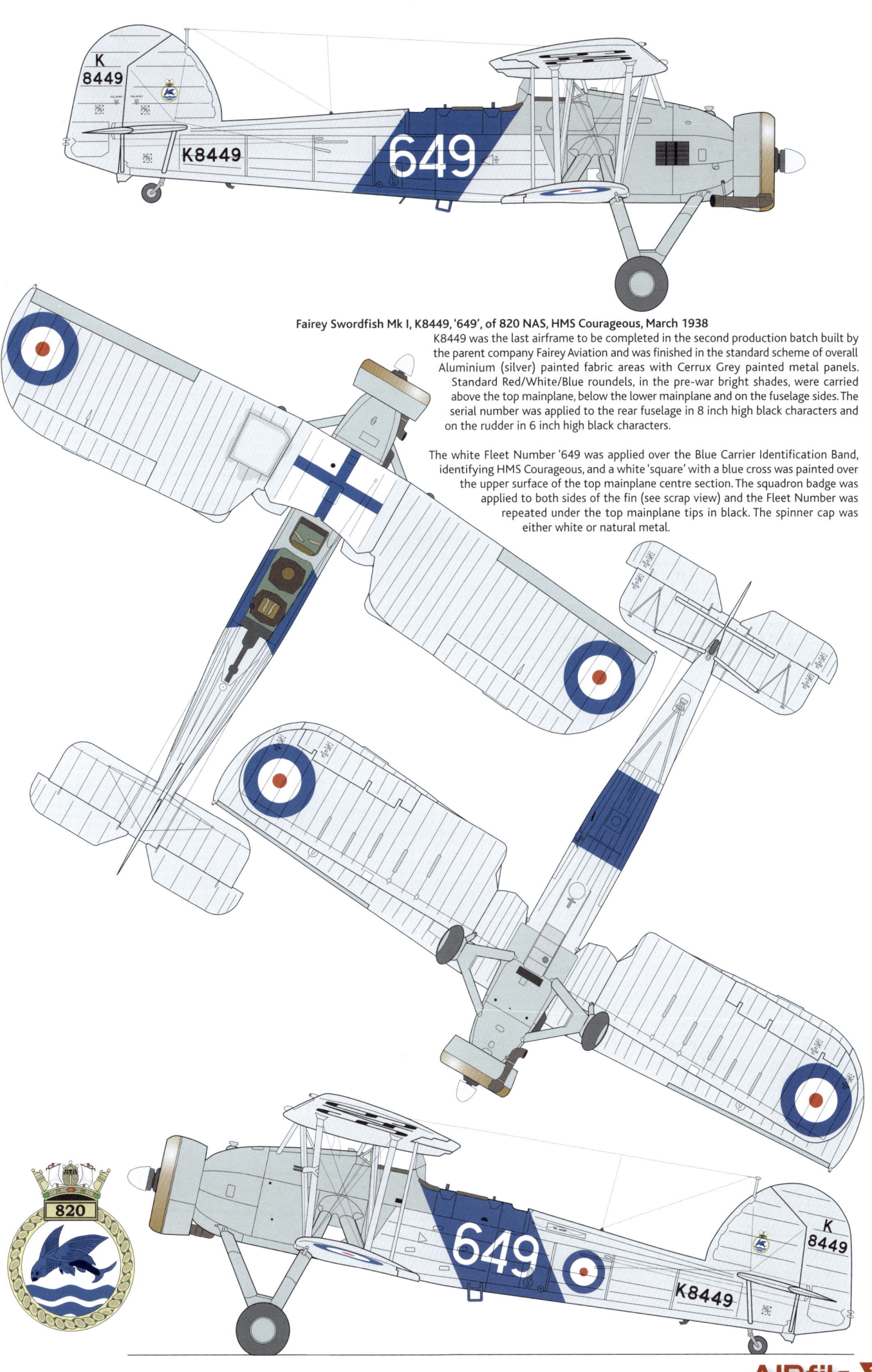

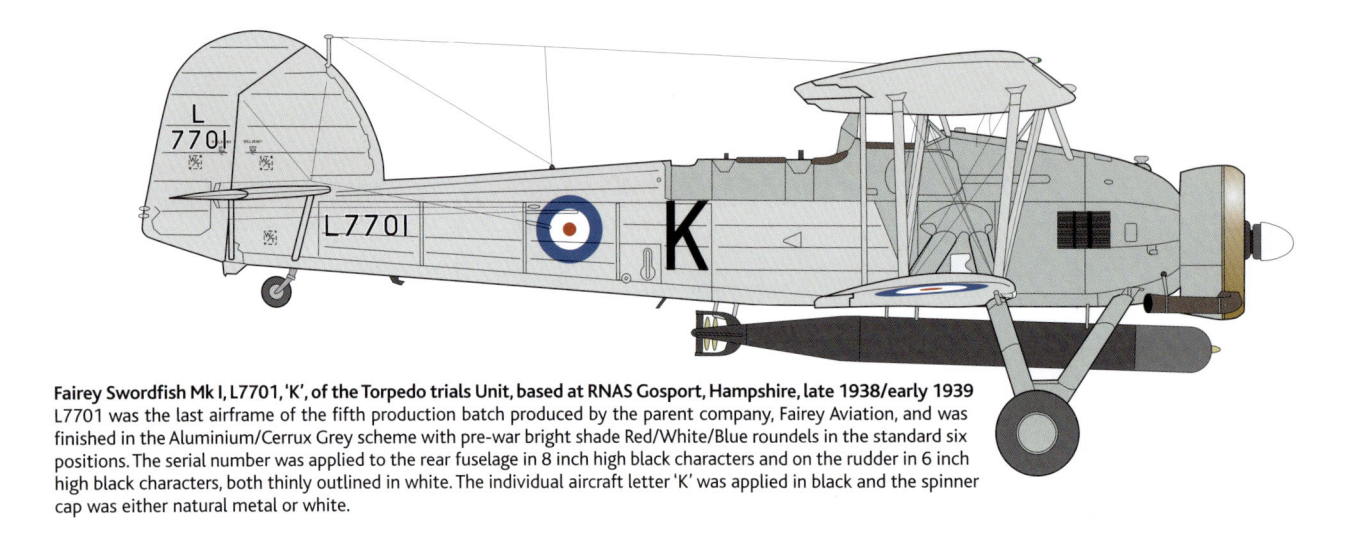

Fairey Swordfish Mk I, L7701, 'K', of the Torpedo trials Unit, based at RNAS Gosport, Hampshire, late 1938/early 1939
L7701 was the last airframe of the fifth production batch produced by the parent company, Fairey Aviation, and was finished in the Aluminium/Cerrux Grey scheme with pre-war bright shade Red/White/Blue roundels in the standard six positions. The serial number was applied to the rear fuselage in 8 inch high black characters and on the rudder in 6 inch high black characters, both thinly outlined in white. The individual aircraft letter 'K' was applied in black and the spinner cap was either natural metal or white.

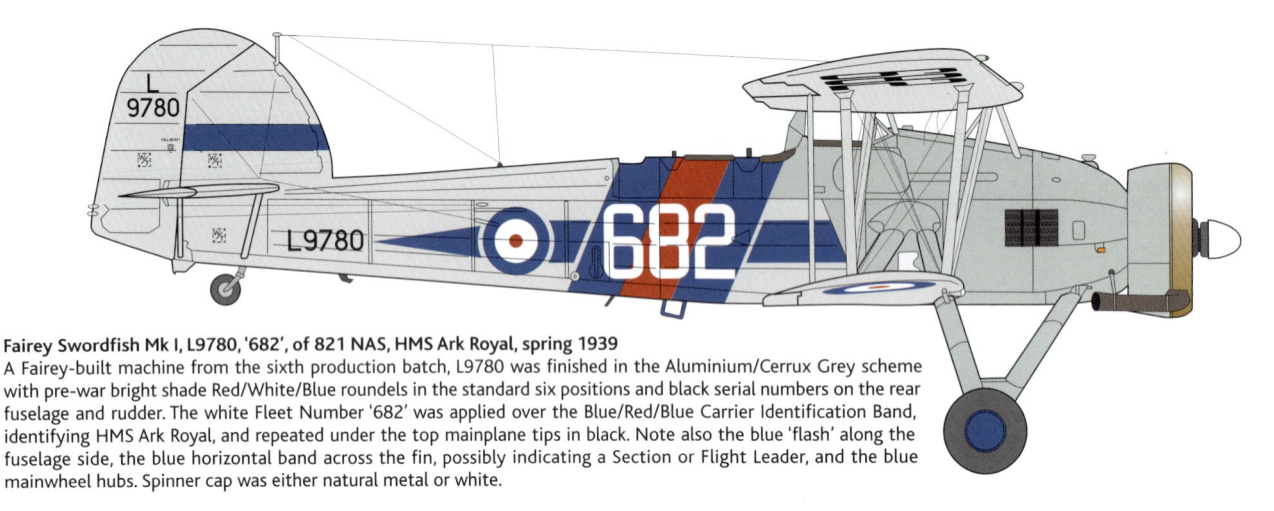

Fairey Swordfish Mk I, L9780, '682', of 821 NAS, HMS Ark Royal, spring 1939
A Fairey-built machine from the sixth production batch, L9780 was finished in the Aluminium/Cerrux Grey scheme with pre-war bright shade Red/White/Blue roundels in the standard six positions and black serial numbers on the rear fuselage and rudder. The white Fleet Number '682' was applied over the Blue/Red/Blue Carrier Identification Band, identifying HMS Ark Royal, and repeated under the top mainplane tips in black. Note also the blue 'flash' along the fuselage side, the blue horizontal band across the fin, possibly indicating a Section or Flight Leader, and the blue mainwheel hubs. Spinner cap was either natural metal or white.

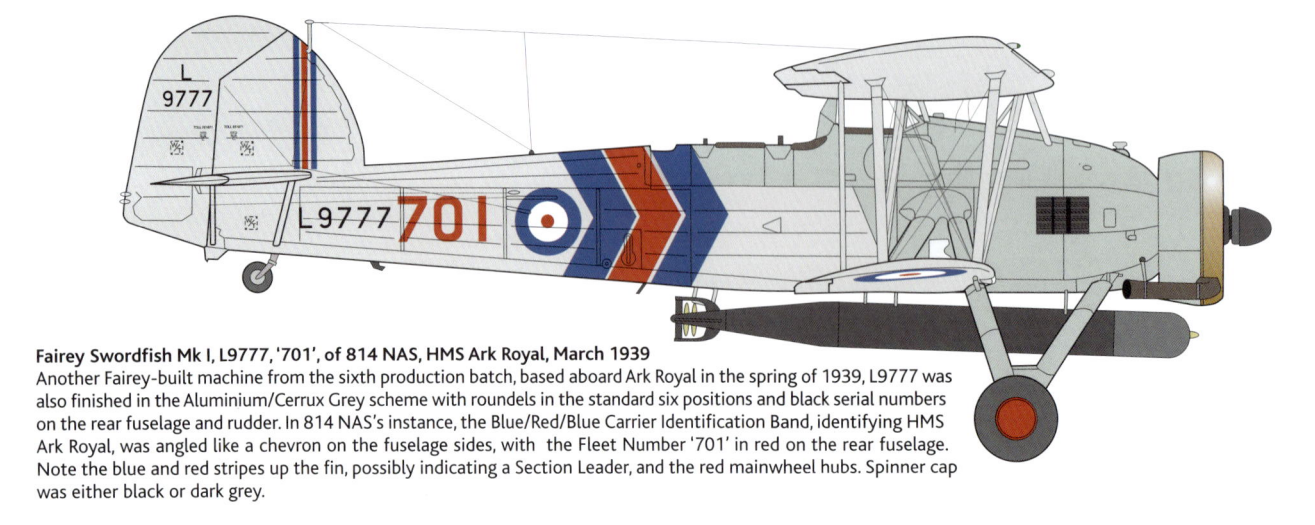

Fairey Swordfish Mk I, L9777, '701', of 814 NAS, HMS Ark Royal, March 1939
Another Fairey-built machine from the sixth production batch, based aboard Ark Royal in the spring of 1939, L9777 was also finished in the Aluminium/Cerrux Grey scheme with roundels in the standard six positions and black serial numbers on the rear fuselage and rudder. In 814 NAS's instance, the Blue/Red/Blue Carrier Identification Band, identifying HMS Ark Royal, was angled like a chevron on the fuselage sides, with the Fleet Number '701' in red on the rear fuselage. Note the blue and red stripes up the fin, possibly indicating a Section Leader, and the red mainwheel hubs. Spinner cap was either black or dark grey.

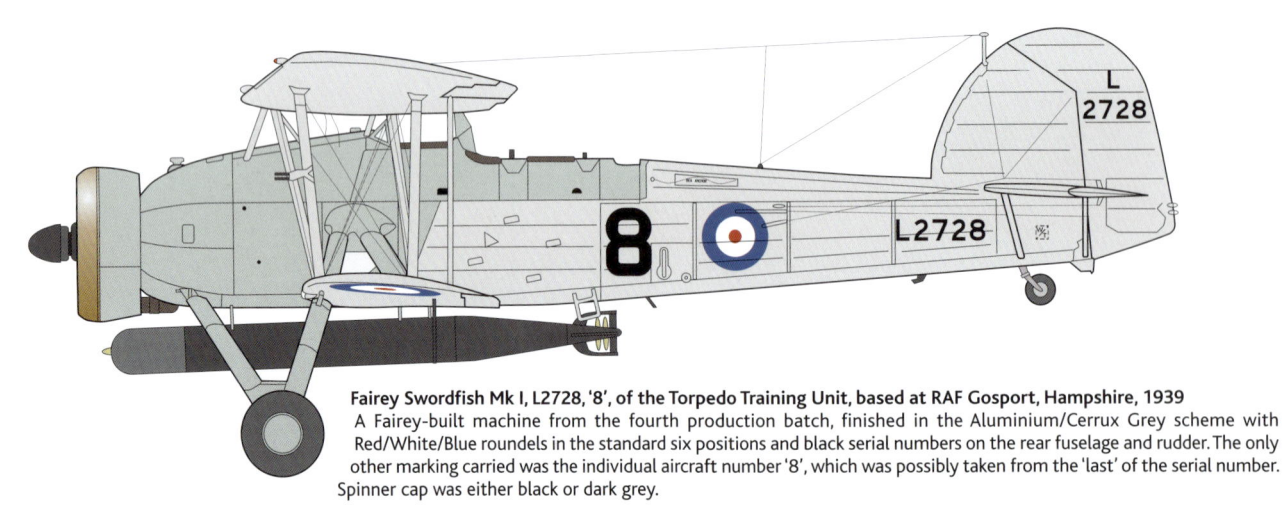

Fairey Swordfish Mk I, L2728, '8', of the Torpedo Training Unit, based at RAF Gosport, Hampshire, 1939
A Fairey-built machine from the fourth production batch, finished in the Aluminium/Cerrux Grey scheme with Red/White/Blue roundels in the standard six positions and black serial numbers on the rear fuselage and rudder. The only other marking carried was the individual aircraft number '8', which was possibly taken from the 'last' of the serial number. Spinner cap was either black or dark grey.

AIRfile

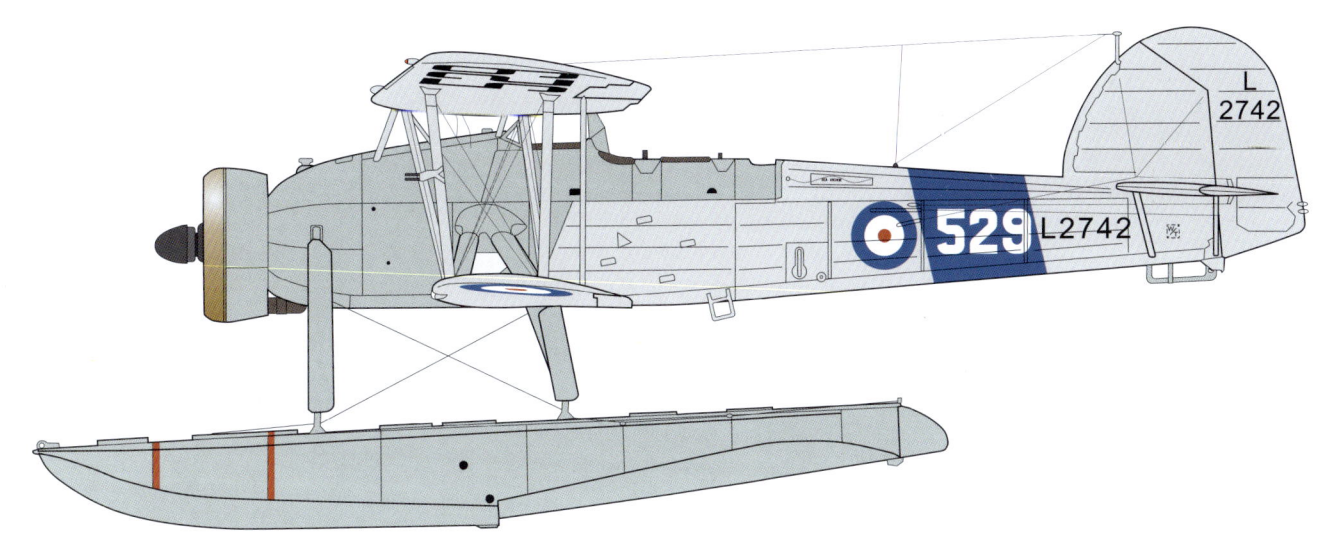

Fairey Swordfish Mk I, L2742, '529', of 701 Ship's Flight, operating off the battleship HMS Hood, 1938
A Fairey-built machine from the fourth production batch, modified in to floatplane configuration for use aboard Royal Navy battleships. Finished in the Aluminium/Cerrux Grey scheme with roundels in the standard six positions. The serial number was applied to the rear fuselage in 8 inch high black characters and on the rudder in 6 inch high black characters. L2742 still carried the Blue Carrier Identification Band and white Fleet Number '529' from its previous service with HMS Courageous, when it served with 810 NAS – see p12. Note the Fleet Number repeated under both top mainplane wing tips in black. Spinner cap was either black or dark grey.

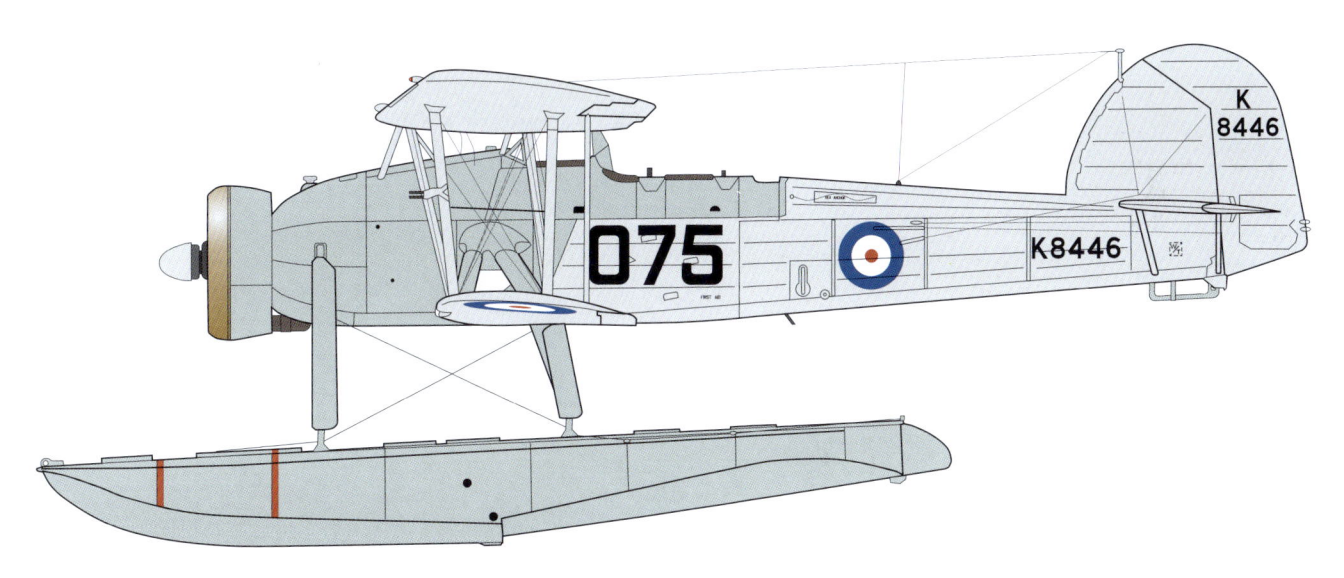

Fairey Swordfish Mk I, K8446, '075', of 701 Ship's Flight, operating off the battleship HMS Warspite, early 1939
A Fairey-built machine from the second production batch, subsequently modified in to floatplane configuration for use aboard Royal Navy battleships. Finished in the Aluminium/Cerrux Grey scheme with roundels in the standard six positions and black 8 inch and 6 inch high serial numbers on the rear fuselage and rudder, the only distinctive marking carried by K8446 was the black Fleet Number '075'. Spinner cap was either natural metal or white.

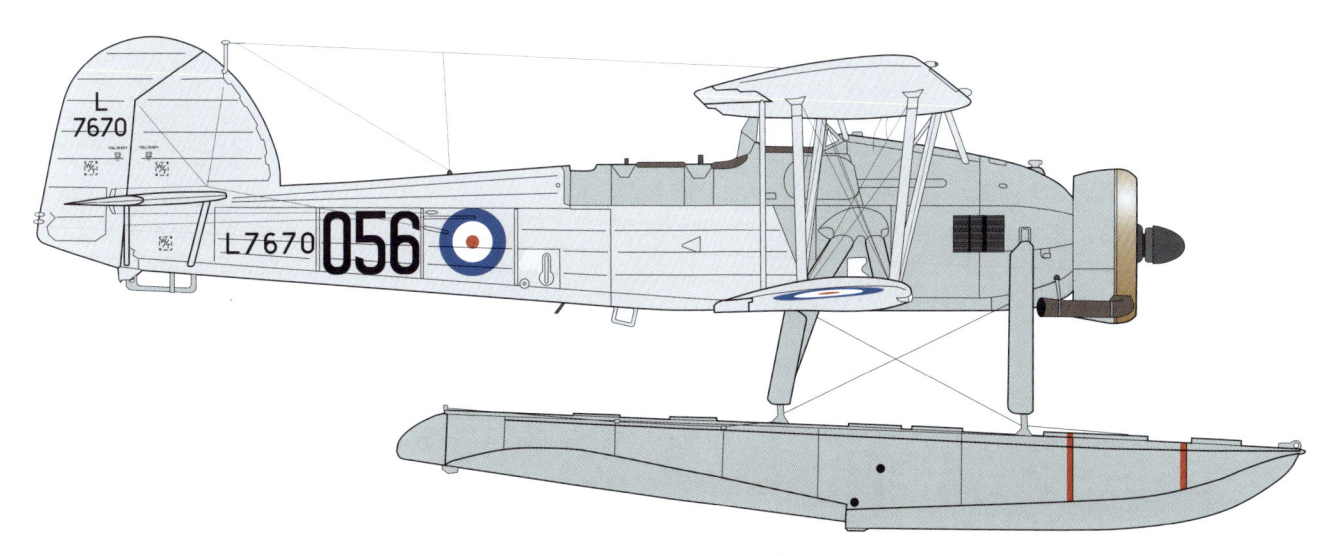

Fairey Swordfish Mk I, L7670, '056', of 702 Catapult Flight, operating off the battleship HMS Rodney, 1939
A Fairey-built machine from the fifth production batch, subsequently modified in to floatplane configuration for use aboard Royal Navy battleships. Finished in the Aluminium/Cerrux Grey scheme with roundels in the standard six positions and black 8 inch and 6 inch high serial numbers on the rear fuselage and rudder, again the only distinctive marking carried by L7670 was the black Fleet Number '056', in this instance, placed on the rear fuselage behind the roundel. Spinner cap was either black or dark grey.

Chapter 2

The early war years
1939 to 1940

Swordfish Mk I, K8869, '968', of 825 NAS, probably photographed at Dekheila, Egypt, in September 1939, prior to embarking on HMS Glorious later in the month for service around the Mediterranean where it was serving in the first few months of World War Two. Finished in the standard Aluminium/Cerrux Grey scheme, the black Fleet Number '968' was applied over the yellow Carrier Identification Band, (for HMS Glorious), which looks dark in this photo due to the type of film used. No 825 NAS's badge was carried on the fin. (see profile on p22)

The Admiralty had regained control of the Fleet Air Arm on 24 May 1939, by which time it had thirteen front-line squadrons equipped with the Swordfish Mark I, eleven flying from aircraft carriers. There were also three Flights of float-equipped Swordfish for use on catapult-equipped warships – one of which, L9767, from HMS Warspite, spotted the fall of shot and radioed gunnery corrections back to the ship during the Second Battle of Narvik in April 1940 and subsequently sank U-boat U-64.

At this time the Swordfish's primary weapon was the 18 inch aerial torpedo, but the low speed of the biplane and the need for a long straight approach made it hazardous to deliver against well-defended targets. Swordfish torpedo doctrine called for an approach at 5,000ft (1,500m) followed by a dive to torpedo release altitude of about 18ft (5.5m). Maximum range of the early Mark XII 18 inch torpedo was 1,500yds (1400m). The torpedo travelled some 200 yards (180m) forward from release to water impact and required another 300 yards (270m) to stabilise at a preset depth and arm itself. Ideal release distance was 1,000 yards (900m) from the target – if the Swordfish survived to that distance.

Armament fits for the Swordfish when it entered service included:
- A single 18 inch, 1610lb (46cm, 730kg) torpedo carried on the centerline.
- A single 1500lb (680kg) mine carried on the centerline.
- 1500lb (680kg) of bombs in configurations such as a single 500lb (225kg) bomb under the fuselage and one each under the wing, or a single 500lb (225kg) bomb under the fuselage and two 250lb (115kg) bombs under each wing, or up to six 250lb (115kg) bombs, three under each wing.
- Up to six 246lb (112kg) Mk VII depth charges – three under each wing.
- Marker flares and smaller bombs could also be carried under the wings.

Production of the Swordfish was moved from the parent company Fairey to Blackburn Aircraft Ltd in early 1940, to allow for the development and production of newer designs such as the Barracuda and Firefly. Blackburn continued production of the Mark I until 1943, when the Mk II was introduced, of which 1,080 were built, the major difference being the strengthening of the structure and metal skinning on the the underside of the lower mainplane to allow underwing rails to be fitted to carry eight 60lb (27kg) Rocket Projectiles (RPs). Later Mark II production also featured an uprated 750hp Pegasus XXX engine replacing the Pegasus IIIM3 and an enlarged oil cooler. An elongated exhaust manifold was also fitted on many later Marks, to help with flame damping.

Swordfish Mk I, L2770 '648' of 820 NAS, having just landed aboard HMS Ark Royal, in early 1939. Still finished in the standard Aluminium/Cerrux Grey scheme, the white Fleet Number '648' was applied over the Carrier Identification Band, (which would have been altered from the all blue band for HMS Courageous, the unit's previous carrier, to the blue/red/blue band for HMS Ark Royal).

Change of coding

Following the transfer of control of the Fleet Air Arm to the Admiralty in early 1939, the aircraft coding system was changed – to a Letter-Numeral-Letter system.

Initially applied to the fuselage sides in the same way as the previous Fleet Numbers, the first letter identified the parent carrier or ship:-

A – HMS Ark Royal

C – HMS Courageous

E – HMS Eagle

F – HMS Formidable

G – HMS Glorious

H – HMS Hermes

L – HMS Illustrious

M – HMS Implacable (under construction at the time)

N – HMS Indomitable (under construction at the time)

U – HMS Furious

Shore bases and second line training units were also allocated Identification Letters:-

R – Fleet Requirements Units

T – Deck Landing Training Units

W – Observer Training Units

Y – Torpedo (and Fighter) Training School

The numeral identified the type or Class of aircraft; in the Swordfish's case the numerals 1 to 5 were allocated to Torpedo-Spotter aircraft. The last letter was the individual aircraft letter.

Initially, this Letter-Numeral-Letter coding was applied over the coloured Aircraft Carrier Identification Bands, applied around the mid fuselage, and replaced the Fleet Number, but later when camouflage was introduced, it was moved on to the fin area.

Introduction of camouflage

Towards the end of 1935, a series of trials had begun to be undertaken by the Royal Aircraft Establishment (RAE) to develop a suitable camouflage scheme for Naval aircraft. Several colours were produced, initially for use on three aircraft types then in FAA service, the Fairey IIIF, Blackburn Shark and Fairey Swordfish.

Under the RAE Trials' collective designation of 'Sea Scheme', five colours were adopted for use on the Swordfish, called the S1E Scheme, (ie the fifth scheme within the Sea Scheme Trials), in a variation of the RAF's Shadow Compensating Scheme for biplanes, with the upper surfaces of the upper mainplane, tailplane and the top half of the fuselage in Extra Dark Sea Grey and Dark Slate Grey, and Dark Sea Grey and Light Slate Grey on the upper surface of the lower mainplanes and on the forward upper fuselage area immediately under the upper mainplane. Sky Grey was used for the entire under surfaces which reached mid-way up the fuselage sides in an undulating line. The fin and rudder were also to be Sky Grey.

The S1E Scheme was promulgated by the Admiralty in Confidential Admiralty Fleet Order (CAFO) 1213/39 issued on 11 May 1939, stating that whilst new aircraft on the production line would be received from the manufacturers already finished in the Scheme, special arrangements would be necessary to ensure that all aircraft already in service or in reserve which were not camouflaged, which meant those aircraft which had previously been delivered in the overall Aluminium/Cerrux Grey finish, would be painted the appropriate colours at the earliest convenient date. CAFO 1213/39 went on to explain that the Admiralty, in conjunction with the Air Ministry, would be issuing the necessary drawings and finishing materials required for each type of aircraft and instructions for its application would be issued in due course.

Two camouflage patterns were shown on the diagram, A Scheme and B Scheme, (see pp32 and 33) which were effectively mirror images of each other, to be applied on alternate aircraft still on the production line or, if already in squadron service, to be applied to equal numbers of aircraft within each squadron, and most Swordfish had been suitably camouflaged by outbreak of war in September 1939.

National markings had gone through a similar progression as those on RAF aircraft, with the Red, White and Blue roundels, in the pre-war 'bright' colours, in the usual six positions – ie above the top mainplane, below the lower mainplanes and on either side of the fuselage. Following the outbreak of war, a few aircraft had the fuselage Red/White/Blue roundels modified in to the Red/Blue style, but with the introduction of the camouflage finish, the roundels above the top mainplane on all FAA aircraft were to be changed to the Red/Blue style, (later known as National Marking i). The Red/White/Blue roundels under the lower wing, (National Marking ii), were to remain but the aircraft serial number, (if applied), was to be omitted from under the wings and reduced in size on the fuselage to a height of 4 inches.

A Yellow outer ring was added around the Red/White/Blue National Marking ii fuselage roundels (to create a Red/White/Blue/Yellow roundel to be henceforth known as National Marking iii) and Red/White/Blue vertical stripes were applied to the fin on all operational British aircraft, including Fleet Air Arm types, to be applied 'at Squadron level' or at the MUs on existing 'in-sevice' machines, and on the manufacturers' production line, as soon as was practical after 1 May 1940.

Following the adoption and introduction of the S1E Camouflage Scheme, the RAE was then asked to create a simplified definitive camouflage scheme for carrier-based Fleet Air Arm aircraft, based upon the colours of the S1E Scheme, to be termed the Temperate Sea Scheme.

Comprising just the Extra Dark Sea Grey and Dark Slate Grey colours on the upper surfaces, and initially retaining the Sky Grey on the under surfaces and fuselage sides, the 'new' Temperate Sea Scheme was gradually introduced on the production line during mid-1940 (see p49).

The introduction of Sky under surfaces to replace the Sky Grey was supposed to have taken place in June 1940, in conjunction with the changeover for RAF aircraft, but, due to shortages of Sky paint, it eventually started to be implemented from around September 1940 for all Fleet Air Arm aircraft types.

These changes appear to have been implemented fairly rapidly, but because no official detail on the specific size of the new markings was given initially, many different interpretations appeared as the individual units tried to comply with the new instructions. Roundels were modified with Yellow outer bands of varying widths whilst the fin flash was also applied in different widths and styles.

Above and below:
Landing, or indeed take-off, accidents were an ever present hazard aboard the rolling and pitching deck of an aircraft carrier and despite the Swordfish's excellent handling qualities, the type was not immune to the odd mishap as these two unidentified examples bear testament to!

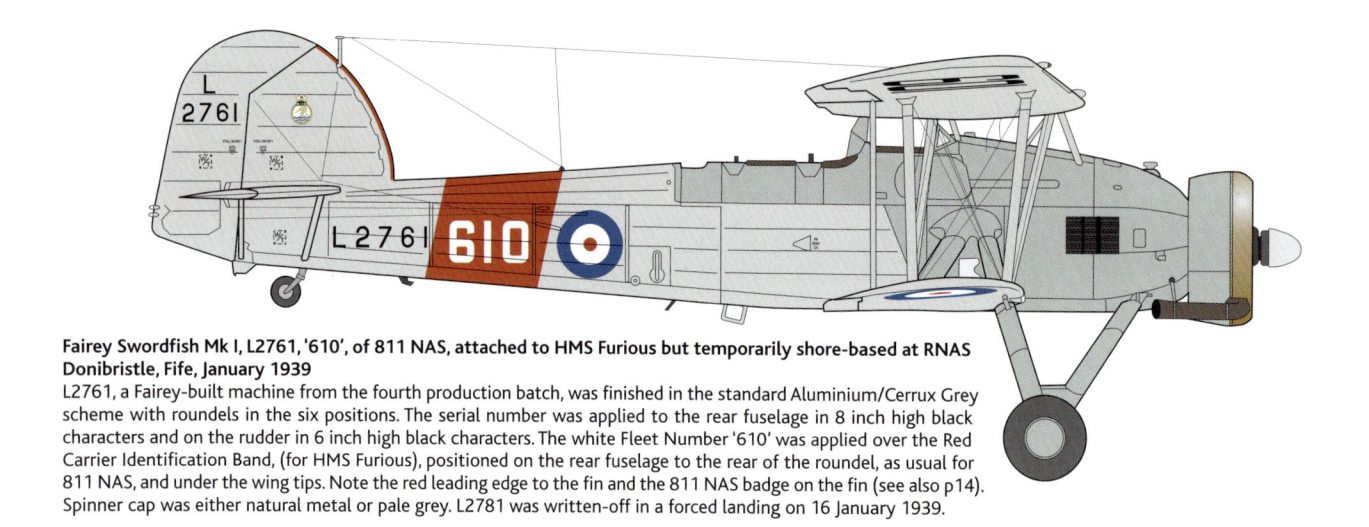

Fairey Swordfish Mk I, L2761, '610', of 811 NAS, attached to HMS Furious but temporarily shore-based at RNAS Donibristle, Fife, January 1939
L2761, a Fairey-built machine from the fourth production batch, was finished in the standard Aluminium/Cerrux Grey scheme with roundels in the six positions. The serial number was applied to the rear fuselage in 8 inch high black characters and on the rudder in 6 inch high black characters. The white Fleet Number '610' was applied over the Red Carrier Identification Band, (for HMS Furious), positioned on the rear fuselage to the rear of the roundel, as usual for 811 NAS, and under the wing tips. Note the red leading edge to the fin and the 811 NAS badge on the fin (see also p14). Spinner cap was either natural metal or pale grey. L2781 was written-off in a forced landing on 16 January 1939.

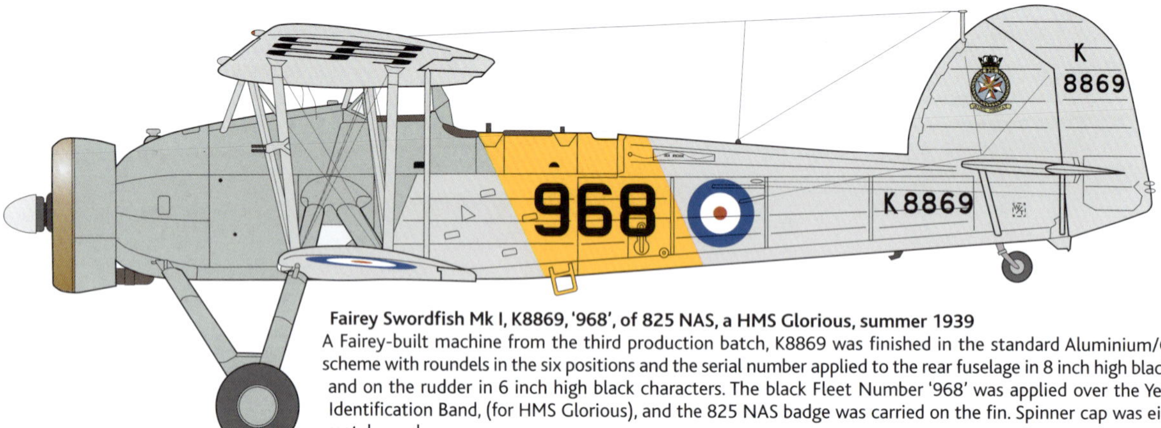

Fairey Swordfish Mk I, K8869, '968', of 825 NAS, a HMS Glorious, summer 1939
A Fairey-built machine from the third production batch, K8869 was finished in the standard Aluminium/Cerrux Grey scheme with roundels in the six positions and the serial number applied to the rear fuselage in 8 inch high black characters and on the rudder in 6 inch high black characters. The black Fleet Number '968' was applied over the Yellow Carrier Identification Band, (for HMS Glorious), and the 825 NAS badge was carried on the fin. Spinner cap was either natural metal or pale grey.

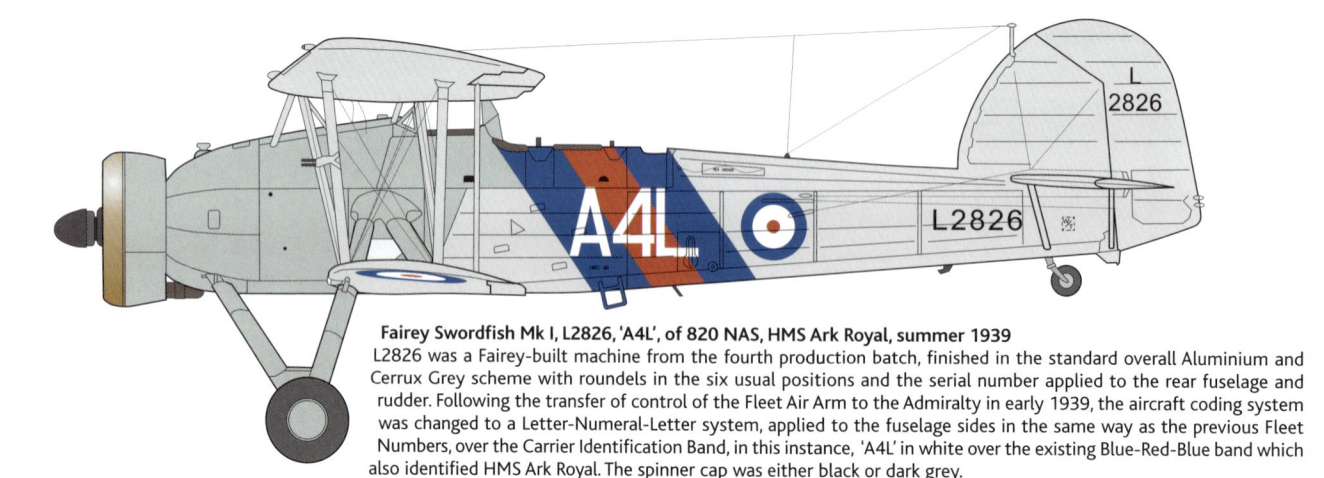

Fairey Swordfish Mk I, L2826, 'A4L', of 820 NAS, HMS Ark Royal, summer 1939
L2826 was a Fairey-built machine from the fourth production batch, finished in the standard overall Aluminium and Cerrux Grey scheme with roundels in the six usual positions and the serial number applied to the rear fuselage and rudder. Following the transfer of control of the Fleet Air Arm to the Admiralty in early 1939, the aircraft coding system was changed to a Letter-Numeral-Letter system, applied to the fuselage sides in the same way as the previous Fleet Numbers, over the Carrier Identification Band, in this instance, 'A4L' in white over the existing Blue-Red-Blue band which also identified HMS Ark Royal. The spinner cap was either black or dark grey.

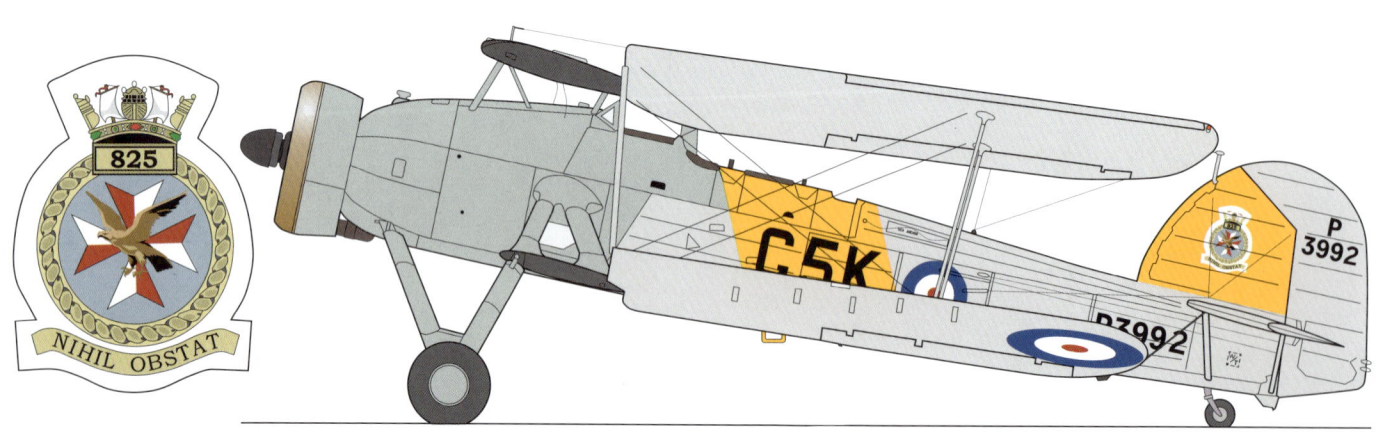

Fairey Swordfish Mk I, P3992, 'G5K', of 825 NAS, a HMS Glorious, summer 1939
A Fairey-built machine from the seventh production batch, P3992 was finished in the standard Aluminium/Cerrux Grey scheme, and was possibly amongst the last aircraft to be produced as such prior to the introduction of the S1E camouflage on the production line. Roundels were in the six usual positions with black serial numbers on the rear fuselage and rudder. The new Letter-Numeral-Letter coding was initially applied over the coloured Aircraft Carrier Identification Bands, in this instance 'G5K' in black over the Yellow band, for HMS Glorious. Note also the Yellow fin, possibly identifying the Squadron Commander or a Flight Leader, and the 825 NAS badge in a 'battleship frame' on the fin (see scrap view). The spinner cap was either black or dark grey.

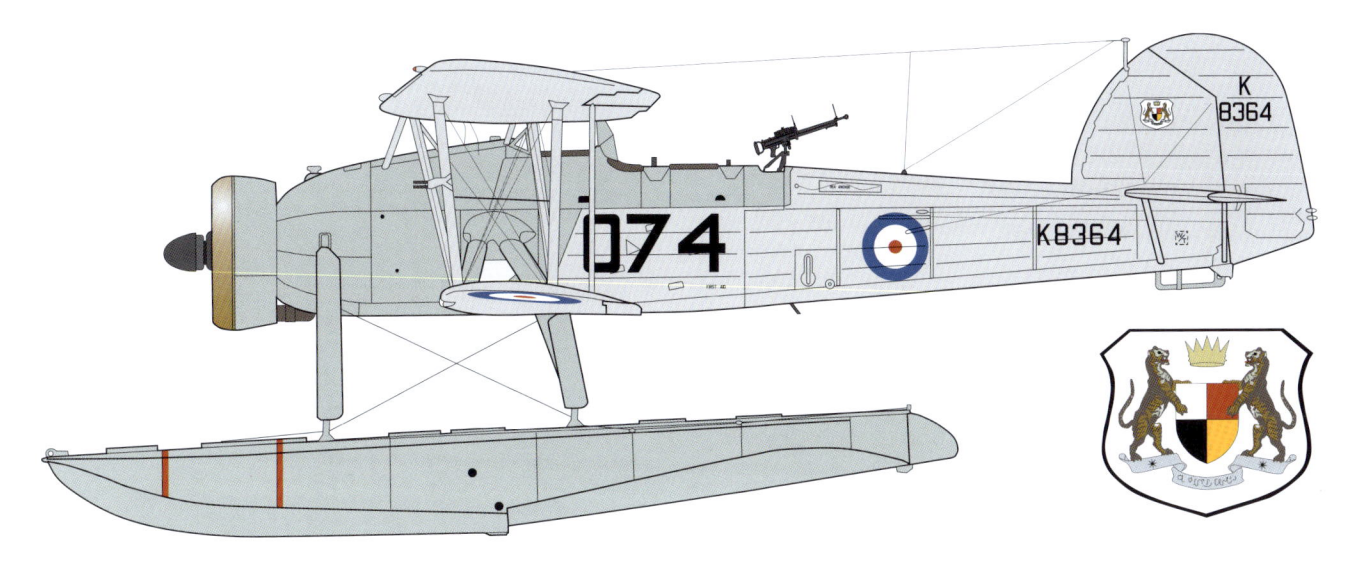

Fairey Swordfish Mk I, K8364, '074', of 701 Ship's Flight, operating off the battleship HMS Malaya, early 1939
A Fairey-built machine from the second production batch, subsequently modified in to floatplane configuration for use aboard Royal Navy battleships. Finished in the Aluminium/Cerrux Grey scheme with roundels in the standard six positions, the serial number was applied to the rear fuselage in 8 inch high black characters and on the rudder in 6 inch high black characters. The original black Fleet Number, '074', was still retained at this stage. Note the crest of the Federated Malay States on the fin. The spinner cap was either black or dark grey.

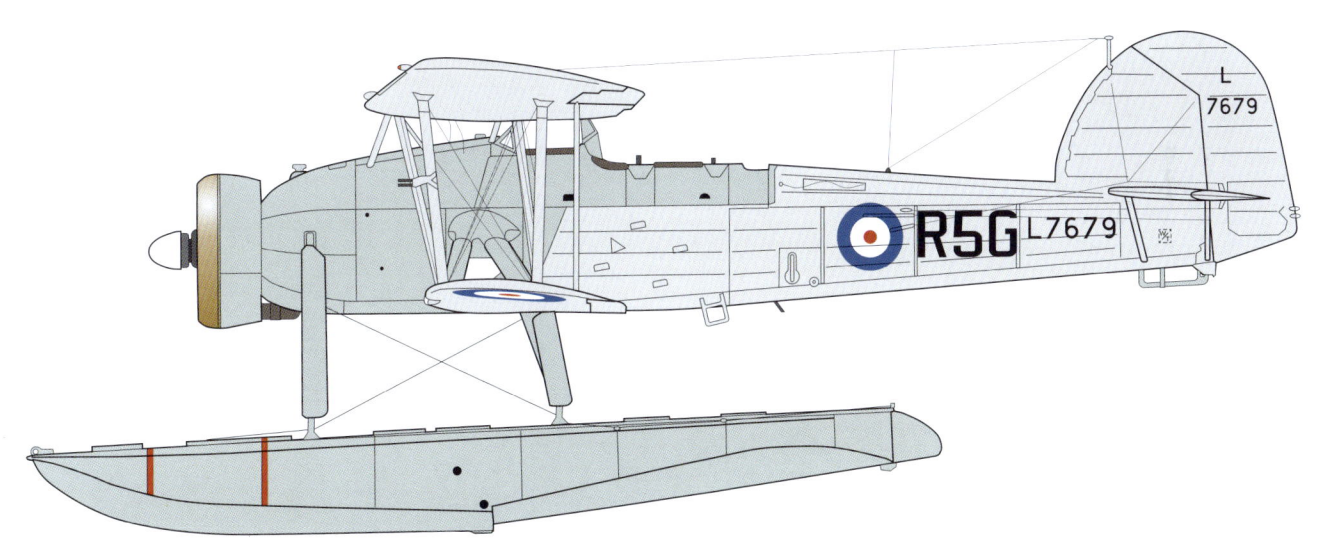

Fairey Swordfish Mk I, L7679, 'R5G', of 771 NAS, a second line squadron, based at RNAS Portland, Dorset, summer 1939
A Fairey-built machine from the fifth production batch, probably built from the outset in floatplane configuration, L7679 was finished in the Aluminium/Cerrux Grey scheme with roundels in the standard six positions and black 8 inch and 6 inch high serial numbers on the rear fuselage and rudder. The 'R' prefix in the Letter-Numeral-Letter system, in this case identified a second line/training Fleet Requirements unit. Spinner cap was either natural metal or white.

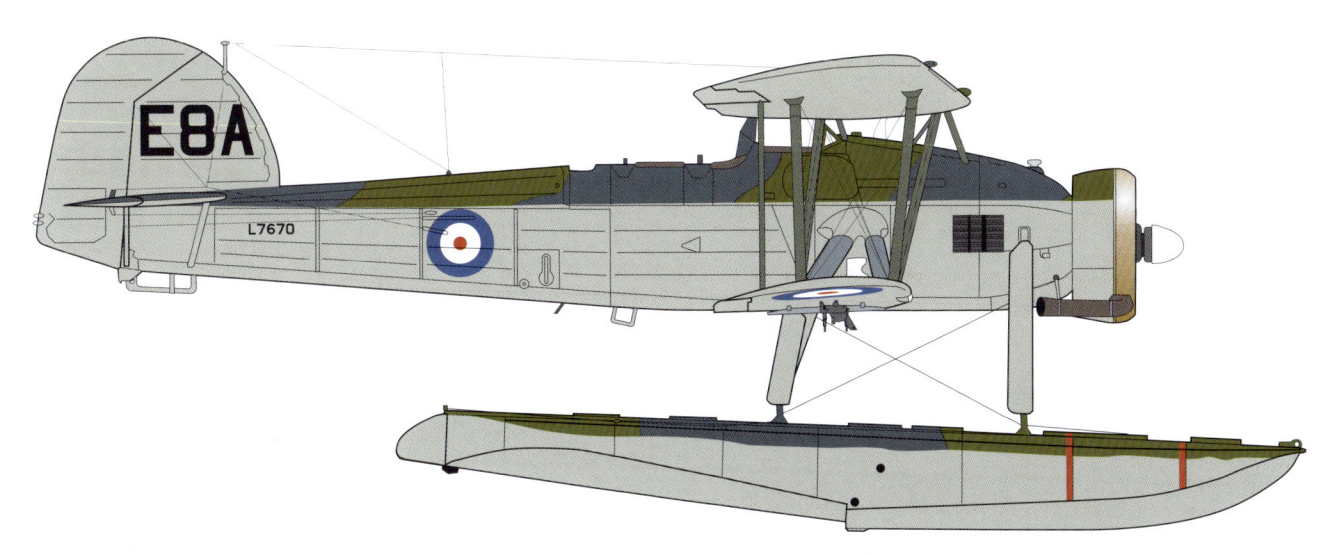

Fairey Swordfish Mk I, L7670, 'E8A', of 702 NAS, Catapult Flight, operating off the battleship HMS Rodney, late 1939
This is the same aircraft as that illustrated on p19. Originally delivered in the Aluminium/Cerrux Grey scheme, L7670 was repainted in-service in the S1E Scheme of Extra Dark Sea Grey/Dark Slate Grey and Dark Sea Grey/Light Slate Grey on the upper surfaces with Sky Grey under surfaces and fuselage sides (see p27). The new Letter-Numeral-Letter coding has been applied to the fin, and although the prefix letter is 'E', (ostensibly for HMS Eagle), the middle 'Aircraft Class' numeral, '8', is the designation for aircraft with convertible undercarriage assigned to catapult ships. Pre-war, bright shade, Red/White/Blue roundels were still carried in the standard six positions but the serial number has been reduced in size, to 4 inches high, and restricted to the rear fuselage only. Spinner cap was either natural metal or white.

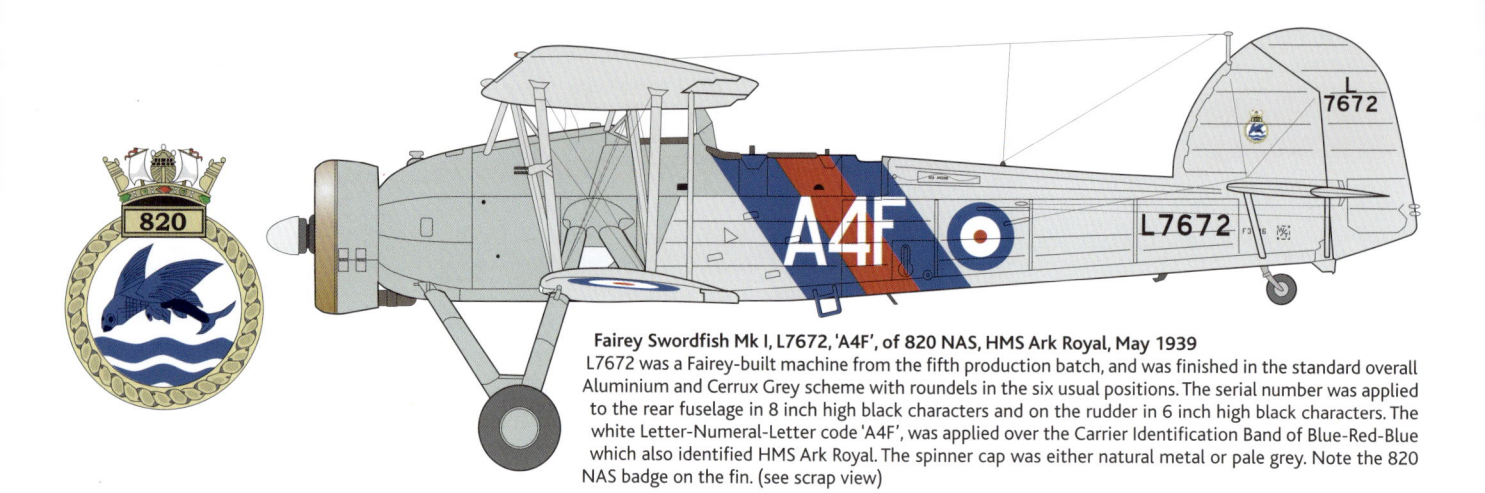

Fairey Swordfish Mk I, L7672, 'A4F', of 820 NAS, HMS Ark Royal, May 1939
L7672 was a Fairey-built machine from the fifth production batch, and was finished in the standard overall Aluminium and Cerrux Grey scheme with roundels in the six usual positions. The serial number was applied to the rear fuselage in 8 inch high black characters and on the rudder in 6 inch high black characters. The white Letter-Numeral-Letter code 'A4F', was applied over the Carrier Identification Band of Blue-Red-Blue which also identified HMS Ark Royal. The spinner cap was either natural metal or pale grey. Note the 820 NAS badge on the fin. (see scrap view)

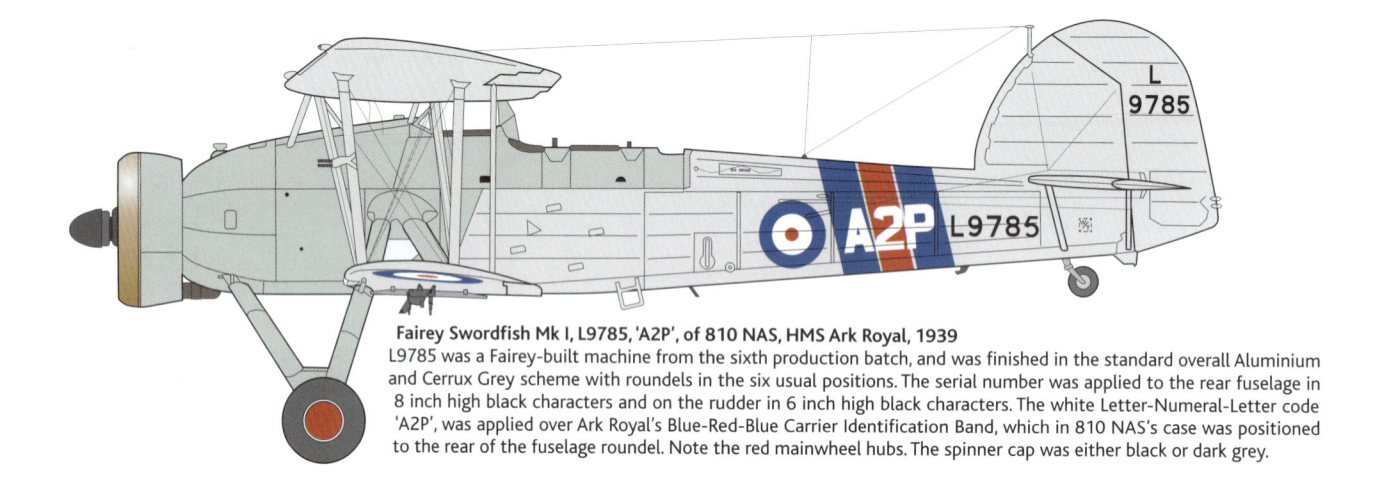

Fairey Swordfish Mk I, L9785, 'A2P', of 810 NAS, HMS Ark Royal, 1939
L9785 was a Fairey-built machine from the sixth production batch, and was finished in the standard overall Aluminium and Cerrux Grey scheme with roundels in the six usual positions. The serial number was applied to the rear fuselage in 8 inch high black characters and on the rudder in 6 inch high black characters. The white Letter-Numeral-Letter code 'A2P', was applied over Ark Royal's Blue-Red-Blue Carrier Identification Band, which in 810 NAS's case was positioned to the rear of the fuselage roundel. Note the red mainwheel hubs. The spinner cap was either black or dark grey.

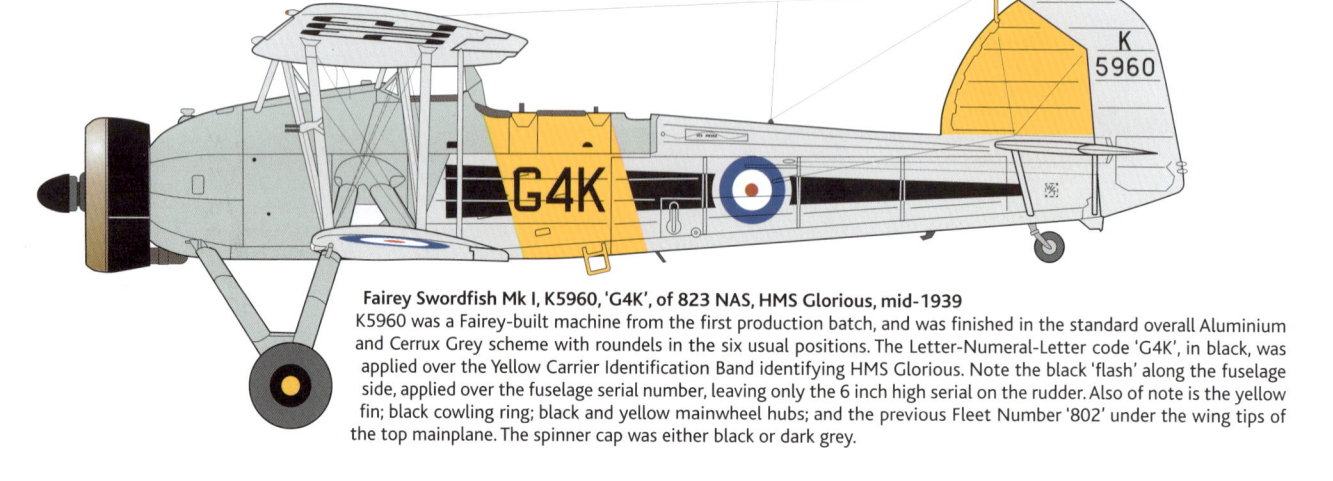

Fairey Swordfish Mk I, K5960, 'G4K', of 823 NAS, HMS Glorious, mid-1939
K5960 was a Fairey-built machine from the first production batch, and was finished in the standard overall Aluminium and Cerrux Grey scheme with roundels in the six usual positions. The Letter-Numeral-Letter code 'G4K', in black, was applied over the Yellow Carrier Identification Band identifying HMS Glorious. Note the black 'flash' along the fuselage side, applied over the fuselage serial number, leaving only the 6 inch high serial on the rudder. Also of note is the yellow fin; black cowling ring; black and yellow mainwheel hubs; and the previous Fleet Number '802' under the wing tips of the top mainplane. The spinner cap was either black or dark grey.

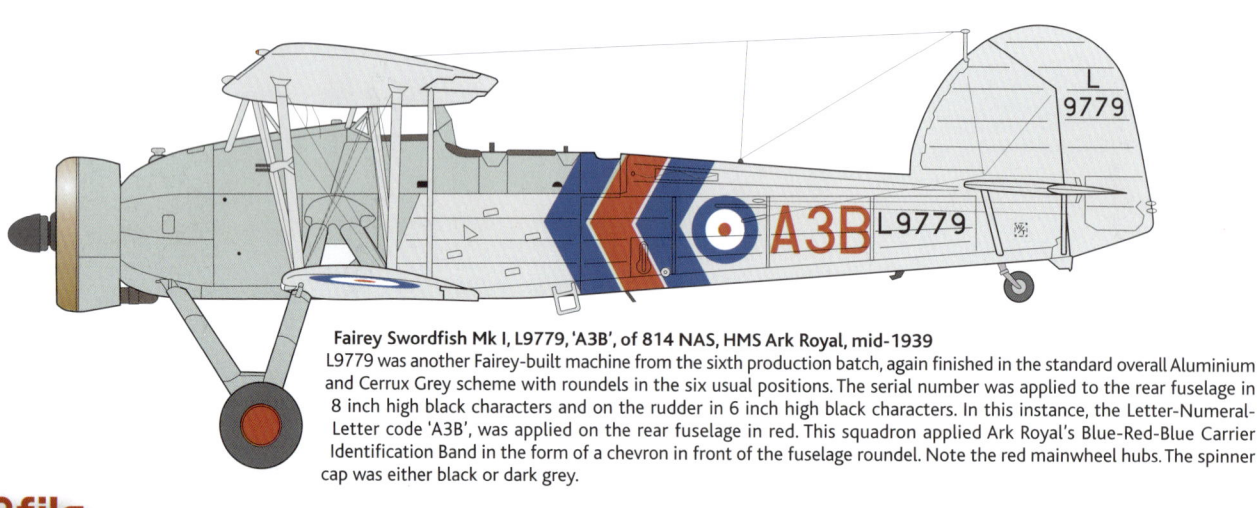

Fairey Swordfish Mk I, L9779, 'A3B', of 814 NAS, HMS Ark Royal, mid-1939
L9779 was another Fairey-built machine from the sixth production batch, again finished in the standard overall Aluminium and Cerrux Grey scheme with roundels in the six usual positions. The serial number was applied to the rear fuselage in 8 inch high black characters and on the rudder in 6 inch high black characters. In this instance, the Letter-Numeral-Letter code 'A3B', was applied on the rear fuselage in red. This squadron applied Ark Royal's Blue-Red-Blue Carrier Identification Band in the form of a chevron in front of the fuselage roundel. Note the red mainwheel hubs. The spinner cap was either black or dark grey.

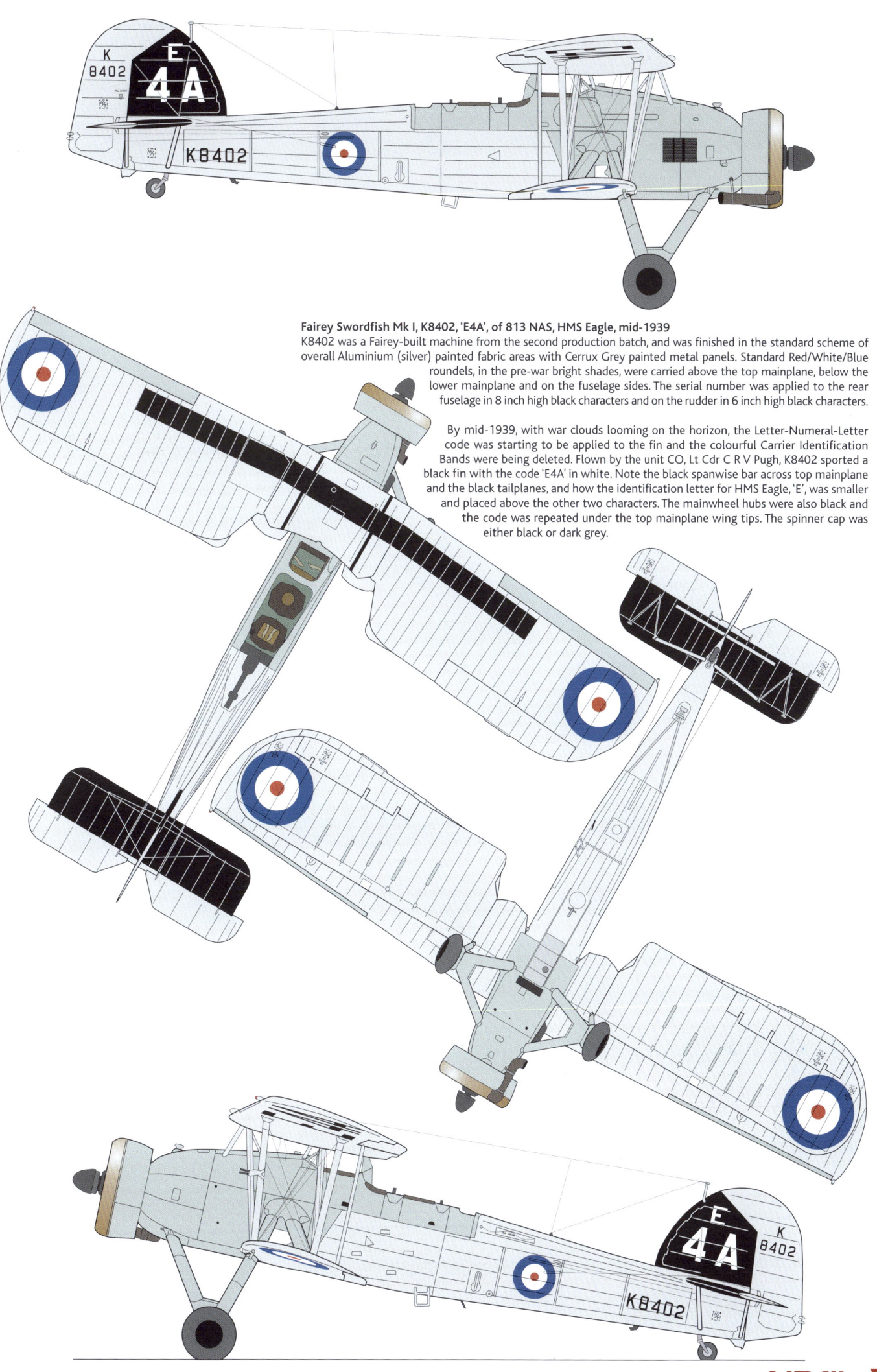

Fairey Swordfish Mk I, K8402, 'E4A', of 813 NAS, HMS Eagle, mid-1939

K8402 was a Fairey-built machine from the second production batch, and was finished in the standard scheme of overall Aluminium (silver) painted fabric areas with Cerrux Grey painted metal panels. Standard Red/White/Blue roundels, in the pre-war bright shades, were carried above the top mainplane, below the lower mainplane and on the fuselage sides. The serial number was applied to the rear fuselage in 8 inch high black characters and on the rudder in 6 inch high black characters.

By mid-1939, with war clouds looming on the horizon, the Letter-Numeral-Letter code was starting to be applied to the fin and the colourful Carrier Identification Bands were being deleted. Flown by the unit CO, Lt Cdr C R V Pugh, K8402 sported a black fin with the code 'E4A' in white. Note the black spanwise bar across top mainplane and the black tailplanes, and how the identification letter for HMS Eagle, 'E', was smaller and placed above the other two characters. The mainwheel hubs were also black and the code was repeated under the top mainplane wing tips. The spinner cap was either black or dark grey.

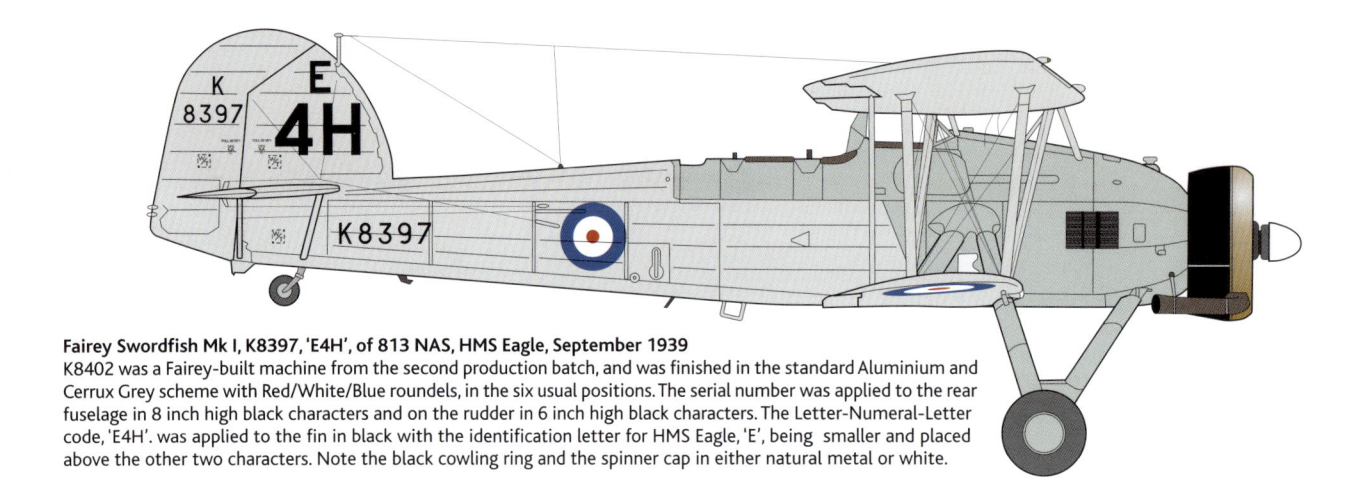

Fairey Swordfish Mk I, K8397, 'E4H', of 813 NAS, HMS Eagle, September 1939
K8402 was a Fairey-built machine from the second production batch, and was finished in the standard Aluminium and Cerrux Grey scheme with Red/White/Blue roundels, in the six usual positions. The serial number was applied to the rear fuselage in 8 inch high black characters and on the rudder in 6 inch high black characters. The Letter-Numeral-Letter code, 'E4H'. was applied to the fin in black with the identification letter for HMS Eagle, 'E', being smaller and placed above the other two characters. Note the black cowling ring and the spinner cap in either natural metal or white.

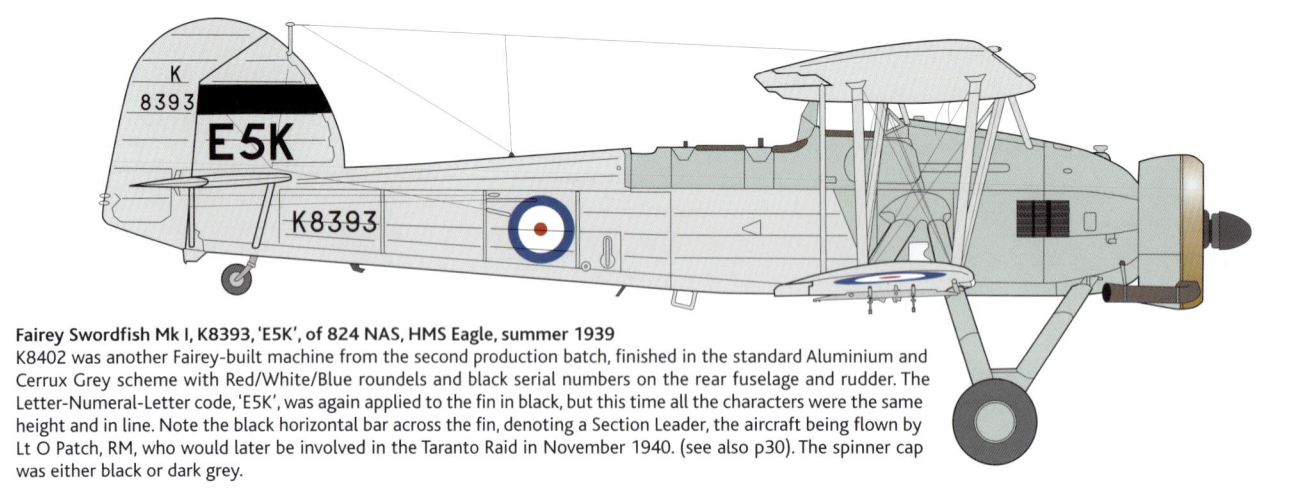

Fairey Swordfish Mk I, K8393, 'E5K', of 824 NAS, HMS Eagle, summer 1939
K8402 was another Fairey-built machine from the second production batch, finished in the standard Aluminium and Cerrux Grey scheme with Red/White/Blue roundels and black serial numbers on the rear fuselage and rudder. The Letter-Numeral-Letter code, 'E5K', was again applied to the fin in black, but this time all the characters were the same height and in line. Note the black horizontal bar across the fin, denoting a Section Leader, the aircraft being flown by Lt O Patch, RM, who would later be involved in the Taranto Raid in November 1940. (see also p30). The spinner cap was either black or dark grey.

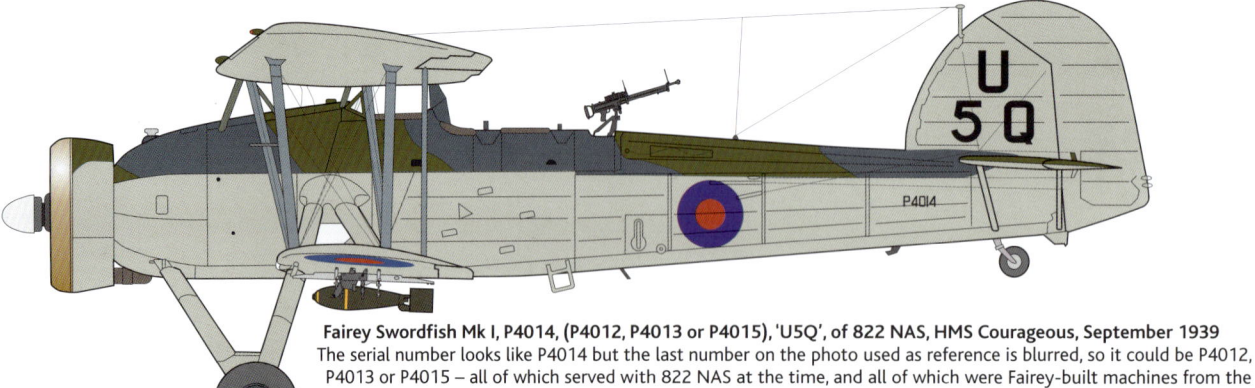

Fairey Swordfish Mk I, P4014, (P4012, P4013 or P4015), 'U5Q', of 822 NAS, HMS Courageous, September 1939
The serial number looks like P4014 but the last number on the photo used as reference is blurred, so it could be P4012, P4013 or P4015 – all of which served with 822 NAS at the time, and all of which were Fairey-built machines from the last production batch completed by the parent company. As with the previous K and L-serial batches, the first of the P-serial aircraft (possibly up to P4061) were still being finished in the Aluminium and Cerrux Grey scheme on delivery and then camouflaged 'in service' by the Fleet Air Arm, in the S1E scheme of Extra Dark Sea Grey/Dark Slate Grey and Dark Sea Grey/Light Slate Grey on the upper surfaces with Sky Grey under surfaces and fuselage sides. The roundels had also been modified in to the Red/Blue style, and the serial number reduced in size to 4 inches high, and restricted to the rear fuselage. The Letter-Numeral-Letter code was applied to the fin in black, with the carrier letter 'U' (for HMS Furious) positioned above the other two characters. No 822 NAS had recently been transferred from HMS Furious to HMS Courageous, which was torpedoed by U-29 on 17 September 1939, with the loss of 518 crewmen and all of the Swordfish from 811 and 822 NASs.

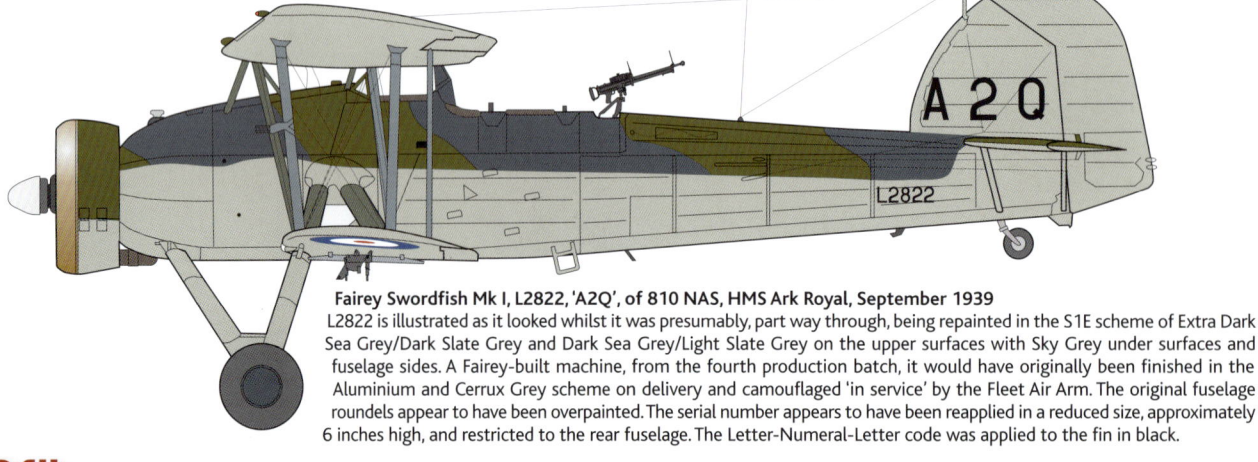

Fairey Swordfish Mk I, L2822, 'A2Q', of 810 NAS, HMS Ark Royal, September 1939
L2822 is illustrated as it looked whilst it was presumably, part way through, being repainted in the S1E scheme of Extra Dark Sea Grey/Dark Slate Grey and Dark Sea Grey/Light Slate Grey on the upper surfaces with Sky Grey under surfaces and fuselage sides. A Fairey-built machine, from the fourth production batch, it would have originally been finished in the Aluminium and Cerrux Grey scheme on delivery and camouflaged 'in service' by the Fleet Air Arm. The original fuselage roundels appear to have been overpainted. The serial number appears to have been reapplied in a reduced size, approximately 6 inches high, and restricted to the rear fuselage. The Letter-Numeral-Letter code was applied to the fin in black.

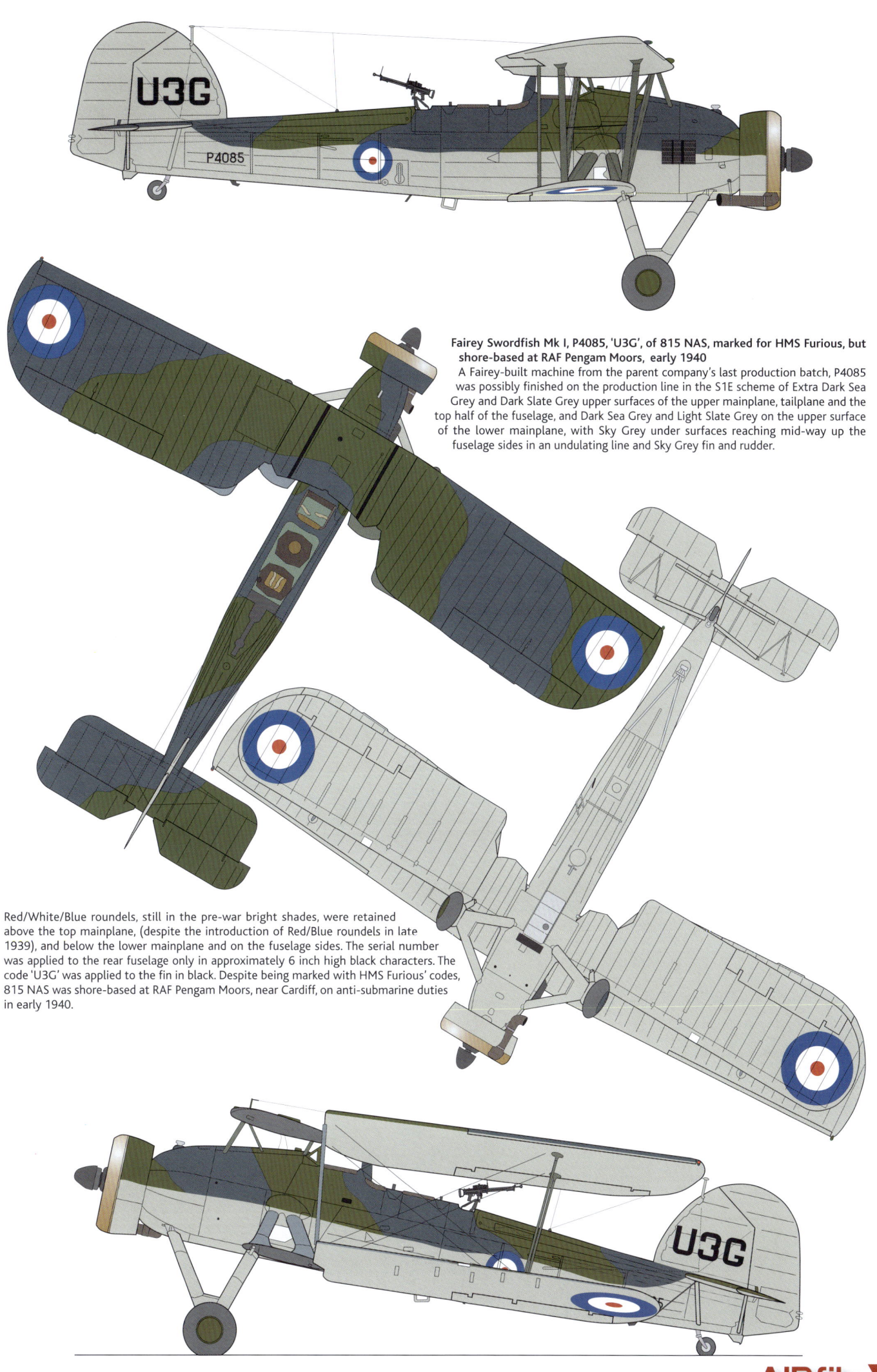

Fairey Swordfish Mk I, P4085, 'U3G', of 815 NAS, marked for HMS Furious, but shore-based at RAF Pengam Moors, early 1940

A Fairey-built machine from the parent company's last production batch, P4085 was possibly finished on the production line in the S1E scheme of Extra Dark Sea Grey and Dark Slate Grey upper surfaces of the upper mainplane, tailplane and the top half of the fuselage, and Dark Sea Grey and Light Slate Grey on the upper surface of the lower mainplane, with Sky Grey under surfaces reaching mid-way up the fuselage sides in an undulating line and Sky Grey fin and rudder.

Red/White/Blue roundels, still in the pre-war bright shades, were retained above the top mainplane, (despite the introduction of Red/Blue roundels in late 1939), and below the lower mainplane and on the fuselage sides. The serial number was applied to the rear fuselage only in approximately 6 inch high black characters. The code 'U3G' was applied to the fin in black. Despite being marked with HMS Furious' codes, 815 NAS was shore-based at RAF Pengam Moors, near Cardiff, on anti-submarine duties in early 1940.

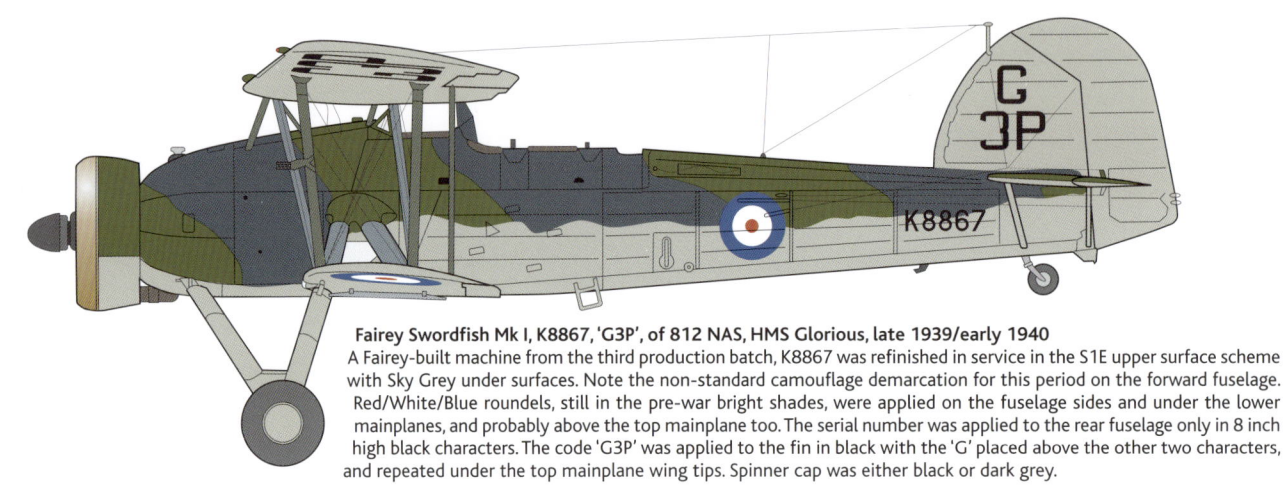

Fairey Swordfish Mk I, K8867, 'G3P', of 812 NAS, HMS Glorious, late 1939/early 1940
A Fairey-built machine from the third production batch, K8867 was refinished in service in the S1E upper surface scheme with Sky Grey under surfaces. Note the non-standard camouflage demarcation for this period on the forward fuselage. Red/White/Blue roundels, still in the pre-war bright shades, were applied on the fuselage sides and under the lower mainplanes, and probably above the top mainplane too. The serial number was applied to the rear fuselage only in 8 inch high black characters. The code 'G3P' was applied to the fin in black with the 'G' placed above the other two characters, and repeated under the top mainplane wing tips. Spinner cap was either black or dark grey.

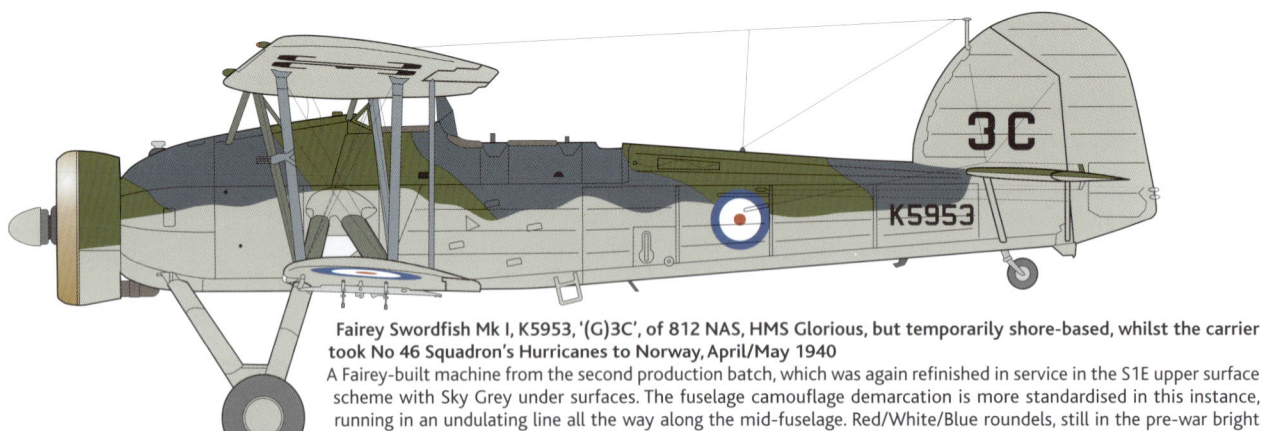

Fairey Swordfish Mk I, K5953, '(G)3C', of 812 NAS, HMS Glorious, but temporarily shore-based, whilst the carrier took No 46 Squadron's Hurricanes to Norway, April/May 1940
A Fairey-built machine from the second production batch, which was again refinished in service in the S1E upper surface scheme with Sky Grey under surfaces. The fuselage camouflage demarcation is more standardised in this instance, running in an undulating line all the way along the mid-fuselage. Red/White/Blue roundels, still in the pre-war bright shades, were retained in on the fuselage sides and under the lower mainplanes, but those above the top mainplanes may have been Red/Blue. The serial number was applied to the rear fuselage only in 8 inch high black characters. The identification code letter 'G' (for HMS Glorious) has either not been applied or overpainted, with just the Aircraft Class numeral and individual aircraft letter (ie 3C) applied to the fin in black, and repeated under the top mainplane wing tips. Spinner cap appears to be Sky Grey.

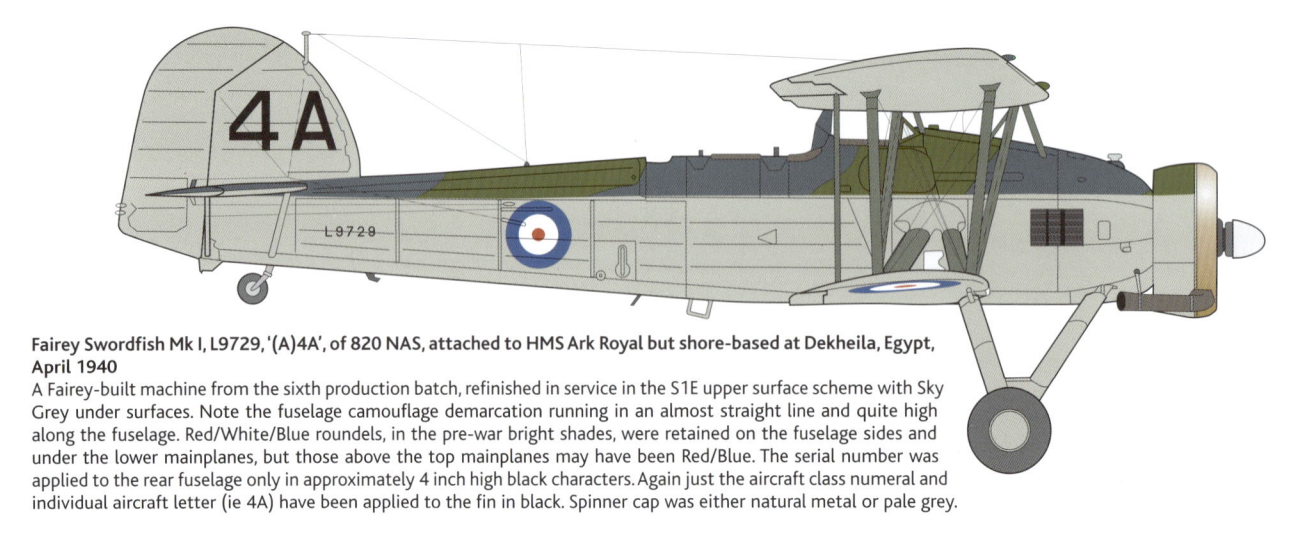

Fairey Swordfish Mk I, L9729, '(A)4A', of 820 NAS, attached to HMS Ark Royal but shore-based at Dekheila, Egypt, April 1940
A Fairey-built machine from the sixth production batch, refinished in service in the S1E upper surface scheme with Sky Grey under surfaces. Note the fuselage camouflage demarcation running in an almost straight line and quite high along the fuselage. Red/White/Blue roundels, in the pre-war bright shades, were retained on the fuselage sides and under the lower mainplanes, but those above the top mainplanes may have been Red/Blue. The serial number was applied to the rear fuselage only in approximately 4 inch high black characters. Again just the aircraft class numeral and individual aircraft letter (ie 4A) have been applied to the fin in black. Spinner cap was either natural metal or pale grey.

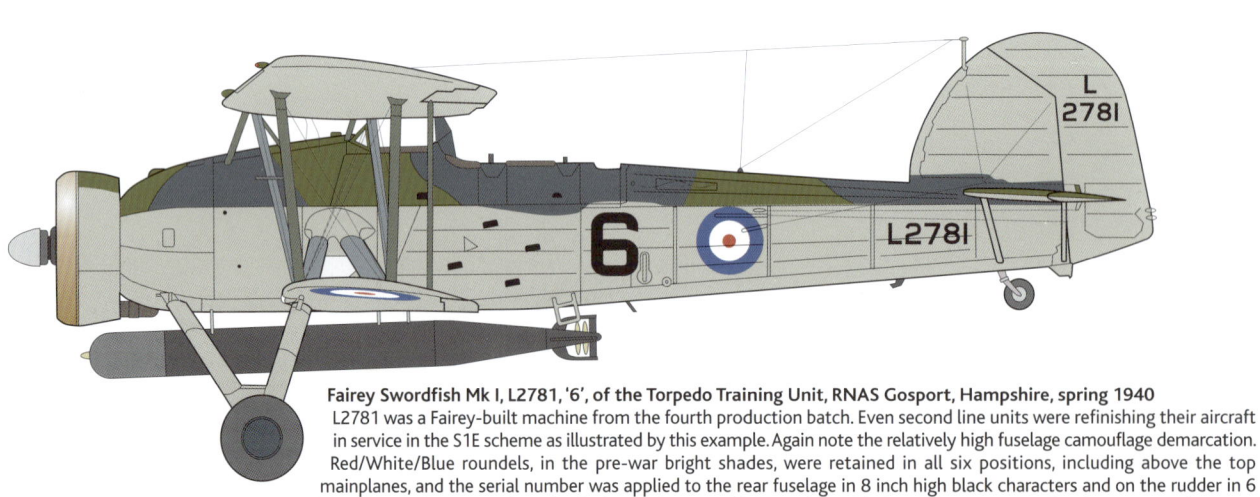

Fairey Swordfish Mk I, L2781, '6', of the Torpedo Training Unit, RNAS Gosport, Hampshire, spring 1940
L2781 was a Fairey-built aircraft from the fourth production batch. Even second line units were refinishing their aircraft in service in the S1E scheme as illustrated by this example. Again note the relatively high fuselage camouflage demarcation. Red/White/Blue roundels, in the pre-war bright shades, were retained in all six positions, including above the top mainplanes, and the serial number was applied to the rear fuselage in 8 inch high black characters and on the rudder in 6 inch high black characters. The individual aircraft numeral '6' was also in black. Spinner appears to be Sky Grey or pale grey.

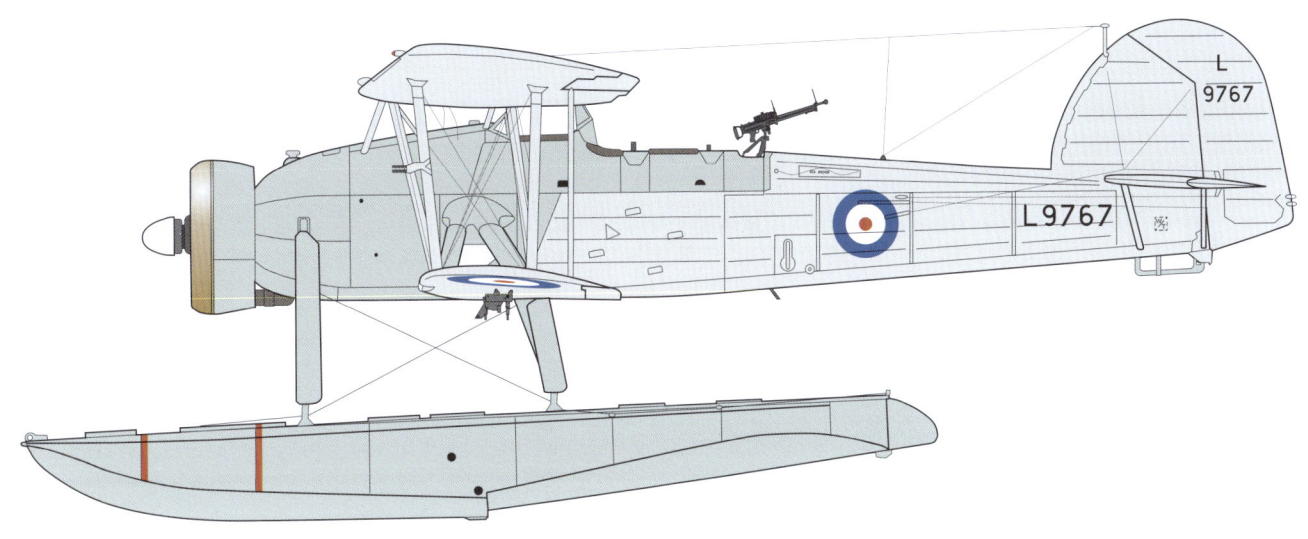

Fairey Swordfish Mk I, L9767, of 701 Ship's Flight, operating off the battleship HMS Warspite, April 1940
A Fairey-built machine from the sixth production batch, and subsequently modified into floatplane configuration for use aboard Royal Navy battleships, L9767 was still finished in the Aluminium/Cerrux Grey scheme with Red/White/Blue roundels in the standard six positions, when it was involved in the Second Battle of Narvik on 13 April 1940. Apart from directing the battleship's gunfire, L9767 also bombed and sank U-64, which was at anchor in the Herjangsfjord. This was the first submarine to be sunk by an aircraft in World War Two. The pilot was Petty Officer F G Rice, the observer Lt Cdr W L M Brown, and the TAG, Leading Airman M G Pacey. The serial number was applied in pre-war fashion to the rear fuselage in 8 inch high black characters and on the rudder in 6 inch high black characters. No other markings appear to have been carried. The spinner cap was either natural metal or white.

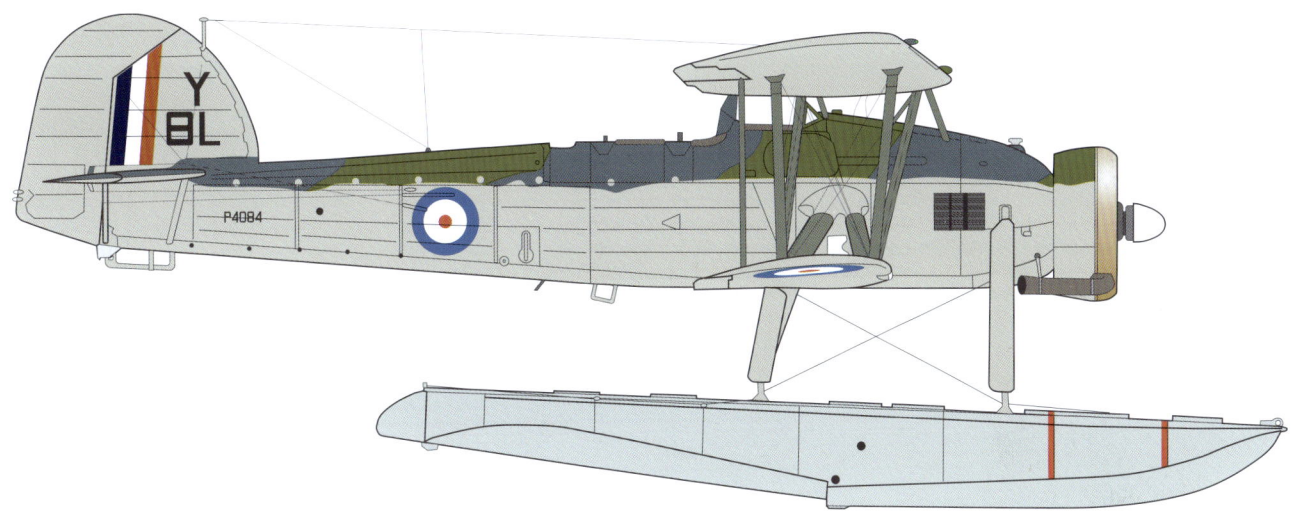

Fairey Swordfish Mk I, P4084, 'Y8L', of 765 NAS, based at RNAS Sandbanks, Poole, Dorset, summer 1940
A machine from the seventh and last production batch produced by the parent company, P4084 may have been built from the outset in floatplane configuration. Although it was probably produced in the S1E upper surface scheme with Sky Grey under surfaces, note that it was still fitted with Cerrux Grey painted floats. Red/White/Blue roundels, still in the pre-war bright shades, were retained on the fuselage sides and under the lower mainplanes, but the roundels above the top mainplane would almost certainly have been the Red/Blue (National Marking i) style, in the darker wartime shades, as was the Red/White/Blue fin flash, angled along the line of the rudder hinge. The serial number was applied to the rear fuselage only, in 4 inch high black characters, and the code 'Y8L' was applied to the fin in black with the 'Y' (identifying a torpedo training function) placed above the other two characters. Spinner cap was either natural metal or white.

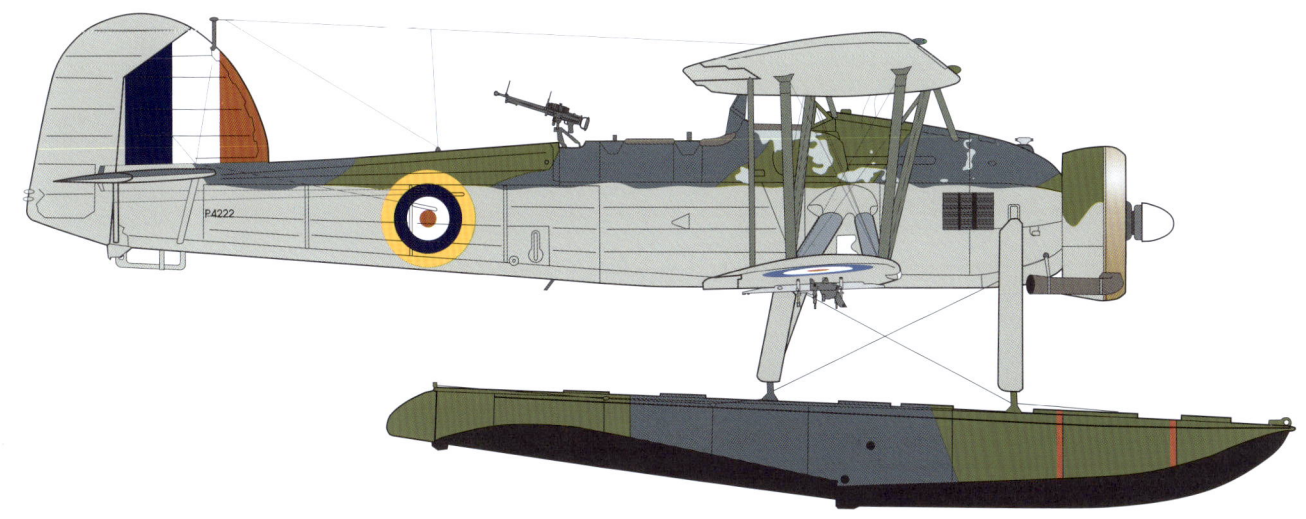

Fairey Swordfish Mk I, P4222, of 700 NAS, Ship's Flight, operating off the battlecruiser HMS Repulse, summer 1940
Another machine from the seventh and last production batch produced by the parent company, P4222 may also have been built from the outset in floatplane configuration. It would almost certainly have been finished in the S1E upper surface scheme with Sky Grey under surfaces, too, with Night (black) paint on their undersides. Red/Blue oundels were carried above the top mainplane with Red/White/Blue/Yellow roundels on the fuselage sides, in the wartime dull shades, as were the Red/White/Blue stripes covering the entire fin area. The Red/White/Blue underwing roundels appear to still be in the pre-war bright shades. The serial number was applied to the rear fuselage only, in approximately 2 inch high black characters. Spinner cap was either natural metal or white. Note the weathering around the cockpit area.

Fairey Swordfish Mk I, P4221, '5L' of 819 NAS, shore-based at RAF Detling, Kent, where it was engaged in anti-U-Boat patrols off the Belgian coast, May 1940
A machine from the seventh and last production batch produced by the parent company, P4221 was almost certainly finished on the production line in the S1E upper surface scheme with Sky Grey under surfaces, with an unevenly undulating fuselage camouflage demarcation. Red/Blue roundels were carried above the top mainplane with Red/White/Blue/Yellow roundels on the fuselage sides, in the wartime darker shades, as was the Red/White/Blue fin flash. Red/White/Blue roundels were carried under the lower mainplanes and the serial number was applied to the rear fuselage only, in approximately 4 inch high black characters. Just the Aircraft Class numeral '5' and individual aircraft letter 'L' have been applied to the fin in black. Spinner cap was either natural metal or pale grey.

Fairey Swordfish Mk I, K8418, '(E)5K' of 824 NAS, HMS Eagle, mid-1940
A Fairey-built machine from the second production batch which had been refinished in service in the S1E upper surface scheme with Sky Grey under surfaces, featuring another unevenly undulating fuselage camouflage demarcation. Red/Blue roundels were carried above the top mainplane with Red/White/Blue/Yellow roundels on the fuselage sides, in the wartime darker shades, as was the Red/White/Blue fin flash. Red/White/Blue roundels were carried under the lower mainplanes and the serial number was applied to the rear fuselage only, in approximately 4 inch high black characters. Just the Aircraft Class numeral '5' and the individual aircraft letter 'K' were applied to the fin, in black, with two black horizontal bars above, denoting the senior pilot in the squadron, Lt O Patch, RM, who would later be involved in the Taranto Raid in November 1940. (see also K8393 p26 and Chapter 3). Spinner cap was either black or dark grey.

Fairey Swordfish Mk I, L2750, of 825 NAS, based at RNAS Worthy Down, Hampshire, summer 1940
A Fairey-built machine from the fourth production batch which had been refinished in service in the S1E upper surface scheme with Sky Grey under surfaces, with a less unevenly undulating fuselage camouflage demarcation. Red/Blue roundels were carried above the top mainplane with Red/White/Blue/Yellow roundels on the fuselage sides and Red/White/Blue roundels under the lower mainplanes, with Red/White/Blue stripes covering the whole of the fin area – the Red and the Blue areas all in the pre-war bright shades. The serial number was applied to the rear fuselage only, in approximately 4 inch high black characters. No other markings appear to have been carried other than red painted tyre walls. Spinner cap was either natural metal or pale grey.

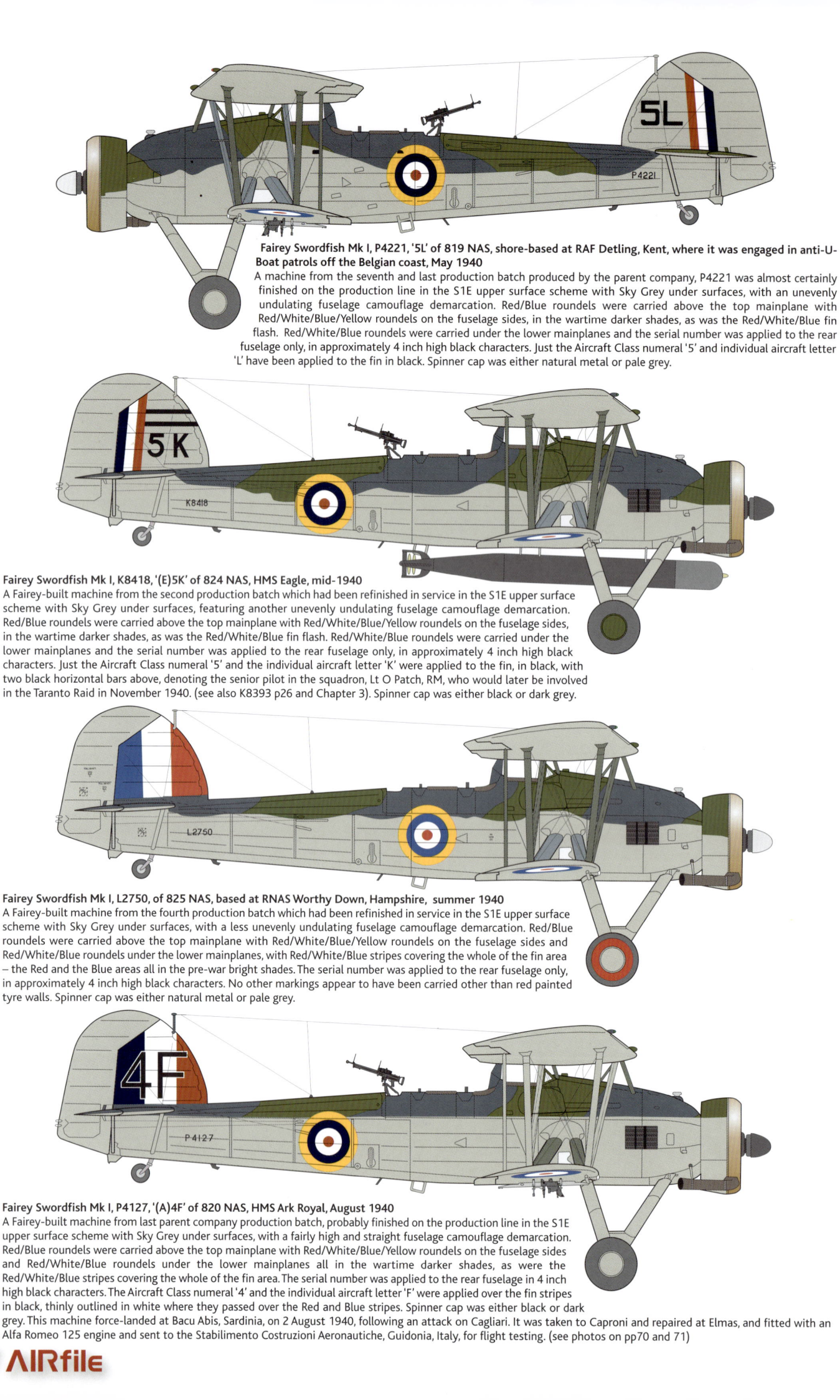

Fairey Swordfish Mk I, P4127, '(A)4F' of 820 NAS, HMS Ark Royal, August 1940
A Fairey-built machine from last parent company production batch, probably finished on the production line in the S1E upper surface scheme with Sky Grey under surfaces, with a fairly high and straight fuselage camouflage demarcation. Red/Blue roundels were carried above the top mainplane with Red/White/Blue/Yellow roundels on the fuselage sides and Red/White/Blue roundels under the lower mainplanes all in the wartime darker shades, as were the Red/White/Blue stripes covering the whole of the fin area. The serial number was applied to the rear fuselage only in 4 inch high black characters. The Aircraft Class numeral '4' and the individual aircraft letter 'F' were applied over the fin stripes in black, thinly outlined in white where they passed over the Red and Blue stripes. Spinner cap was either black or dark grey. This machine force-landed at Bacu Abis, Sardinia, on 2 August 1940, following an attack on Cagliari. It was taken to Caproni and repaired at Elmas, and fitted with an Alfa Romeo 125 engine and sent to the Stabilimento Costruzioni Aeronautiche, Guidonia, Italy, for flight testing. (see photos on pp70 and 71)

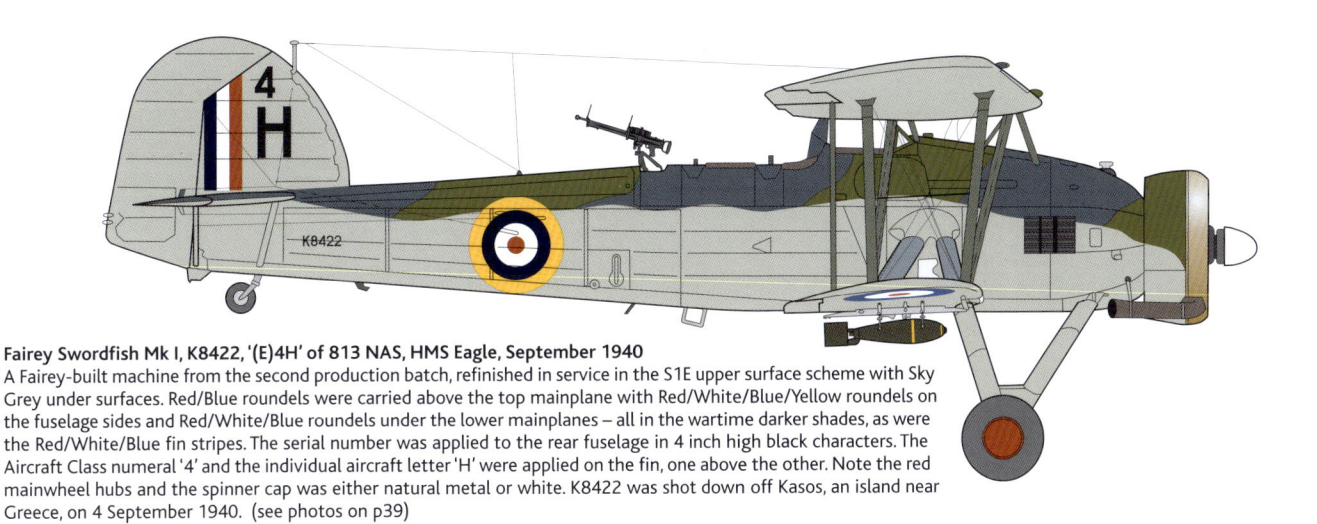

Fairey Swordfish Mk I, K8422, '(E)4H' of 813 NAS, HMS Eagle, September 1940
A Fairey-built machine from the second production batch, refinished in service in the S1E upper surface scheme with Sky Grey under surfaces. Red/Blue roundels were carried above the top mainplane with Red/White/Blue/Yellow roundels on the fuselage sides and Red/White/Blue roundels under the lower mainplanes – all in the wartime darker shades, as were the Red/White/Blue fin stripes. The serial number was applied to the rear fuselage in 4 inch high black characters. The Aircraft Class numeral '4' and the individual aircraft letter 'H' were applied on the fin, one above the other. Note the red mainwheel hubs and the spinner cap was either natural metal or white. K8422 was shot down off Kasos, an island near Greece, on 4 September 1940. (see photos on p39)

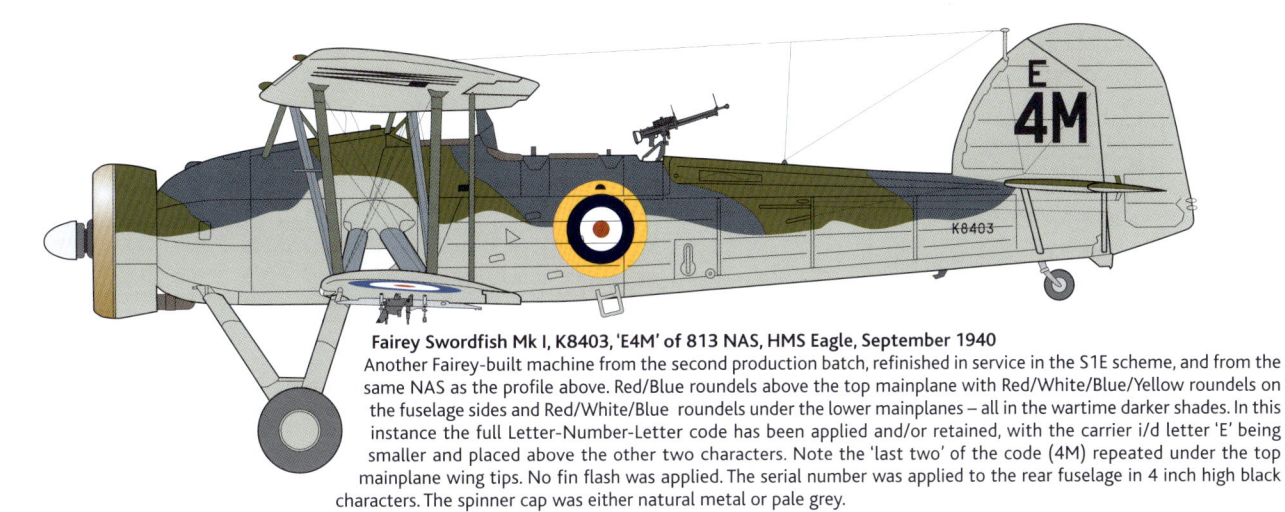

Fairey Swordfish Mk I, K8403, 'E4M' of 813 NAS, HMS Eagle, September 1940
Another Fairey-built machine from the second production batch, refinished in service in the S1E scheme, and from the same NAS as the profile above. Red/Blue roundels above the top mainplane with Red/White/Blue/Yellow roundels on the fuselage sides and Red/White/Blue roundels under the lower mainplanes – all in the wartime darker shades. In this instance the full Letter-Number-Letter code has been applied and/or retained, with the carrier i/d letter 'E' being smaller and placed above the other two characters. Note the 'last two' of the code (4M) repeated under the top mainplane wing tips. No fin flash was applied. The serial number was applied to the rear fuselage in 4 inch high black characters. The spinner cap was either natural metal or pale grey.

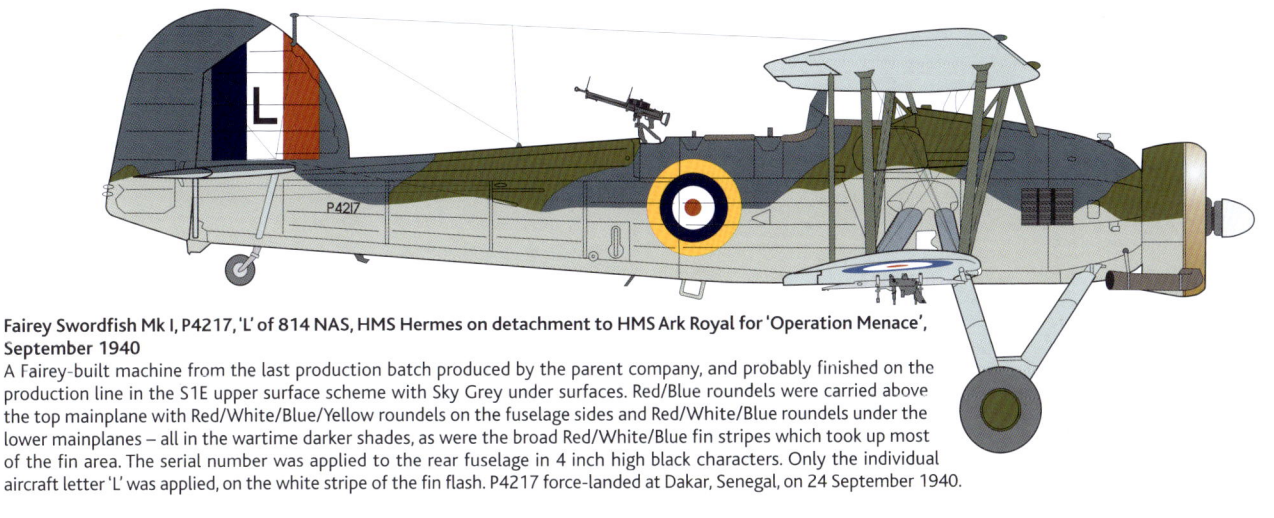

Fairey Swordfish Mk I, P4217, 'L' of 814 NAS, HMS Hermes on detachment to HMS Ark Royal for 'Operation Menace', September 1940
A Fairey-built machine from the last production batch produced by the parent company, and probably finished on the production line in the S1E upper surface scheme with Sky Grey under surfaces. Red/Blue roundels were carried above the top mainplane with Red/White/Blue/Yellow roundels on the fuselage sides and Red/White/Blue roundels under the lower mainplanes – all in the wartime darker shades, as were the broad Red/White/Blue fin stripes which took up most of the fin area. The serial number was applied to the rear fuselage in 4 inch high black characters. Only the individual aircraft letter 'L' was applied, on the white stripe of the fin flash. P4217 force-landed at Dakar, Senegal, on 24 September 1940.

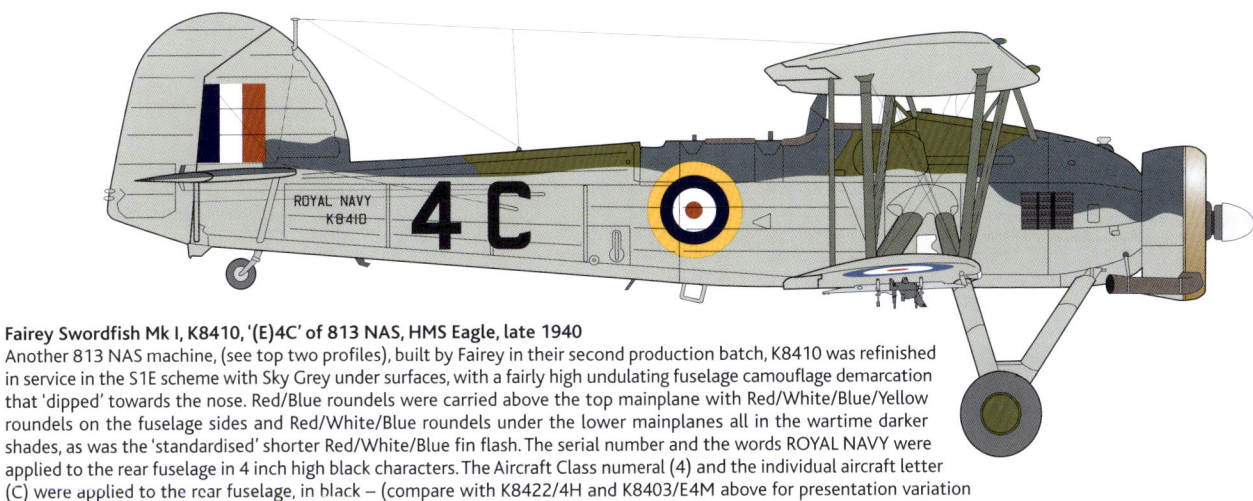

Fairey Swordfish Mk I, K8410, '(E)4C' of 813 NAS, HMS Eagle, late 1940
Another 813 NAS machine, (see top two profiles), built by Fairey in their second production batch, K8410 was refinished in service in the S1E scheme with Sky Grey under surfaces, with a fairly high undulating fuselage camouflage demarcation that 'dipped' towards the nose. Red/Blue roundels were carried above the top mainplane with Red/White/Blue/Yellow roundels on the fuselage sides and Red/White/Blue roundels under the lower mainplanes all in the wartime darker shades, as was the 'standardised' shorter Red/White/Blue fin flash. The serial number and the words ROYAL NAVY were applied to the rear fuselage in 4 inch high black characters. The Aircraft Class numeral (4) and the individual aircraft letter (C) were applied to the rear fuselage, in black – (compare with K8422/4H and K8403/E4M above for presentation variation within the same squadron). Spinner cap was natural metal or pale grey.

Original five-colour S1E Scheme
A Scheme

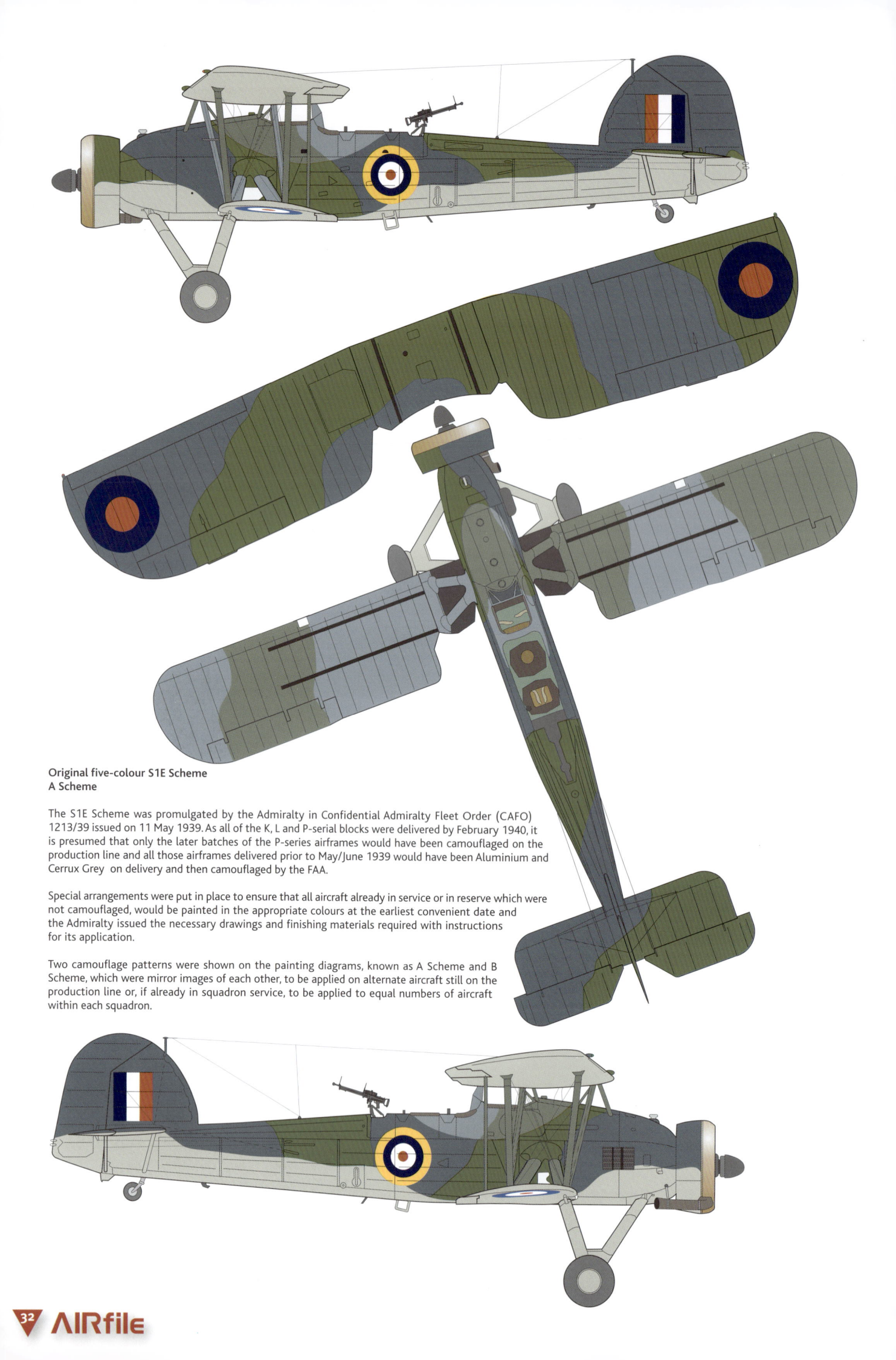

The S1E Scheme was promulgated by the Admiralty in Confidential Admiralty Fleet Order (CAFO) 1213/39 issued on 11 May 1939. As all of the K, L and P-serial blocks were delivered by February 1940, it is presumed that only the later batches of the P-series airframes would have been camouflaged on the production line and all those airframes delivered prior to May/June 1939 would have been Aluminium and Cerrux Grey on delivery and then camouflaged by the FAA.

Special arrangements were put in place to ensure that all aircraft already in service or in reserve which were not camouflaged, would be painted in the appropriate colours at the earliest convenient date and the Admiralty issued the necessary drawings and finishing materials required with instructions for its application.

Two camouflage patterns were shown on the painting diagrams, known as A Scheme and B Scheme, which were mirror images of each other, to be applied on alternate aircraft still on the production line or, if already in squadron service, to be applied to equal numbers of aircraft within each squadron.

Original five-colour S1E Scheme
B Scheme

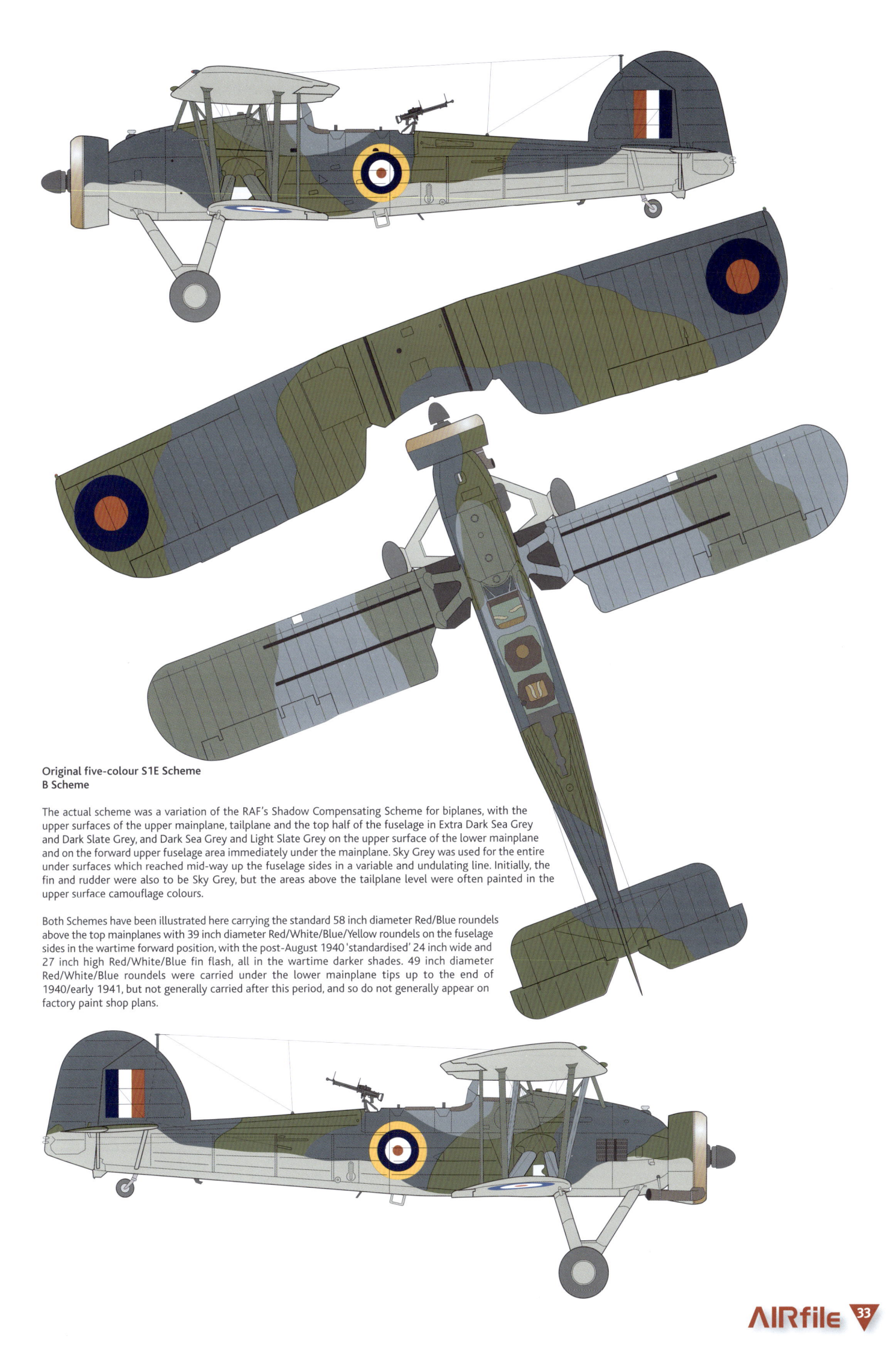

The actual scheme was a variation of the RAF's Shadow Compensating Scheme for biplanes, with the upper surfaces of the upper mainplane, tailplane and the top half of the fuselage in Extra Dark Sea Grey and Dark Slate Grey, and Dark Sea Grey and Light Slate Grey on the upper surface of the lower mainplane and on the forward upper fuselage area immediately under the mainplane. Sky Grey was used for the entire under surfaces which reached mid-way up the fuselage sides in a variable and undulating line. Initially, the fin and rudder were also to be Sky Grey, but the areas above the tailplane level were often painted in the upper surface camouflage colours.

Both Schemes have been illustrated here carrying the standard 58 inch diameter Red/Blue roundels above the top mainplanes with 39 inch diameter Red/White/Blue/Yellow roundels on the fuselage sides in the wartime forward position, with the post-August 1940 'standardised' 24 inch wide and 27 inch high Red/White/Blue fin flash, all in the wartime darker shades. 49 inch diameter Red/White/Blue roundels were carried under the lower mainplane tips up to the end of 1940/early 1941, but not generally carried after this period, and so do not generally appear on factory paint shop plans.

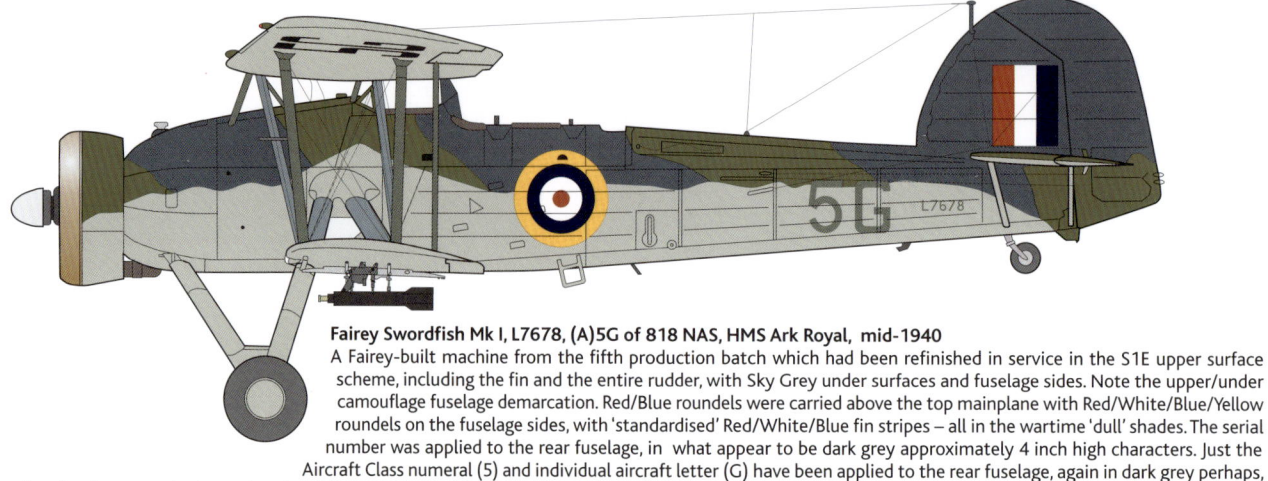

Fairey Swordfish Mk I, L7678, (A)5G of 818 NAS, HMS Ark Royal, mid-1940
A Fairey-built machine from the fifth production batch which had been refinished in service in the S1E upper surface scheme, including the fin and the entire rudder, with Sky Grey under surfaces and fuselage sides. Note the upper/under camouflage fuselage demarcation. Red/Blue roundels were carried above the top mainplane with Red/White/Blue/Yellow roundels on the fuselage sides, with 'standardised' Red/White/Blue fin stripes – all in the wartime 'dull' shades. The serial number was applied to the rear fuselage, in what appear to be dark grey approximately 4 inch high characters. Just the Aircraft Class numeral (5) and individual aircraft letter (G) have been applied to the rear fuselage, again in dark grey perhaps, and repeated under the top mainplane wing tips. Spinner cap was either natural metal or pale grey.

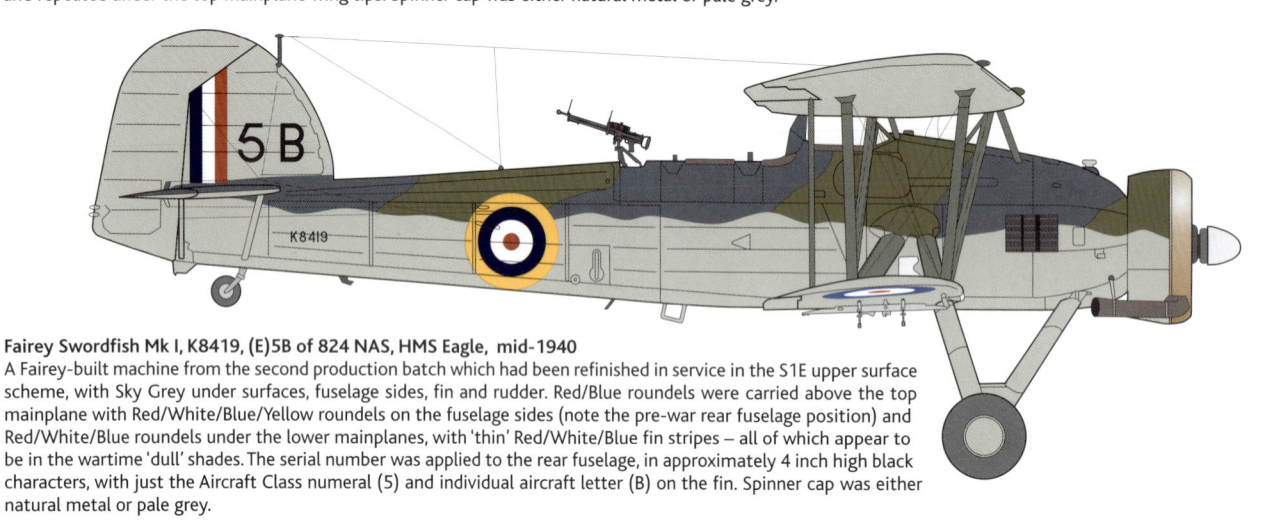

Fairey Swordfish Mk I, K8419, (E)5B of 824 NAS, HMS Eagle, mid-1940
A Fairey-built machine from the second production batch which had been refinished in service in the S1E upper surface scheme, with Sky Grey under surfaces, fuselage sides, fin and rudder. Red/Blue roundels were carried above the top mainplane with Red/White/Blue/Yellow roundels on the fuselage sides (note the pre-war rear fuselage position) and Red/White/Blue roundels under the lower mainplanes, with 'thin' Red/White/Blue fin stripes – all of which appear to be in the wartime 'dull' shades. The serial number was applied to the rear fuselage, in approximately 4 inch high black characters, with just the Aircraft Class numeral (5) and individual aircraft letter (B) on the fin. Spinner cap was either natural metal or pale grey.

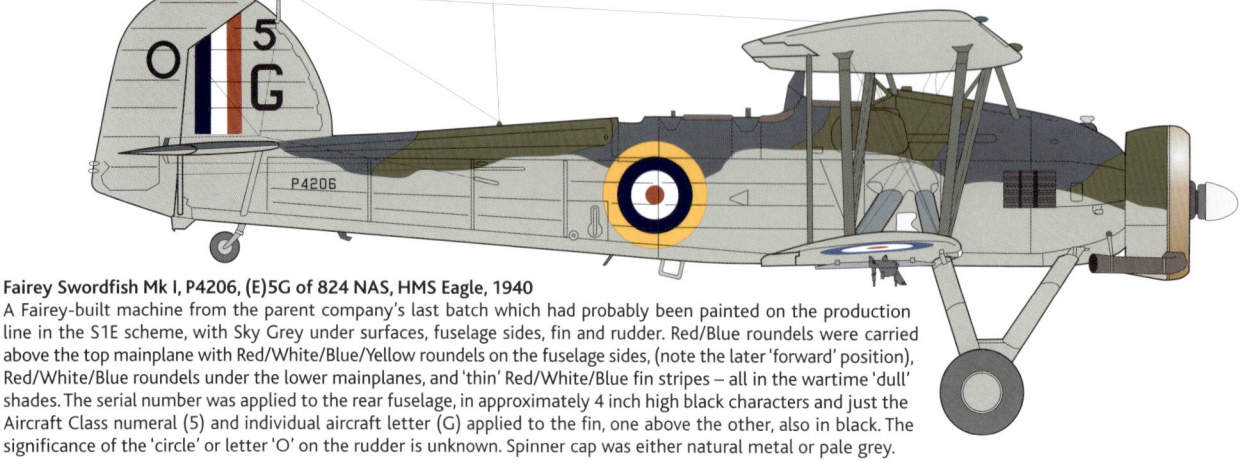

Fairey Swordfish Mk I, P4206, (E)5G of 824 NAS, HMS Eagle, 1940
A Fairey-built machine from the parent company's last batch which had probably been painted on the production line in the S1E scheme, with Sky Grey under surfaces, fuselage sides, fin and rudder. Red/Blue roundels were carried above the top mainplane with Red/White/Blue/Yellow roundels on the fuselage sides, (note the later 'forward' position), Red/White/Blue roundels under the lower mainplanes, and 'thin' Red/White/Blue fin stripes – all in the wartime 'dull' shades. The serial number was applied to the rear fuselage, in approximately 4 inch high black characters and just the Aircraft Class numeral (5) and individual aircraft letter (G) applied to the fin, one above the other, also in black. The significance of the 'circle' or letter 'O' on the rudder is unknown. Spinner cap was either natural metal or pale grey.

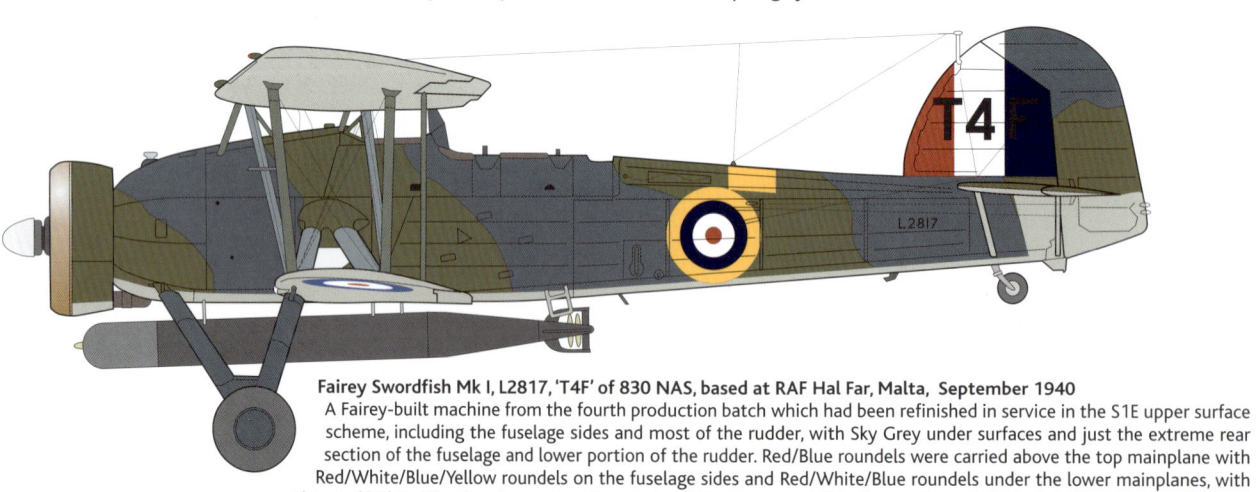

Fairey Swordfish Mk I, L2817, 'T4F' of 830 NAS, based at RAF Hal Far, Malta, September 1940
A Fairey-built machine from the fourth production batch which had been refinished in service in the S1E upper surface scheme, including the fuselage sides and most of the rudder, with Sky Grey under surfaces and just the extreme rear section of the fuselage and lower portion of the rudder. Red/Blue roundels were carried above the top mainplane with Red/White/Blue/Yellow roundels on the fuselage sides and Red/White/Blue roundels under the lower mainplanes, with the Red/White/Blue bands covering the whole of the fin area – all in the wartime 'dull' shades. The serial number was applied to the rear fuselage, in 8 inch high black characters, with the code 'T4F' positioned across the fin bands ('T' identified Deck Landing Training Aircraft). Note the yellow (?) area just above the fuselage roundel. Spinner cap was either natural metal or pale grey.

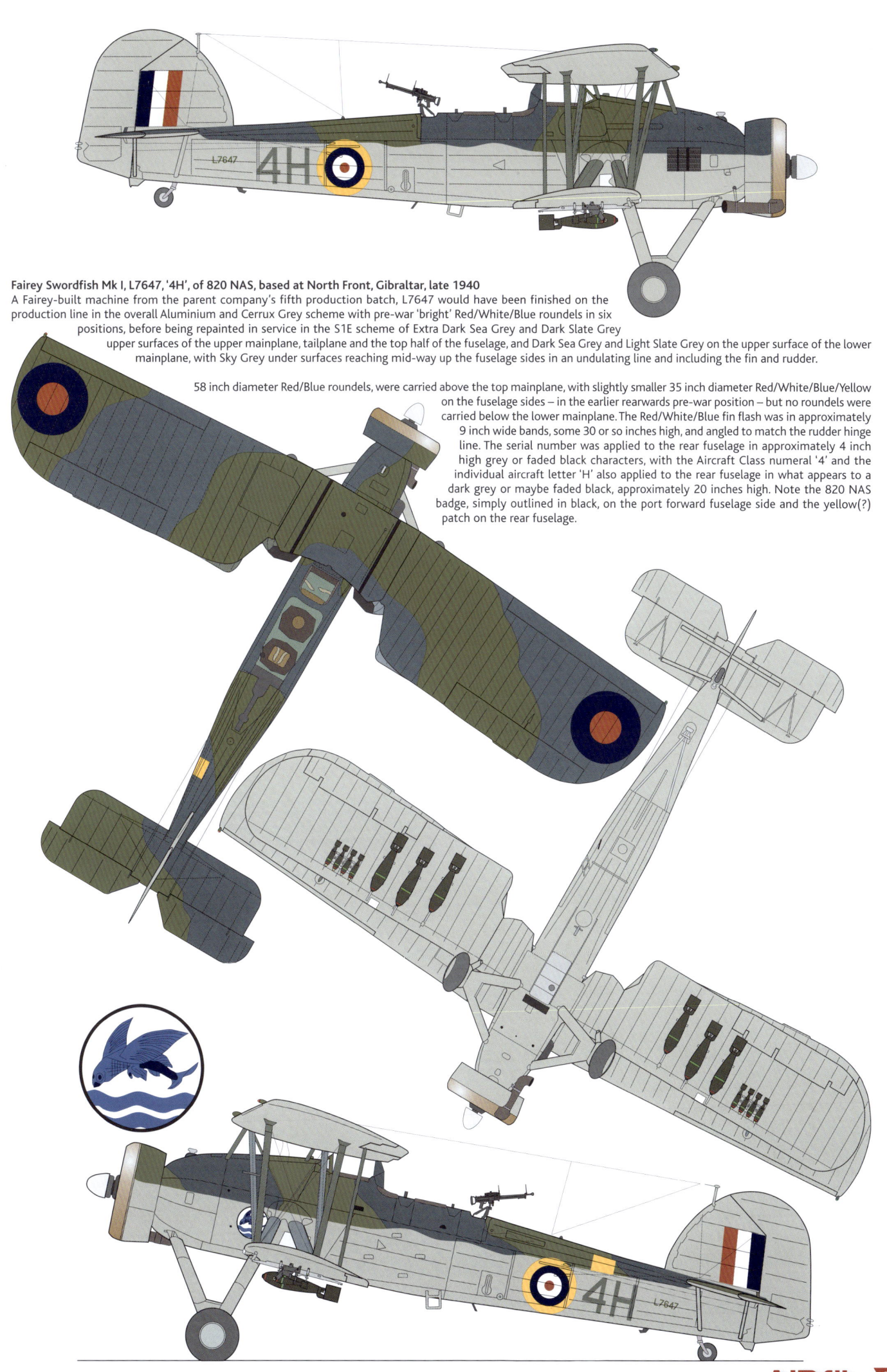

Fairey Swordfish Mk I, L7647, '4H', of 820 NAS, based at North Front, Gibraltar, late 1940
A Fairey-built machine from the parent company's fifth production batch, L7647 would have been finished on the production line in the overall Aluminium and Cerrux Grey scheme with pre-war 'bright' Red/White/Blue roundels in six positions, before being repainted in service in the S1E scheme of Extra Dark Sea Grey and Dark Slate Grey upper surfaces of the upper mainplane, tailplane and the top half of the fuselage, and Dark Sea Grey and Light Slate Grey on the upper surface of the lower mainplane, with Sky Grey under surfaces reaching mid-way up the fuselage sides in an undulating line and including the fin and rudder.

58 inch diameter Red/Blue roundels, were carried above the top mainplane, with slightly smaller 35 inch diameter Red/White/Blue/Yellow on the fuselage sides – in the earlier rearwards pre-war position – but no roundels were carried below the lower mainplane. The Red/White/Blue fin flash was in approximately 9 inch wide bands, some 30 or so inches high, and angled to match the rudder hinge line. The serial number was applied to the rear fuselage in approximately 4 inch high grey or faded black characters, with the Aircraft Class numeral '4' and the individual aircraft letter 'H' also applied to the rear fuselage in what appears to a dark grey or maybe faded black, approximately 20 inches high. Note the 820 NAS badge, simply outlined in black, on the port forward fuselage side and the yellow(?) patch on the rear fuselage.

Chapter 3

Taranto!

Possibly the most famous action the Fairey Swordfish was involved in, on the night of 11/12 November 1940 against the Italian navy berthed in Taranto Harbour, Italy.

The strike was originally to be launched from the older carrier, HMS *Eagle*, and was scheduled to take place on 21 October 1940, Trafalgar Day, but a hangar fire destroyed two Swordfish, then *Eagle* suffered a fuel system breakdown, so the brand-new carrier, HMS *Illustrious*, based at Alexandria, took over the role and five Swordfish and crews from Nos 813 and 824 Naval Air Squadrons from HMS *Eagle* were transferred to Illustrious for the operation.

The twenty-one Swordfish from *Eagle*'s Nos 813 and 824 NASs and *Illusrious*'s Nos 815 and 819 NASs were fitted with 60 gallon (273 litre) auxiliary fuel tanks in the open cockpit area behind the pilot, replacing the observer, to extend the type's operating range. Half the strike force was armed with 18 inch Mk XII torpedoes as the primary strike aircraft, with the other half carrying 250lb SAP bombs and parachute flares to carry out diversions.

Aerial torpedo experts had thought that torpedo attacks against ships could only be made in deep water of at least 100ft (30m). Taranto's harbour had a depth of only about 40ft (12m), however the Royal Navy modified their torpedoes and dropped them from a very low height. The torpedoes were fitted with Duplex magnetic/contact exploders, which were extremely sensitive, especially in rough seas, as the attacks on the German battleship *Bismarck* showed (see next section).

Following several reconaissance flights by RAF Martin Marylands of No 431 (GR) Sqn flying from Malta confirming the location of the Italian fleet, the first wave of twelve Swordfish, six armed with torpedoes and six with bombs, left *Illustrious* just before 2100hrs, followed by the second wave about an hour and a half later. Of the nine aircraft of the second wave, one turned back, L5Q crewed by Lt(A) W D Morford and Sub Lt(A) R A Green, when the auxiliary fuel tank broke loose and fell overboard, and one aircraft, L5F crewed by Lts E W Clifford and G R M Going, launched 20 minutes late, after requiring emergency repairs to damage from a minor taxiing accident with the ill-fated L5Q, which may have accounted for the damage to the auxiliary fuel tank mountings.

The main group approached the harbour at 2258hrs and one bomb-carrying aircraft, L4P, crewed by Lts Kiggell and Janvrin set fire to the harbour oil tanks. Then three aircraft led by Lt Cdr Williamson and Lt Scarlett of 815 Squadron in L4A, attacked over San Pietro Island, and hit the battleship *Conte di Cavour* with a torpedo that blasted a 27ft (8.2m) wide hole in her side below the waterline. Unfortunately, L4A was shot down by flak and both Lt Cdr Williamson and Lt Scarlett were taken prisoner.

The two remaining aircraft in this sub-flight (L4C and L4R) continued, dodging the balloon barrage and heavy anti-aircraft fire, to press home an unsuccessful attack on the battleship *Andrea Doria*. The next sub-flight of three (L4R, L4M and E4F) attacked from a more northerly direction, attacking the battleship *Littorio*, hitting it with two torpedoes and launching one torpedo at the flagship *Vittorio Veneto* which failed to hit its target. The bomber force then attacked two cruisers from 1,500ft (460m) and straddled four destroyers.

In the second wave five were armed with torpedoes and the remaining three with bombs. Two aircraft (L5A and E4H) aimed their torpedoes at the *Littorio*, one of which hit home, (from L5A), whilst another aircraft, (E5H), despite having been hit twice by anti-aircraft fire, aimed a torpedo at the *Vittorio Veneto* but missed. Another aircraft (L5H) hit the battleship *Caio Duilio* with a torpedo blowing a large hole in her hull and flooding both of her forward magazines but the aircraft, crewed by Lt G W L A Bayly RN and Lt J H Slaughter, E4H, was shot down by flak and both crew tragically killed.

The final aircraft to arrive on the scene, L5F, 15 minutes behind the others made a dive bombing attack on the Italian cruiser *Trento* despite heavy anti-aircraft fire, and then made a safe getaway, returning to *Illustrious* at 0239 hours.

Three Italian battleships received very heavy damage. *Conti de Cavour* had a huge hole in the hull and was effectively sunk. (She was raised later and partially repaired, but never regained service, so in effect was lost that night; *Caio Duilio* was also holed and was only saved by running her aground; and *Littorio* had considerable flooding caused by the three torpedo strikes, was totally disabled and was only saved by running her aground. Despite this, in the morning the ship's bows were totally submerged. The cruiser *Trento* was also damaged by a 250lb bomb from L5F which failed to detonate.

The Italian fleet had suffered heavily, and the next day the *Regia Marina* transferred its undamaged ships from Taranto to Naples to protect them from similar attacks. Repairs to the *Littorio* took about five months and to the *Caio Duilio* six, but the *Conte di Cavour* required extensive salvage work and her repairs were still incomplete when Italy surrendered in 1943. The Italian battleship fleet had effectively lost about half of its strength in one night.

In the aftermath, Taranto Harbour was visited by the Japanese naval attache from Berlin, who later briefed the Imperial Japanese Navy's planning staff who carefully studied the Taranto attack when planning their attack on Pearl Harbor on 7 December 1941.

First Wave

L4A, 815 NAS crewed by Lt Cdr K Williamson RN and Lt N Scarlett RN (torpedo)

L4C, 815 NAS crewed by Sub Lt(A) P Sparke and Sub Lt(A) J Neale (torpedo)

L4R, 815 NAS crewed by Sub Lt(A) A S D Macauley RN and Sub Lt(A) A L O Wray RNVR (torpedo)

L4K, 815 NAS crewed by Lt N M Kemp RN and Sub Lt(A) R A Bailey RN (torpedo)

L4M, P4154, 815 NAS crewed by Sub Lt(A) H I A Swayne RN and Sub Lt(A) J Buscall RNVR (torpedo)

E4F, 813 NAS crewed by Lt M R Maund RN and Sub Lt(A) W A Bull RN (torpedo)

E5A, K8393, 824 NAS crewed by Capt O Patch RM and Lt D G Goodwinn RN (bombs)

L4L, 815 NAS crewed by Sub Lt(A) W C Sarra RN and Mid(A) J Bowker RN (bombs)

L4H, 815 NAS crewed by Sub Lt(A) A J B Forde RN and Sub Lt(A) A Mardel-Ferreira RN (bombs)

L4P, 815 NAS crewed by Lt(A) L J Kiggell RN and Lt H R B Janvrin RN (bombs and flares)

L5B, 819 NAS crewed by Lt(A) C B Lamb RN and Lt K C Grieve RN (bombs and flares)

E5Q, 824 NAS crewed by Lt(A) J B Murray RN and Sub Lt(A) S M Paine RN (bombs)

Second wave

L5A, 819 NAS crewed by Lt Cdr J W Hale RN and Lt G A carline RN (torpedo)

E4H, 813 NAS crewed by Lt G W L A Bayley RN and Lt H J Slaughter RN (torpedo)

L5H, 819 NAS crewed by Lt(A) C S E Lea RN and Sub Lt(A) P D Jones RN (torpedo)

L5K, 819 NAS crewed by Lt F M A Torrens-Spence RN and Lt A W F Sutton RN (torpedo)

E5H, P3999, 824 NAS crewed by Lt(A) J W G Wellham RN and Lt P Humphreys RN (torpedo)

L5R, P4224, 819 NAS crewed by Lt R W V Hamilton RN and Sub Lt(A) J R Weekes RN (bombs and flares)

L4F, 815 NAS crewed by Lt(A) R G Skelton RN and Sub Lt(A) E A perkins RNVR (bombs and flares)

L5F, 819 NAS crewed by Lt E W Clifford RN and Lt G R M Going RN (bombs and flares)

L5Q, 819 NAS crewed by Lt(A) W D Morford RN and Sub Lt(A) R A Green RN (bombs)

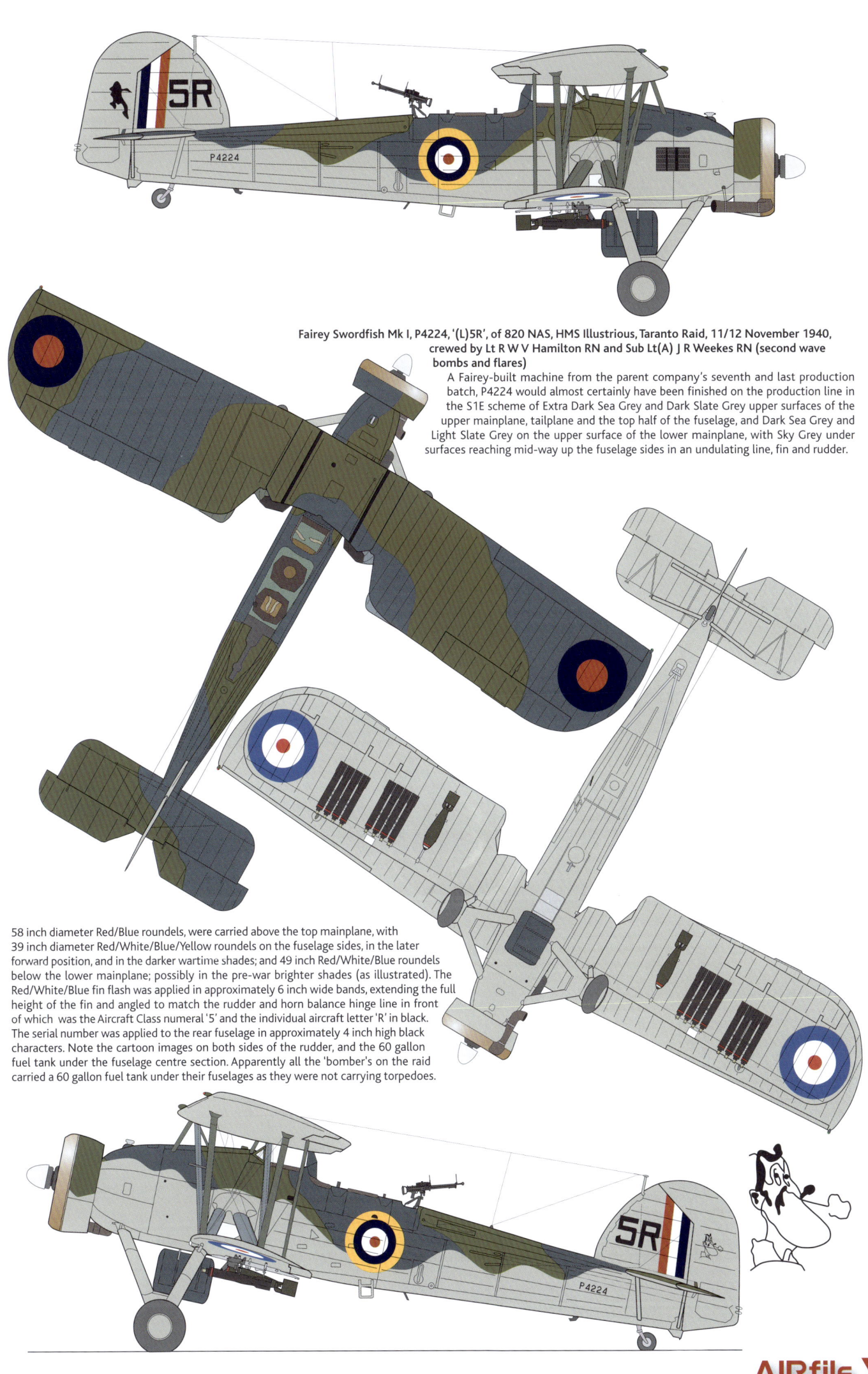

Fairey Swordfish Mk I, P4224, '(L)5R', of 820 NAS, HMS Illustrious, Taranto Raid, 11/12 November 1940, crewed by Lt R W V Hamilton RN and Sub Lt(A) J R Weekes RN (second wave bombs and flares)

A Fairey-built machine from the parent company's seventh and last production batch, P4224 would almost certainly have been finished on the production line in the S1E scheme of Extra Dark Sea Grey and Dark Slate Grey upper surfaces of the upper mainplane, tailplane and the top half of the fuselage, and Dark Sea Grey and Light Slate Grey on the upper surface of the lower mainplane, with Sky Grey under surfaces reaching mid-way up the fuselage sides in an undulating line, fin and rudder.

58 inch diameter Red/Blue roundels, were carried above the top mainplane, with 39 inch diameter Red/White/Blue/Yellow roundels on the fuselage sides, in the later forward position, and in the darker wartime shades; and 49 inch Red/White/Blue roundels below the lower mainplane; possibly in the pre-war brighter shades (as illustrated). The Red/White/Blue fin flash was applied in approximately 6 inch wide bands, extending the full height of the fin and angled to match the rudder and horn balance hinge line in front of which was the Aircraft Class numeral '5' and the individual aircraft letter 'R' in black. The serial number was applied to the rear fuselage in approximately 4 inch high black characters. Note the cartoon images on both sides of the rudder, and the 60 gallon fuel tank under the fuselage centre section. Apparently all the 'bomber's on the raid carried a 60 gallon fuel tank under their fuselages as they were not carrying torpedoes.

AIRfile 37

Fairey Swordfish Mk I, P4154, '(L)4M', of 815 NAS, HMS Illustrious, Taranto Raid, 11/12 November 1940, crewed by Lt I H Swayne RN and Sub Lt(A) J Buscall RNVR (first wave torpedo)
A Fairey-built machine from the parent company's seventh and last production batch, P4154 would almost certainly have been finished on the production line in the S1E scheme with Sky Grey under surfaces, fuselage sides, fin and rudder. However, it would appear from photographs of this machine taken well before the Taranto raid, that it had the upper surface camouflage colours extended down the fuselage sides, and all the under surfaces – including both mainplanes, the tailplanes and the fuselage – overpainted in Night (black). Red/Blue roundels, were carried above the top mainplane, with Red/White/Blue/Yellow roundels on the fuselage sides, and Red/White/Blue roundels below the lower mainplane. The Red/White/Blue fin flash was applied in approximately 6 inch wide bands, extending the full height of the fin and angled to match the rudder and horn balance hinge line. The Aircraft Class numeral '4' and the individual aircraft letter 'M' was also applied to the fin in white. The serial number was applied to the rear fuselage in approximately 4 inch high black characters on what appears to be a masked-out section of the original Sky Grey. Black spinner cap. Note the 60 gallon fuel tank in the observer's cockpit.

Fairey Swordfish Mk I, (serial number unknown), '(L)4A', of 815 NAS, HMS Illustrious, Taranto Raid, 11/12 November 1940, crewed by Lt Cdr K Williamson RN (first wave leader) and Lt N Scarlett
Despite being the First Wave Leader's aircraft, the serial number of Lt Cdr Williamson's Swordfish is unfortunately unknown, however, it would have been a Fairey-built machine, and, like P4154/4M immediately above, appears to have had its upper surface camouflage colours extended down the fuselage sides, and all the under surfaces overpainted in Night. Red/Blue roundels, were carried above the top mainplane, with Red/White/Blue/Yellow roundels on the fuselage sides, and Red/White/Blue roundels below the lower mainplane. The Red/White/Blue fin flash was applied in approximately 6 inch wide bands, extending the full height of the fin and angled to match the rudder and horn balance hinge line. The Aircraft Class numeral '4' and the individual aircraft letter 'A' was also applied to the fin in white. The serial number was probably applied to the rear fuselage in 4 inch high black characters. Black spinner cap. This aircraft torpedoed the Italian battleship *'Conte di Cavour'* which settled on to Taranto harbour's bottom, but was shot down immediately afterwards. The crew survived and were taken prisoner – Lt Cdr Williamson was awarded the DSO and Lt Scarlett the DSC. Note the 60 gallon fuel tank in the observer's cockpit. (see photos opposite)

Fairey Swordfish Mk I, P3999, '(E)5H', of 824 NAS, HMS Illustrious, Taranto Raid, 11/12 November 1940, crewed by Lt(A) J W G Wellham RN and Lt P Humphreys RN (second wave torpedo)
A Fairey-built machine from the parent company's seventh and last production batch, finished on the production line in the S1E scheme with Sky Grey under surfaces reaching midway up the fuselage sides in an undulating line and on the fin and rudder. Red/Blue roundels above the top mainplane, Red/White/Blue/Yellow roundels on the fuselage sides and Red/White/Blue roundels below the lower mainplane. The Red/White/Blue fin flash was applied in approximately 6 inch wide bands, extending the full height of the fin and angled to match the rudder and horn balance hinge line, in front of which was the Aircraft Class numeral '5' and the individual aircraft letter 'H' in black. The serial number was applied to the rear fuselage in approximately 4 inch high black characters. Black spinner cap. Note the 60 gallon fuel tank in the observer's cockpit. This Swordfish, from 824 NAS and on temporary loan from HMS *Eagle* for the raid, attacked, but missed the battleship *'Vittorio Veneto'*, and was severely damaged during the run-in, but returned safely to HMS *Illustrious*.

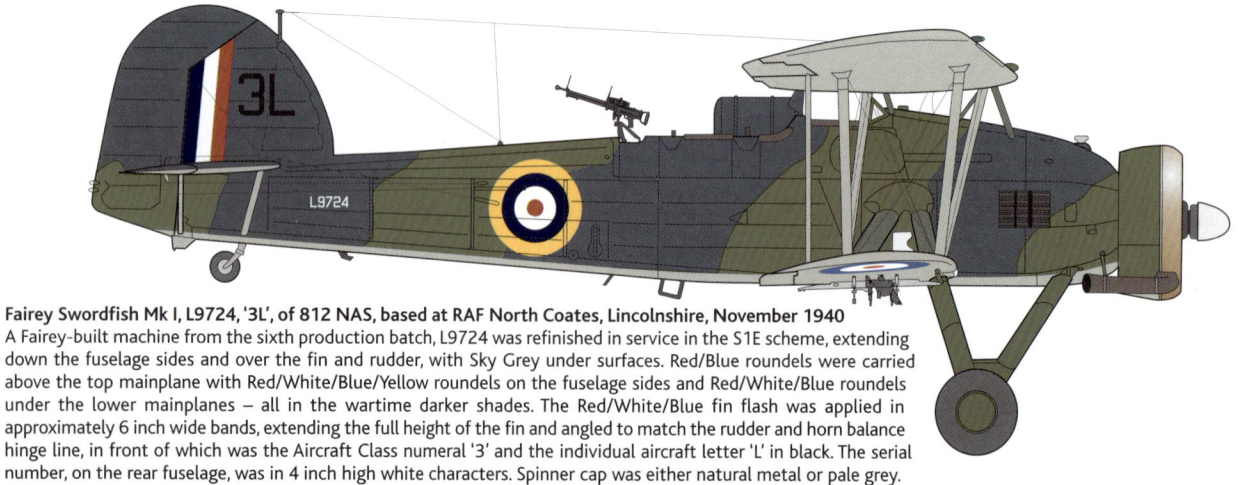

Fairey Swordfish Mk I, L9724, '3L', of 812 NAS, based at RAF North Coates, Lincolnshire, November 1940
A Fairey-built machine from the sixth production batch, L9724 was refinished in service in the S1E scheme, extending down the fuselage sides and over the fin and rudder, with Sky Grey under surfaces. Red/Blue roundels were carried above the top mainplane with Red/White/Blue/Yellow roundels on the fuselage sides and Red/White/Blue roundels under the lower mainplanes – all in the wartime darker shades. The Red/White/Blue fin flash was applied in approximately 6 inch wide bands, extending the full height of the fin and angled to match the rudder and horn balance hinge line, in front of which was the Aircraft Class numeral '3' and the individual aircraft letter 'L' in black. The serial number, on the rear fuselage, was in 4 inch high white characters. Spinner cap was either natural metal or pale grey.

Above:
A selection of photographs of the remains of Swordfish Mk I, (serial number is unfortunately unknown), coded '4A', of 815 NAS, flown off HMS Illustrious for the Taranto Raid, on the night of 11/12 November 1940, crewed by Lt Cdr K Williamson RN (first wave leader) and Lt N Scarlett. After they had torpedoed the Italian battleship 'Conte di Cavour', '4A' was shot down immediately afterwards, but the crew survived and were taken prisoner. Note the black under surfaces, applied for the raid. (see profile opposite)

Below:
Another selection of photographs, this time taken of K8422, coded '4H' which, when serving with 813 NAS, aboard HMS Eagle, was forced down off Kasos, an island near Greece, after a night raid on Maritza, on the mainland, on 4 September 1940, the crew becoming PoWs. The aircraft was repaired by the Italians and is thought to have been flown by 68ª Squadriglia, 34° Gruppo BT, an SM.79 bomber unit, for liaison duties until June 1941. (see profile on p31)

Chapter 4

Sink the Bismarck!

Although not involved in the attacks on *Bismarck*, DK785, '3Q' of 825 NAS is typical of the finish and markings carried by the Swordfish that were involved. In this photo, DK785 is seen after hitting the island aboard HMS Illustrious on 13 March 1942 while operating off Madagascar, in the Indian Ocean. Note the lower camouflage demarcation on the fuselage sides that was starting to be introduced during this period.

By the end of 1940 and in to the beginning of the new year Swordfish were regularly flying anti-shipping sorties from Malta and in May 1941, the Swordfish was again involved in a major naval action, this time against the German battleship *Bismarck*.

The *Bismarck* was one of the most famous warships of World War Two. She displaced more than 50,000 tonnes fully loaded and was the largest warship then commissioned. However, she took part in only one operation (lasting 135 hours) during her brief career. She and the heavy cruiser *Prinz Eugen* left Gotenhafen (Gdynia) on the morning of 19 May 1941 for *Unternehmen 'Rheinübung'* (Operation 'Rhine'), during which she was to have attempted to intercept and destroy convoys in transit between North America and the United Kingdom. When the two ships attempted to break out into the Atlantic, they were discovered and brought to battle in the Denmark Strait. During a short engagement with HMS *Hood* and HMS *Prince of Wales*, the battlecruiser HMS *Hood*, flagship of the Home Fleet and pride of the Royal Navy, was sunk after several minutes of firing with only three survivors from the ship's company of 1,422.

Two days later, in the evening of 24 May, nine Swordfish of 825 NAS, led by Lt Cdr(A) Eugene Esmonde RN, were launched from the carrier HMS *Victorious*. The aircraft were fitted with ASV (Air-to-Surface Vessel) radar, and made contact with *Bismarck* at 2327hrs, it still being light at that time in those northerly latitudes, and despite intense and accurate anti-aircraft fire, they managed to get one good torpedo strike, albeit the blast from which, only caused superficial damage to *Bismarck*'s armoured belt, but the effect reopened an earlier 'wound' received during the engagement with HMS *Hood* and HMS *Prince of Wales*, and caused the collision mats, used to block flooding in the bow region, to come loose due to the constant jarring from evasive action and the firing of the anti-aircraft guns. The packing around the damaged bulkheads was also loosened and led to the flooding of the forward port boiler room, which had to be abandoned. This caused the bow to drop down further, forcing the ship's speed to be reduced to 16 knots while repairs were effected.

In this instance, the slow airspeed of the Fairey Swordfish may have acted in the type's favour, as, despite the barrage of anti-aircraft fire, *Bismarck*'s gunners experienced difficulty predicting their attacker's positions and many shells exploded well in front of the aircraft, reducing the threat of shrapnel damage, and all nine aircraft returned safely back to *Victorious*. The Swordfish also flew so low that many of the *Bismarck*'s anti-aircraft weapons were unable to depress low enough to hit them.

Following this action, contact was lost with *Bismarck* for a few nerve-racking hours, but then the British had a stroke of luck, in the mid-morning of 26 May, an RAF Coastal Command Catalina reconnaissance aircraft from No 209 Sqn spotted the *Bismarck* from an oil slick she was trailing and reported her position to the Admiralty.

After an earlier, potentially disastrous, attack in the afternoon by Swordfish from HMS *Ark Royal* on HMS *Sheffield*, which was now shadowing *Bismarck*, which, although losing precious time, actually proved to be beneficial in that the magnetic detonators on the torpedoes used against *Sheffield* were seen to be defective, and for the following actual attack on '*Bismarck*', were replaced by contact detonators.

At 1925hrs, in atrocious weather conditions, *Ark Royal* launched fourteen aircraft from Nos 810, 818 and 820 NASs for a strike against *Bismarck*. The actual attack was made at 2105hrs, in failing light, but two hits were scored, one which did little damage, but the other from Swordfish A5C of 818 NAS, piloted by Sub-Lieutenant John Moffat with Sub Lt(A) Miller (Observer) and L/A Hayman (Telegraphist/Air Gunner), jammed *Bismarck*'s rudder and disabled her steering gear, rendering her virtually unmanoeuvrable and causing her to steam in a large circle, with an increased list to port – in the general direction of HMS *King George V* and HMS *Rodney*, two frontline battleships that had been in pursuit from the west.

Throughout the night of 26/27 May, *Bismarck* came under incessant torpedo attacks by the Tribal Class destroyers HMS *Cossack*, *Sikh*, *Maori* and *Zulu*, until around 0800hrs on 27 May, when *Rodney* and *King George V* closed in on her. They opened fire at 0847hrs and although *Bismarck* returned fire, her inability to steer and her list to port affected her accuracy. Her low speed of 7 knots made her a relatively easy target, and she was hit several more times. The heavy cruisers, HMS *Norfolk* and HMS *Dorsetshire*, added their firepower, and an 8 inch shell from *Norfolk* hit the main gun director, knocking it out of action, and a heavy shell from HMS *Rodney* hit both of *Bismarck*'s forward turrets disabling them; this was followed by another salvo which destroyed the forward control post. The aft turrets continued to fire until they too were eventually knocked out.

However, the British ships' fuel and shell supplies were getting low, a demonstration of how difficult it was to sink a battleship of *Bismarck*'s size. One of the reasons *King George V* and *Rodney* failed to sink *Bismarck* was that they had closed to 4 miles range, so their shellfire was virtually horizontal to the German ship's armour. If they had pulled back to 11 miles (or more) range, the shellfire would have become 'plunging shot', and would have been much more likely to penetrate the deck armour and explode within.

Despite the unequal struggle, even though it became obvious that she could not reach port, the *Bismarck* continued to fly her ensign, and with no sign of surrender, HMS *Dorsetshire* launched three 21 inch torpedoes at comparatively short range. By this time, the German battleship's upper works were almost completely destroyed and with her engines still functioning, *Bismarck* finally slipped below the waves, stern first, at 1039hrs that morning.

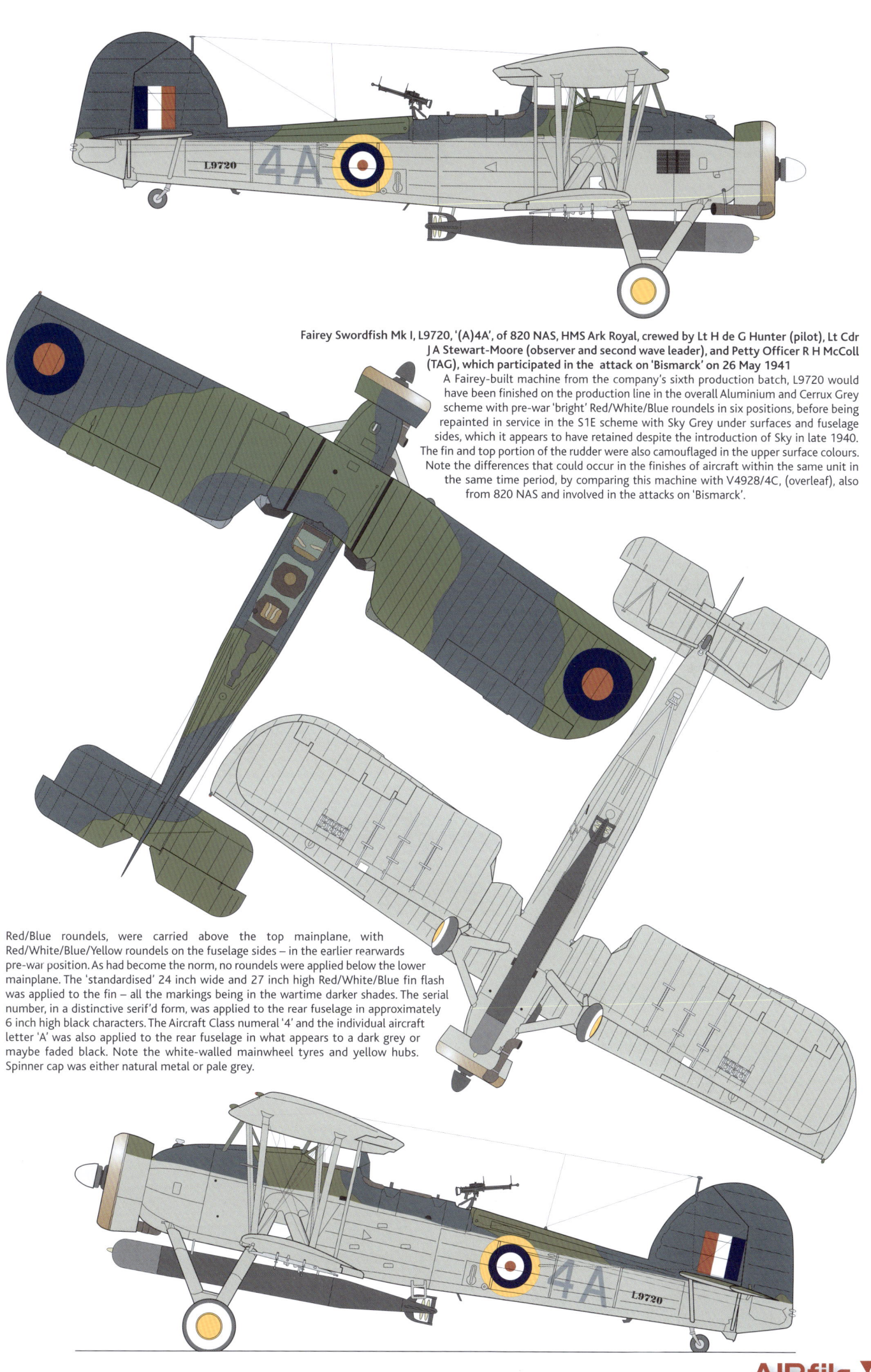

Fairey Swordfish Mk I, L9720, '(A)4A', of 820 NAS, HMS Ark Royal, crewed by Lt H de G Hunter (pilot), Lt Cdr J A Stewart-Moore (observer and second wave leader), and Petty Officer R H McColl (TAG), which participated in the attack on 'Bismarck' on 26 May 1941

A Fairey-built machine from the company's sixth production batch, L9720 would have been finished on the production line in the overall Aluminium and Cerrux Grey scheme with pre-war 'bright' Red/White/Blue roundels in six positions, before being repainted in service in the S1E scheme with Sky Grey under surfaces and fuselage sides, which it appears to have retained despite the introduction of Sky in late 1940. The fin and top portion of the rudder were also camouflaged in the upper surface colours. Note the differences that could occur in the finishes of aircraft within the same unit in the same time period, by comparing this machine with V4928/4C, (overleaf), also from 820 NAS and involved in the attacks on 'Bismarck'.

Red/Blue roundels, were carried above the top mainplane, with Red/White/Blue/Yellow roundels on the fuselage sides – in the earlier rearwards pre-war position. As had become the norm, no roundels were applied below the lower mainplane. The 'standardised' 24 inch wide and 27 inch high Red/White/Blue fin flash was applied to the fin – all the markings being in the wartime darker shades. The serial number, in a distinctive serif'd form, was applied to the rear fuselage in approximately 6 inch high black characters. The Aircraft Class numeral '4' and the individual aircraft letter 'A' was also applied to the rear fuselage in what appears to a dark grey or maybe faded black. Note the white-walled mainwheel tyres and yellow hubs. Spinner cap was either natural metal or pale grey.

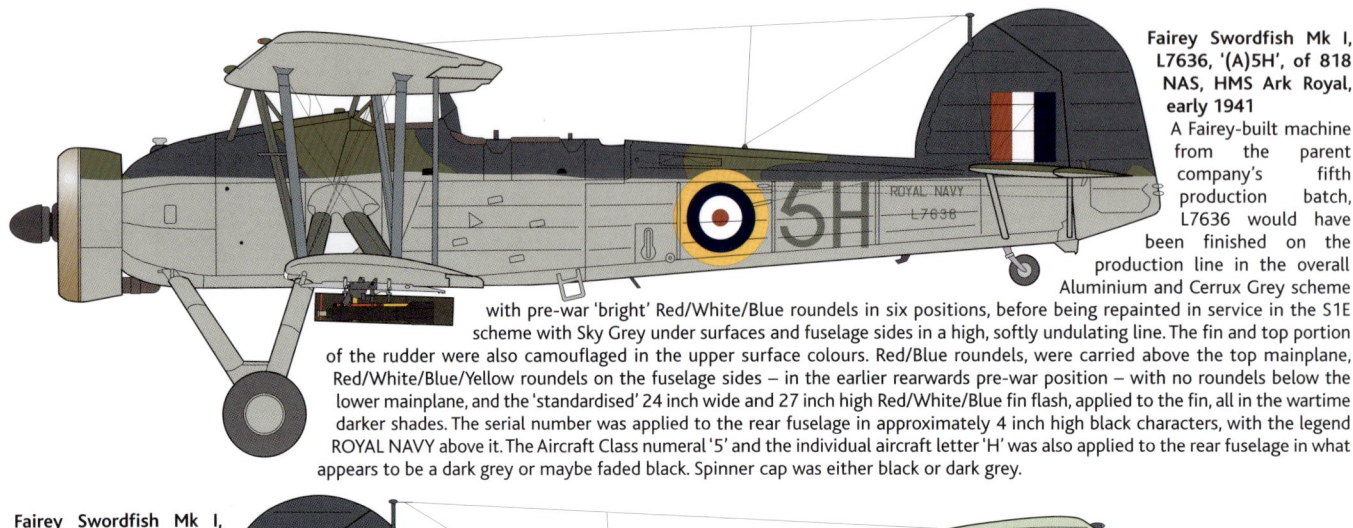

Fairey Swordfish Mk I, L7636, '(A)5H', of 818 NAS, HMS Ark Royal, early 1941

A Fairey-built machine from the parent company's fifth production batch, L7636 would have been finished on the production line in the overall Aluminium and Cerrux Grey scheme with pre-war 'bright' Red/White/Blue roundels in six positions, before being repainted in service in the S1E scheme with Sky Grey under surfaces and fuselage sides in a high, softly undulating line. The fin and top portion of the rudder were also camouflaged in the upper surface colours. Red/Blue roundels, were carried above the top mainplane, Red/White/Blue/Yellow roundels on the fuselage sides – in the earlier rearwards pre-war position – with no roundels below the lower mainplane, and the 'standardised' 24 inch wide and 27 inch high Red/White/Blue fin flash, applied to the fin, all in the wartime darker shades. The serial number was applied to the rear fuselage in approximately 4 inch high black characters, with the legend ROYAL NAVY above it. The Aircraft Class numeral '5' and the individual aircraft letter 'H' was also applied to the rear fuselage in what appears to be a dark grey or maybe faded black. Spinner cap was either black or dark grey.

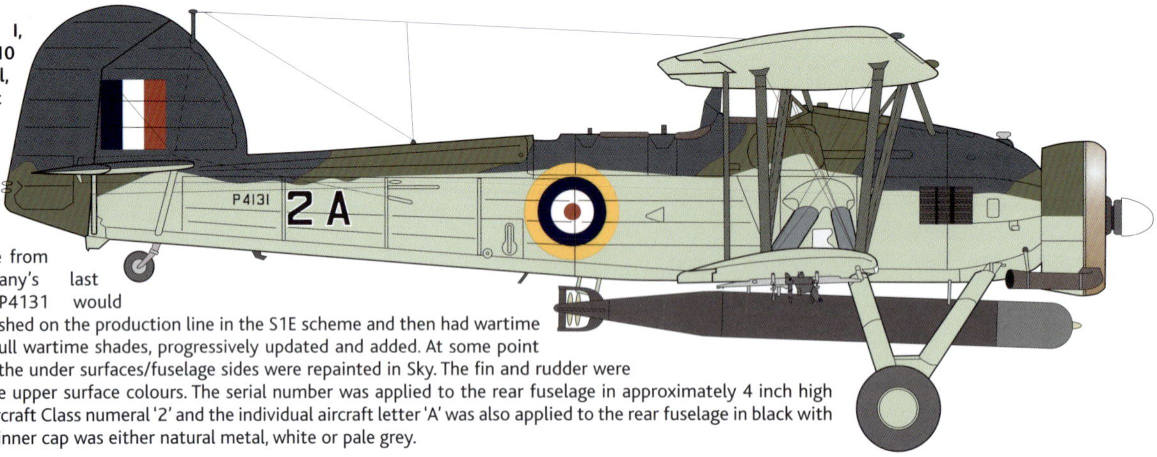

Fairey Swordfish Mk I, P4131, '(A)2A', of 810 NAS, HMS Ark Royal, crewed by Sub Lt Pattison, Sub Lt Meadway and Leadng Airman Mulley, which participated in the attack on 'Bismarck' on 26 May 1941

A Fairey-built machine from the parent company's last production batch, P4131 would probably have been finished on the production line in the S1E scheme and then had wartime style roundels, in the dull wartime shades, progressively updated and added. At some point after September 1940, the under surfaces/fuselage sides were repainted in Sky. The fin and rudder were also camouflaged in the upper surface colours. The serial number was applied to the rear fuselage in approximately 4 inch high black characters. The Aircraft Class numeral '2' and the individual aircraft letter 'A' was also applied to the rear fuselage in black with a thin white outline. Spinner cap was either natural metal, white or pale grey.

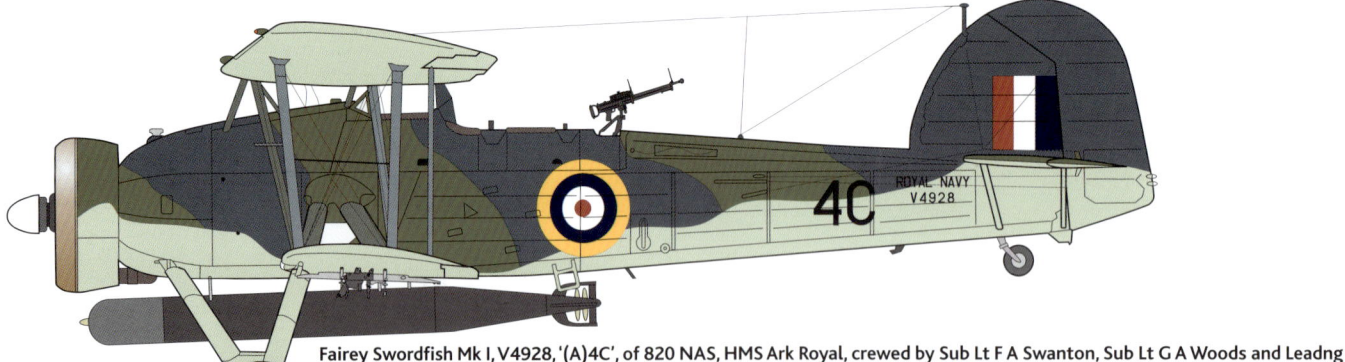

Fairey Swordfish Mk I, V4928, '(A)4C', of 820 NAS, HMS Ark Royal, crewed by Sub Lt F A Swanton, Sub Lt G A Woods and Leadng Airman J R Seager, which participated in the attack on 'Bismarck' on 26 May 1941

One of the first Blackburn-built machines from the company's first production batch, V4928 would probably have been finished on the production line in the S1E scheme possibly still with Sky Grey under surfaces, although they may have had the newly introduced Sky under surfaces applied. Note the distinctive Blackburn fuselage demarcation line which 'dropped' down to the lower mainplane roots. The fin and top portion of the rudder were also camouflaged in the upper surface colours. Red/Blue roundels, were carried above the top mainplane, Red/White/Blue/Yellow roundels on the fuselage sides – in the forward wartime position – with no roundels below the lower mainplane, and the 'standardised' fin flash, all in the wartime darker shades. The serial number was applied to the rear fuselage in approximately 4 inch high black characters, with the legend ROYAL NAVY above it. The Aircraft Class numeral '4' and the individual aircraft letter 'C' were also applied to the rear fuselage in black. Spinner cap was either natural metal or white. This aircraft was badly damaged by flak on the 26 May attack on 'Bismarck' in which Sub Lt Swanton (pilot) and Sub Lt Woods (observer) were wounded but L/A Seager (TAG) was unhurt.

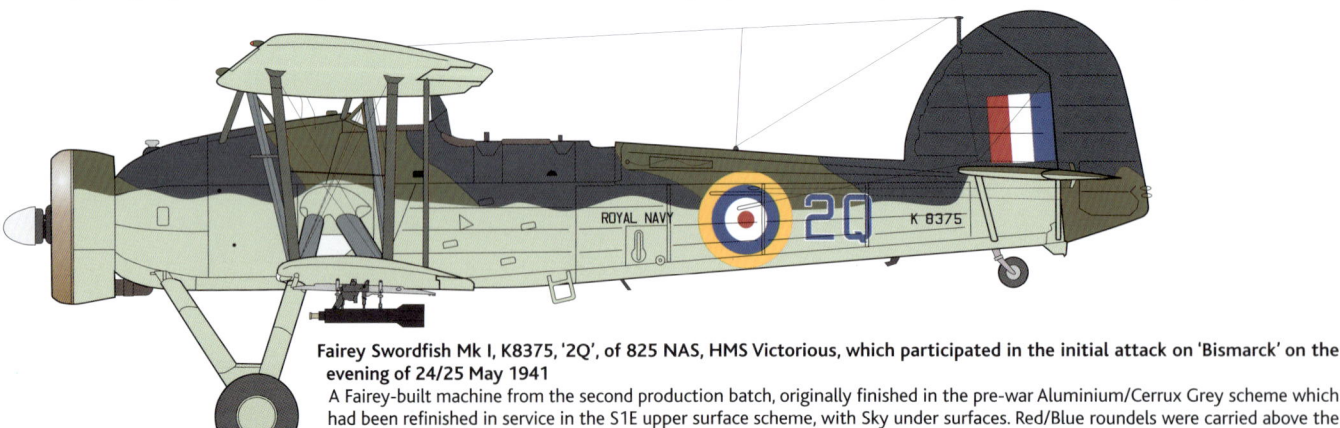

Fairey Swordfish Mk I, K8375, '2Q', of 825 NAS, HMS Victorious, which participated in the initial attack on 'Bismarck' on the evening of 24/25 May 1941

A Fairey-built machine from the second production batch, originally finished in the pre-war Aluminium/Cerrux Grey scheme which had been refinished in service in the S1E upper surface scheme, with Sky under surfaces. Red/Blue roundels were carried above the top mainplane in the wartime 'dull' shades, with Red/White/Blue/Yellow roundels on the fuselage sides in the earlier rearwards pre-war position, and possibly in the bright pre-war shades, with the 'standardised' 24 x 27 inch Red/White/Blue fin flash, also in the bright colours. The serial number was applied to the rear fuselage, in 4 inch high black characters, with the legend ROYAL NAVY positioned in front of the fuselage roundel. The Aircraft Class numeral '2' and the individual aircraft letter 'Q' were also applied to the rear fuselage in bright pre-war roundel blue, thinly outlined in white. Spinner cap was either natural metal or pale grey. This aircraft is believed to have been the machine that scored the torpedo hit on 'Bismarck' on 825 NAS's 24 May attack, which caused her to slow down.

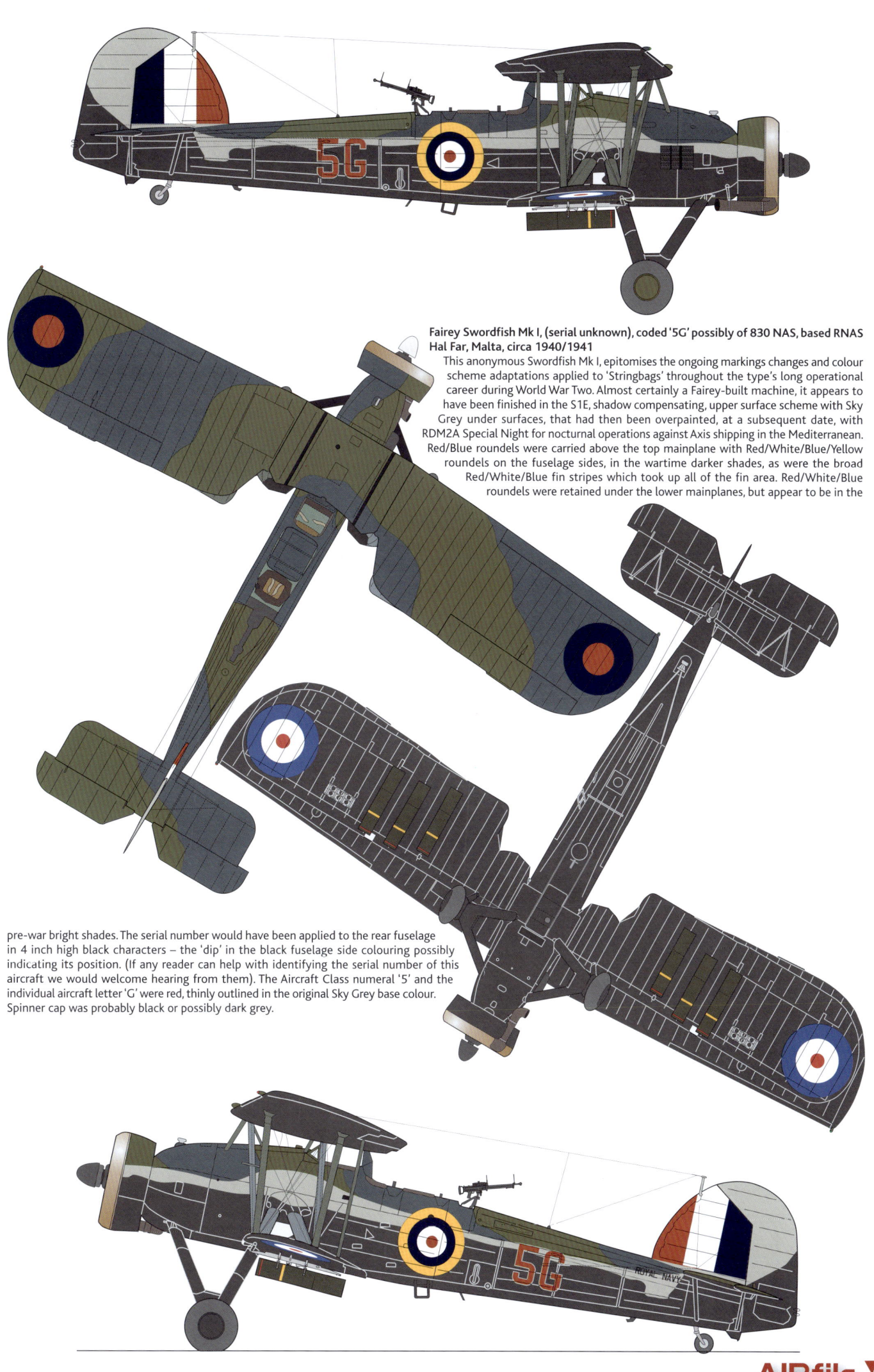

Fairey Swordfish Mk I, (serial unknown), coded '5G' possibly of 830 NAS, based RNAS Hal Far, Malta, circa 1940/1941

This anonymous Swordfish Mk I, epitomises the ongoing markings changes and colour scheme adaptations applied to 'Stringbags' throughout the type's long operational career during World War Two. Almost certainly a Fairey-built machine, it appears to have been finished in the S1E, shadow compensating, upper surface scheme with Sky Grey under surfaces, that had then been overpainted, at a subsequent date, with RDM2A Special Night for nocturnal operations against Axis shipping in the Mediterranean. Red/Blue roundels were carried above the top mainplane with Red/White/Blue/Yellow roundels on the fuselage sides, in the wartime darker shades, as were the broad Red/White/Blue fin stripes which took up all of the fin area. Red/White/Blue roundels were retained under the lower mainplanes, but appear to be in the pre-war bright shades. The serial number would have been applied to the rear fuselage in 4 inch high black characters – the 'dip' in the black fuselage side colouring possibly indicating its position. (If any reader can help with identifying the serial number of this aircraft we would welcome hearing from them). The Aircraft Class numeral '5' and the individual aircraft letter 'G' were red, thinly outlined in the original Sky Grey base colour. Spinner cap was probably black or possibly dark grey.

Chapter 5

The Channel Dash...
... and camouflage and markings changes through to 1943

Formation of Swordfish Mk Is of C Flight, Y Squadron of the Torpedo Trials Unit, based at RNAS Abbotsinch, Renfrewshire, circa 1941, with L9715, 'M' in the foreground. A Fairey-built machine from the parent company's sixth production batch, L9715 would have started life finished in the overall Aluminium and Cerrux Grey scheme before being repainted in service in the Dark Sea Grey and Dark Slate Grey S1E scheme, which extended down the fuselage sides, with Sky Grey under surfaces. (see profile on p46)

The Channel Dash

Despite its success in *Bismarck*'s demise, problems with the Swordfish were starkly demonstrated in February 1942 when a strike on the German battleships *Scharnhorst* and *Gneisenau*, in company with the battle cruiser *Prinz Eugen*, during the so called 'Channel Dash' resulted in the loss of all the attacking Swordfish aircraft.

On 11 February 1942, in an operation code named *Unternehmen 'Cerberus'*, (Operation 'Cerberus'), a German *Kriegsmarine* squadron consisting of *Scharnhorst, Gneisenau* and *Prinz Eugen*, supported by a number of smaller ships, ran a British blockade and successfully sailed from Brest in Brittany to their home bases in Germany through the English Channel. The ships left Brest at 2115hrs and escaped detection for more than 12 hours, approaching the Straits of Dover without check. Despite attacks by the Royal Air Force, the Fleet Air Arm and Coastal Artillery, by 13 February all the ships had completed their transit. Supporting the German naval operation, the *Luftwaffe* launched *Unternehmen 'Donnerkeil'*, (Operation Thunderbolt), to provide air superiority for the passage of the ships.

Scharnhorst and *Gneisenau* had arrived at Brest on 22 March 1941 after operations against Allied shipping in the Atlantic Ocean, and *Prinz Eugen* appeared on 1 June 1941 at Brest Harbour after participating in the ill-fated *Unternehmen 'Rheinübung'* (Operation 'Rhine'), with the *Bismarck*. Here the ships were able to repair, refit and refuel in comparative safety, but were subject to frequent air attacks. In light of this, Hitler ordered the *Kriegsmarine* to move the ships to their home bases.

As the operation had been ordered personally by Hitler, resources were made available for mine sweeping; additional radar jamming stations were set up, and U-boats sent out fto collect meteorological observations. Several *Kriegsmarine* destroyers steamed westward down the Channel to Brest to strengthen the escort screen, and the *Luftwaffe* was closely involved, with JG 26's *Geschwader Kommodore*, fighter 'ace' Adolf Galland attending many of the planning sessions to assure day and night fighter cover along the route.

Vice-Admiral Bertram Ramsay was in command of the Royal Navy's local Home Defences. Available to him were six destroyers, which should have been on 4-hour standby in the Thames Estuary – but were not. There were also three Hunt Class Destroyer Escorts, but they had no torpedo tubes fitted and so posed little threat to the well-armoured German ships, whilst the thirty-two Motor Torpedo Boats of the Dover and Ramsgate Flotillas under Ramsay's command were counterbalanced by the German flotilla of some thirty-four S-Boats.

The Fleet Air Arm, Coastal Command and Bomber Command all expected the Germans to time their dash through the Channel so that the most dangerous point, at Dover-Calais where the ships would need to move within range of British coastal batteries, would be passed at night. However the Germans considered it far more important to maintain the element of surprise for as long as possible by slipping out of Brest unnoticed at night, thus avoiding the 12-hour warning that an early daytime departure would have given the British. Essentially, the British were wrong-footed by this audacious move.

Fleet Air Arm night reconnaissance patrols did not notice the departure of the ships from Brest and the first indication that something was happening came from RAF radar operators who noticed an unusually high level of *Luftwaffe* air-activity over the Channel. The German ships were then spotted in the Channel by RAF Fighter Command Spitfires, but as they were under strict orders not to break radio silence and had not been briefed to look for the German fleet, they did not inform their superiors until they landed back at their base.

Fighter Command was not expected to be the first to spot the German fleet in the Channel, and valuable time was lost reporting the sighting up the chain of command and on to the Royal Navy and Bomber Command.

There then followed several uncoordinated attacks, by Motor Torpedo Boats and the Swordfish from 825 NAS based at Manston, in an operation formally referred to as Operation 'Fuller', all of which failed to inflict any damage. All six aircraft of 825 NAS, led by Lt Cdr Eugene Esmonde, a veteran of the first torpedo attack on *Bismarck*, were lost – only five crew members surviving out of the eighteen.

825 NAS aircraft and crews that took part in the strike against *Scharnhorst, Gneisenau* and *Prinz Eugen* on the afternoon of 12 February 1942 were...

W5984 'H'
Lt Cdr(A) E Esmonde DSO, Lt W H Williams, P/O(A) W J Clinton

W5983 'G'
Sub Lt(A) B W Rose, Sub Lt(A) E F Lee, P/O(A) A L Johnson DSM

W5907 'L'
Sub Lt C M Kingsmill, Sub Lt R McC Samples, L/A A L Bunce

V4523 'F'
Lt J C Thompson, Sub Lt(A) E H F Wright, L/A E Tapping

W5978 'L'
Sub Lt(A) P Bligh, Sub Lt(A) W Benyon, L/A W G Smith

W5985 'K'
Sub Lt C R Wood, Sub Lt(A) R L Parkinson, L/A H T A Wheeler

Lt Cdr Esmonde, was awarded the Victoria Cross, posthumously. Of the five aircrew that survived, Rose, Lee, Kingsmill and Samples got the DSO and Bunce got the CGM. All the others got a posthumous Mention in Despatches. The courage of the Swordfish crews was noted by friend and foe alike. Admiral Ramsay later wrote, *"In my opinion the gallant sortie of these six Swordfish aircraft constitutes one of the finest exhibitions of self-sacrifice and devotion to duty the war had ever witnessed"*, whilst the German Admiral Ciliax said: *"The attack by a handful of ancient biplanes, was crewed by men whose bravery surpassed any other action undertaken by either side that day"*.

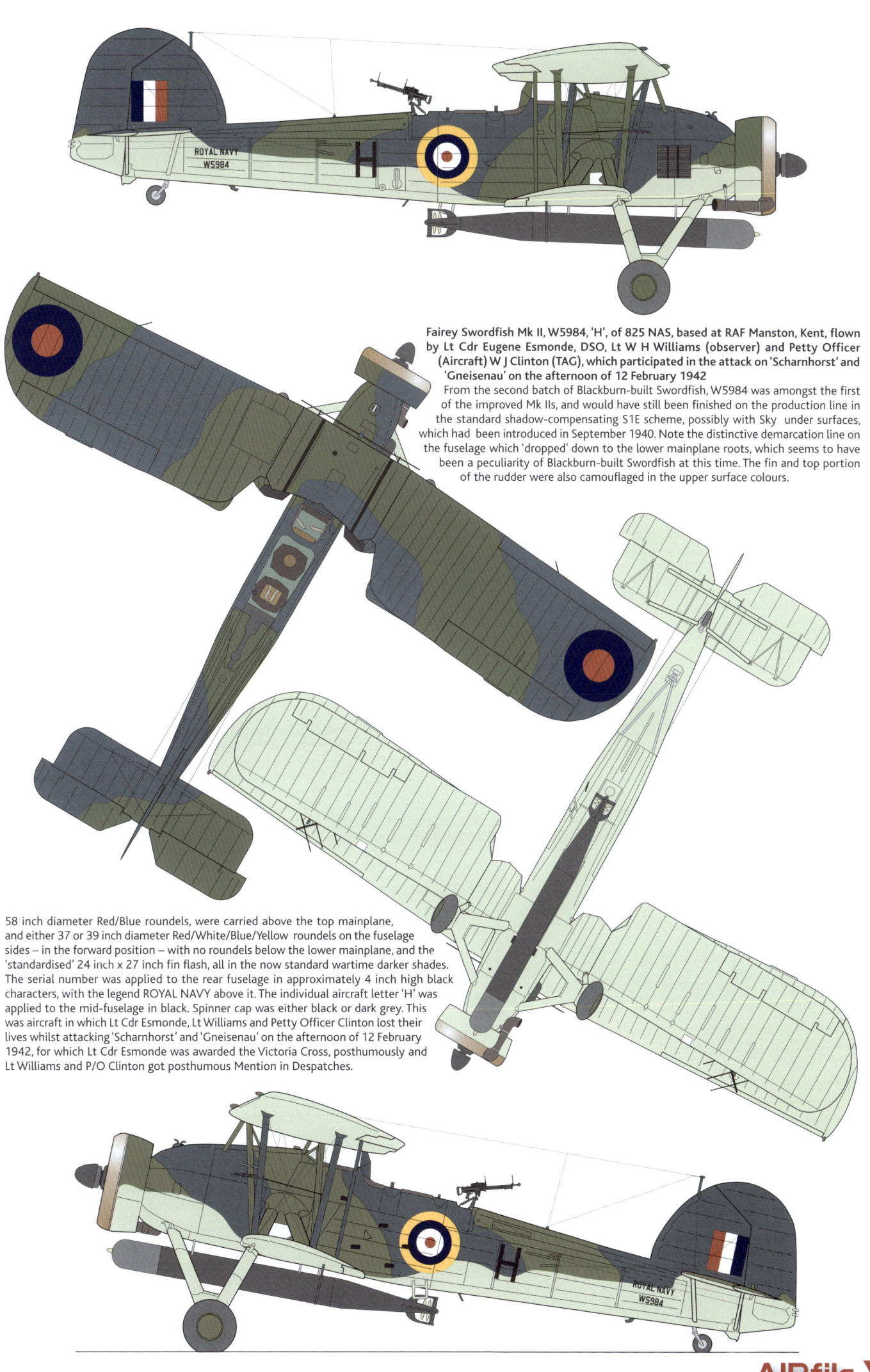

Fairey Swordfish Mk II, W5984, 'H', of 825 NAS, based at RAF Manston, Kent, flown by Lt Cdr Eugene Esmonde, DSO, Lt W H Williams (observer) and Petty Officer (Aircraft) W J Clinton (TAG), which participated in the attack on 'Scharnhorst' and 'Gneisenau' on the afternoon of 12 February 1942

From the second batch of Blackburn-built Swordfish, W5984 was amongst the first of the improved Mk IIs, and would have still been finished on the production line in the standard shadow-compensating S1E scheme, possibly with Sky under surfaces, which had been introduced in September 1940. Note the distinctive demarcation line on the fuselage which 'dropped' down to the lower mainplane roots, which seems to have been a peculiarity of Blackburn-built Swordfish at this time. The fin and top portion of the rudder were also camouflaged in the upper surface colours.

58 inch diameter Red/Blue roundels, were carried above the top mainplane, and either 37 or 39 inch diameter Red/White/Blue/Yellow roundels on the fuselage sides – in the forward position – with no roundels below the lower mainplane, and the 'standardised' 24 inch x 27 inch fin flash, all in the now standard wartime darker shades. The serial number was applied to the rear fuselage in approximately 4 inch high black characters, with the legend ROYAL NAVY above it. The individual aircraft letter 'H' was applied to the mid-fuselage in black. Spinner cap was either black or dark grey. This was aircraft in which Lt Cdr Esmonde, Lt Williams and Petty Officer Clinton lost their lives whilst attacking 'Scharnhorst' and 'Gneisenau' on the afternoon of 12 February 1942, for which Lt Cdr Esmonde was awarded the Victoria Cross, posthumously and Lt Williams and P/O Clinton got posthumous Mention in Despatches.

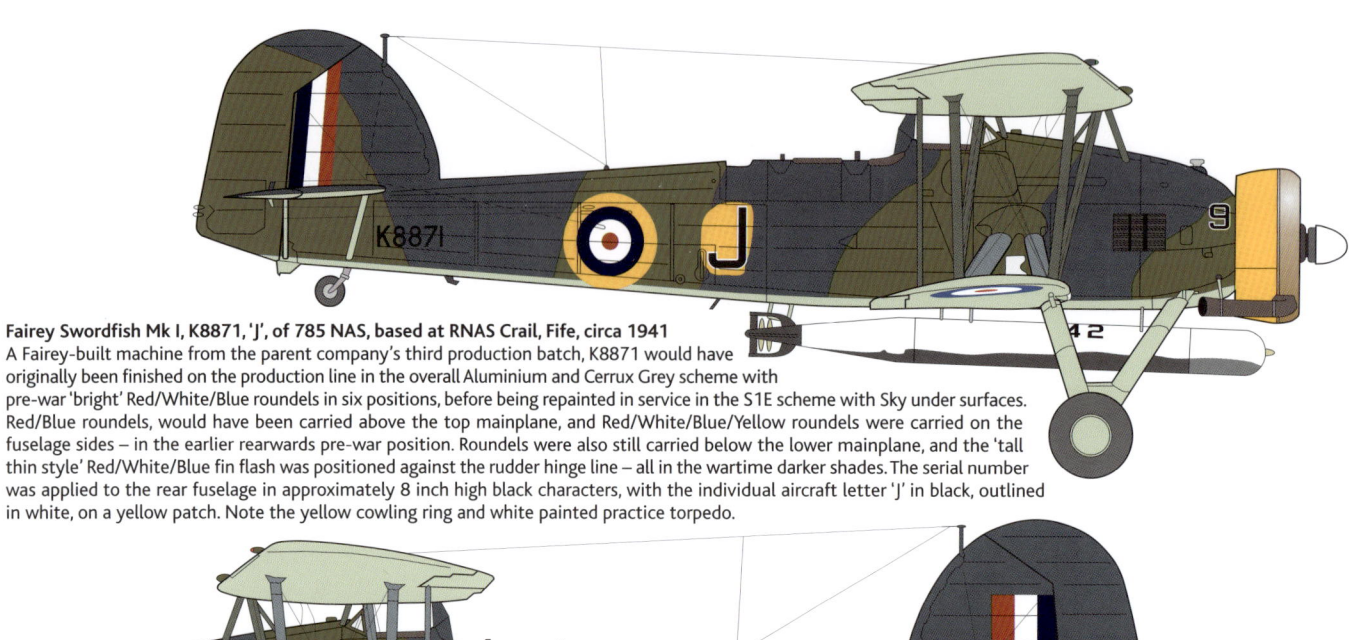

Fairey Swordfish Mk I, K8871, 'J', of 785 NAS, based at RNAS Crail, Fife, circa 1941
A Fairey-built machine from the parent company's third production batch, K8871 would have originally been finished on the production line in the overall Aluminium and Cerrux Grey scheme with pre-war 'bright' Red/White/Blue roundels in six positions, before being repainted in service in the S1E scheme with Sky under surfaces. Red/Blue roundels, would have been carried above the top mainplane, and Red/White/Blue/Yellow roundels were carried on the fuselage sides – in the earlier rearwards pre-war position. Roundels were also still carried below the lower mainplane, and the 'tall thin style' Red/White/Blue fin flash was positioned against the rudder hinge line – all in the wartime darker shades. The serial number was applied to the rear fuselage in approximately 8 inch high black characters, with the individual aircraft letter 'J' in black, outlined in white, on a yellow patch. Note the yellow cowling ring and white painted practice torpedo.

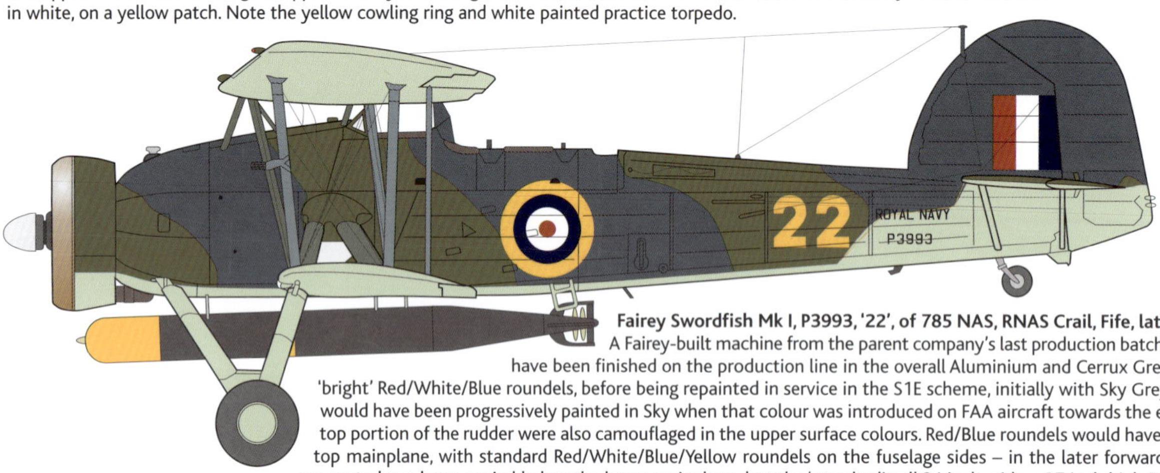

Fairey Swordfish Mk I, P3993, '22', of 785 NAS, RNAS Crail, Fife, late 1941
A Fairey-built machine from the parent company's last production batch, P3993 would probably have been finished on the production line in the overall Aluminium and Cerrux Grey scheme with pre-war 'bright' Red/White/Blue roundels, before being repainted in service in the S1E scheme, initially with Sky Grey under surfaces, which would have been progressively painted in Sky when that colour was introduced on FAA aircraft towards the end of 1940. The fin and top portion of the rudder were also camouflaged in the upper surface colours. Red/Blue roundels would have been carried above the top mainplane, with standard Red/White/Blue/Yellow roundels on the fuselage sides – in the later forward position. No roundels appear to have been carried below the lower mainplane, but the 'standardised' 24 inch wide x 27 inch high Red/White/Blue fin flash was applied to the fin – all of which appear to have been in the wartime darker shades. The serial number was applied to the rear fuselage in approximately 4 inch high black characters, with the legend ROYAL NAVY above it. The individual aircraft numeral '22' was also applied to the rear fuselage in yellow. Note the yellow tip to the practice torpedo. Spinner cap was either natural metal or white.

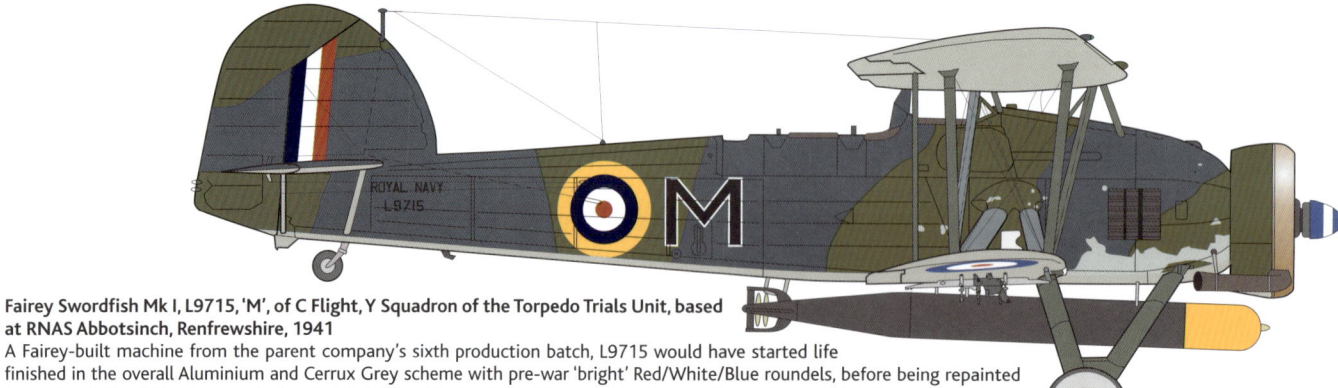

Fairey Swordfish Mk I, L9715, 'M', of C Flight, Y Squadron of the Torpedo Trials Unit, based at RNAS Abbotsinch, Renfrewshire, 1941
A Fairey-built machine from the parent company's sixth production batch, L9715 would have started life finished in the overall Aluminium and Cerrux Grey scheme with pre-war 'bright' Red/White/Blue roundels, before being repainted in service in the S1E scheme, which extended down the fuselage sides, and Sky Grey under surfaces, which it appears to have retained well in to 1941. Red/Blue roundels, were carried above the top mainplane with Red/White/Blue/Yellow roundels on the fuselage sides – in the earlier rearwards pre-war position – and Red/White/Blue roundels below the lower mainplane. The Red/White/Blue fin flash was applied in approximately 6 inch wide bands, extending the full height of the fin and angled to match the rudder and horn balance hinge line. The serial number was applied to the rear fuselage in approximately 4 inch high black characters, with the legend ROYAL NAVY above it. The individual aircraft letter 'M' was applied to the mid fuselage in black thinly outlined in white. Spinner cap appears to be blue with a white band around it. Note the yellow tip to the practice torpedo, the white-walled mainwheel tyres and yellow hubs.

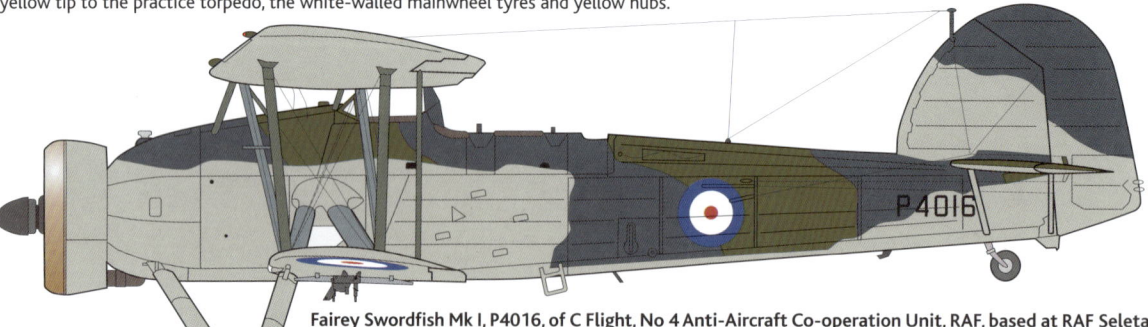

Fairey Swordfish Mk I, P4016, of C Flight, No 4 Anti-Aircraft Co-operation Unit, RAF, based at RAF Seletar, Singapore, late 1941
A Fairey-built machine from the parent company's last production batch, P4016 could possibly have been amongst the last Swordfish airframes to be finished in the overall Aluminium and Cerrux Grey scheme with pre-war 'bright' Red/White/Blue roundels before the production line changeover to camouflage. It would no doubt have been repainted in service, in the S1E scheme on the upper surfaces, with Sky Grey under surfaces, fuselage sides, fin and rudder. However, areas of the upper surface camouflage colour appear to have been applied to the mid fuselage section and across the top of the fin and rudder – although this may just be how the aircraft looked part way through being repainted? Red/Blue roundels, were probably carried above the top mainplane with Red/White/Blue roundels on the fuselage sides – in the earlier rearwards pre-war position – and Red/White/Blue roundels below the lower mainplane – all in the pre-war bright shades. No fin flash was carried and the serial number was only applied to the rear fuselage in 8 inch high black characters. No other markings appear to have been carried. Spinner cap appears to be black or dark grey.

Fairey Swordfish Mk I, V4367, of 701 Ship's Flight, operating off the battleship HMS Malaya, summer 1941

From the first batch of Blackburn-built Mk Is, V4367 may well have been built as a 'wheeled' variant and modified in to floatplane configuration at a subsequent date. Finished in the shadow-compensating S1E scheme of Extra Dark Sea Grey, Dark Slate Grey, Dark Sea Grey and Light Slate Grey on the upper surfaces, it appears to have retained Sky Grey under surfaces, despite the introduction of Sky under surfaces almost a year earlier. Note the distinctive 'Blackburn' demarcation line on the fuselage which 'dropped' down to the lower mainplane roots. The floats were Extra Dark Sea Grey and Dark Slate Grey on their upper surfaces, (and very weathered) with Night under surfaces.

58 inch diameter Red/Blue roundels, were carried above the top mainplane, and possibly 37 inch diameter Red/White/Blue/Yellow roundels on the fuselage sides – in the forward position – with no roundels below the lower mainplane, and the 'standardised' 24 inch x 27 inch fin flash, all in the now standard wartime darker shades. The serial number was applied to the rear fuselage in approximately 4 inch high black characters, with the legend ROYAL NAVY above it. No other markings appear to have been carried. Spinner cap was either black or dark grey. Note this aircraft was fitted with ASV (Air-to-Surface Vessel) radar with the aerials mounted on the outer leading interplane struts.

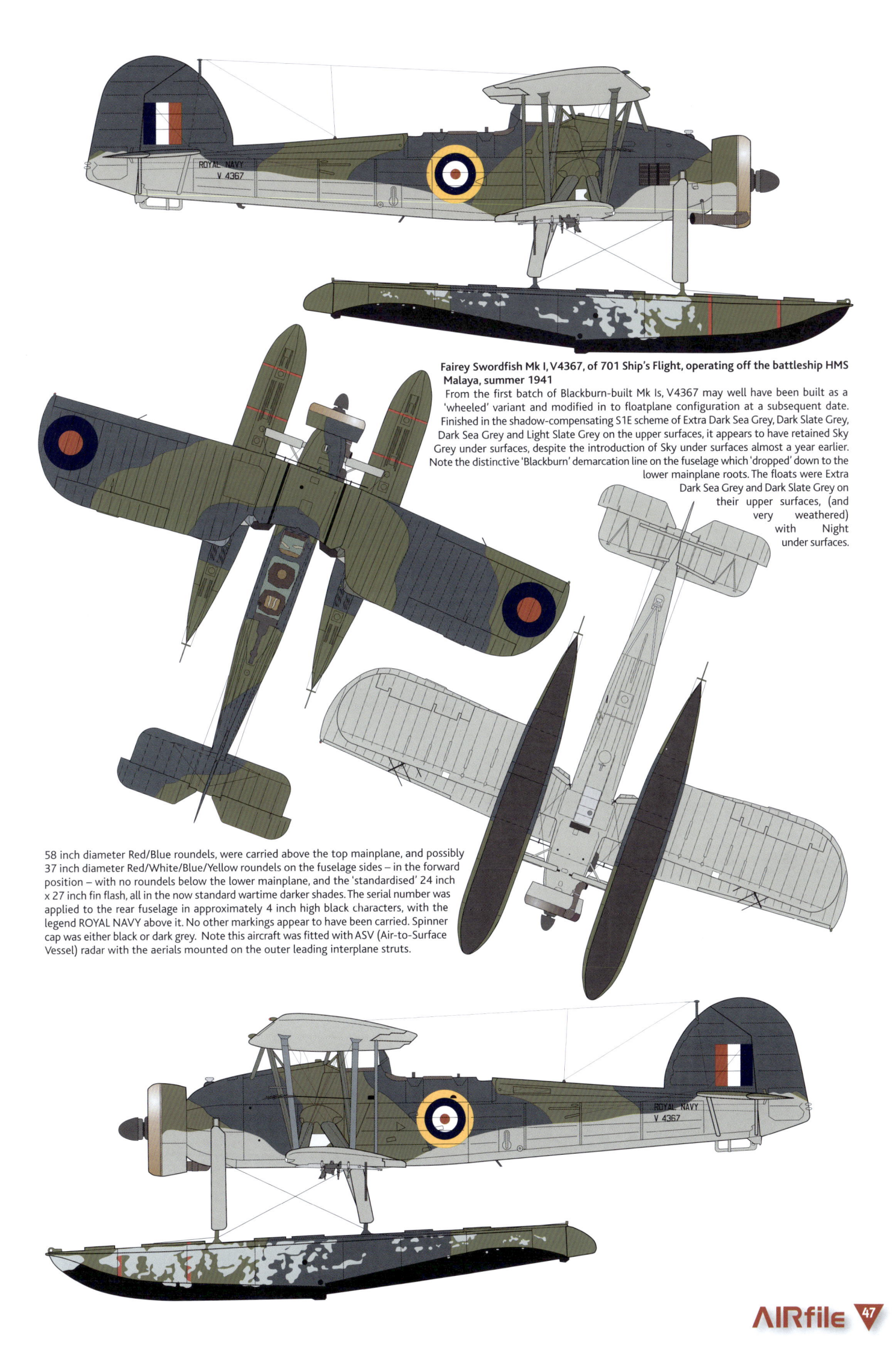

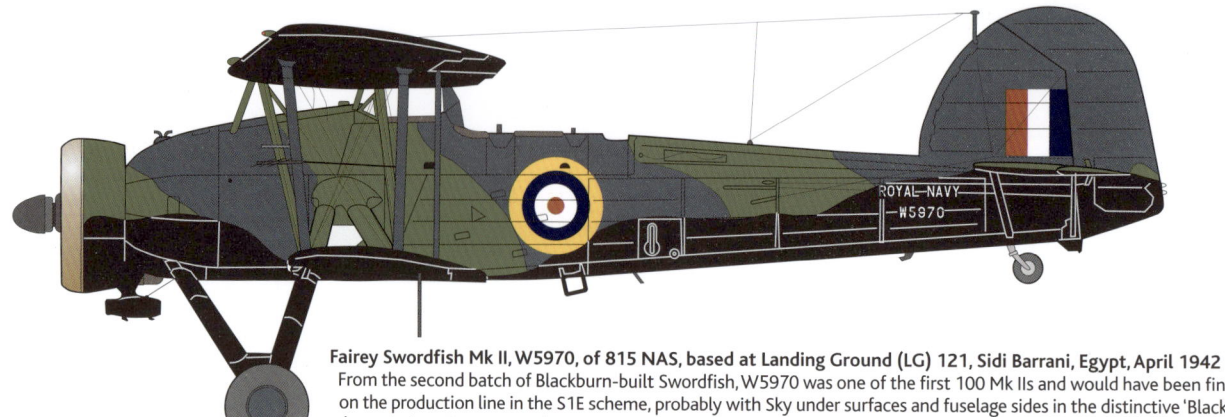

Fairey Swordfish Mk II, W5970, of 815 NAS, based at Landing Ground (LG) 121, Sidi Barrani, Egypt, April 1942
From the second batch of Blackburn-built Swordfish, W5970 was one of the first 100 Mk IIs and would have been finished on the production line in the S1E scheme, probably with Sky under surfaces and fuselage sides in the distinctive 'Blackburn' demarcation. For nocturnal operations, the under surfaces were overpainted in Night. Red/Blue roundels, were carried above the top mainplane, Red/White/Blue/Yellow roundels on the fuselage sides – in the forward wartime position – with no roundels below the lower mainplane – and the 'standardised' fin flash, all in the wartime darker shades. The serial number was applied to the rear fuselage in approximately 4 inch high characters, with the legend ROYAL NAVY above it – all repainted in white, presumably when the NIght under surfaces were applied. Spinner cap also appears to be in Night. Note the Vokes tropical carburettor filter.

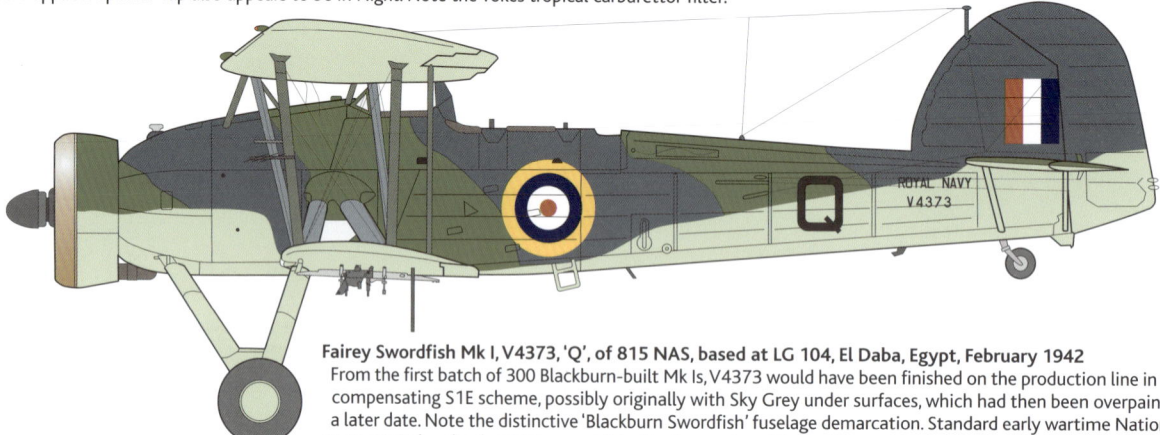

Fairey Swordfish Mk I, V4373, 'Q', of 815 NAS, based at LG 104, El Daba, Egypt, February 1942
From the first batch of 300 Blackburn-built Mk Is, V4373 would have been finished on the production line in the shadow-compensating S1E scheme, possibly originally with Sky Grey under surfaces, which had then been overpainted in Sky at a later date. Note the distinctive 'Blackburn Swordfish' fuselage demarcation. Standard early wartime National Markings were carried – the fuselage roundel in the forward position with no roundels below the lower mainplane, and the 'standardised' 24 inch by 27 inch fin flash, all in the darker shades. The serial number was applied to the rear fuselage in approximately 4 inch high black characters, with the legend ROYAL NAVY above it. The individual aircraft letter 'Q' was applied to the mid-fuselage in black. Spinner cap was either black or dark grey.

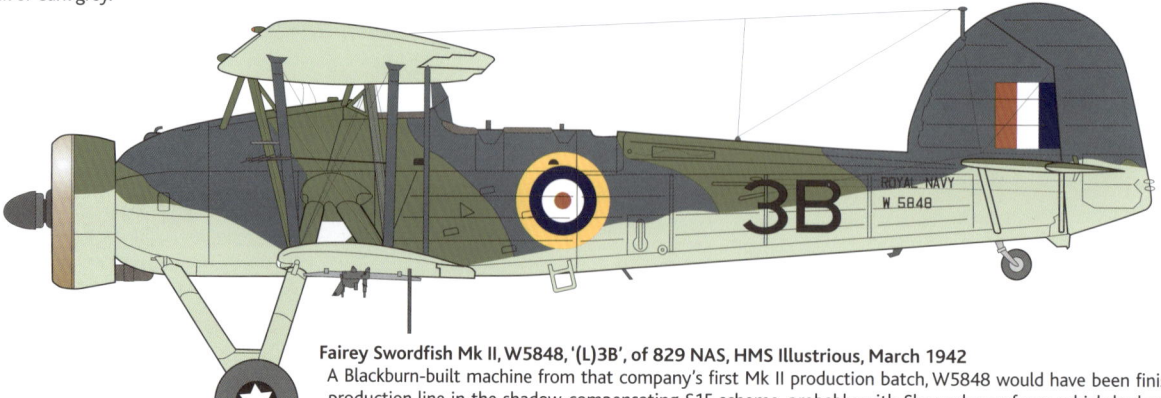

Fairey Swordfish Mk II, W5848, '(L)3B', of 829 NAS, HMS Illustrious, March 1942
A Blackburn-built machine from that company's first Mk II production batch, W5848 would have been finished on the production line in the shadow-compensating S1E scheme, probably with Sky under surfaces, which had possibly been introduced on the production line by the time of the aircraft's manufacture. Standard early wartime National Markings were carried – the fuselage roundel in the forward position with no roundels below the lower mainplane, and the 'standardised' 24 inch by 27 inch fin flash, all in the darker shades. The serial number was applied to the rear fuselage in approximately 4 inch high black characters, with the legend ROYAL NAVY above it. The Aircraft Class numeral '3' and the individual aircraft letter 'B' were positioned on the rear fuselage in black. Spinner cap was either black or dark grey. Note the white, six-pointed star on the black mainwheel hubs.

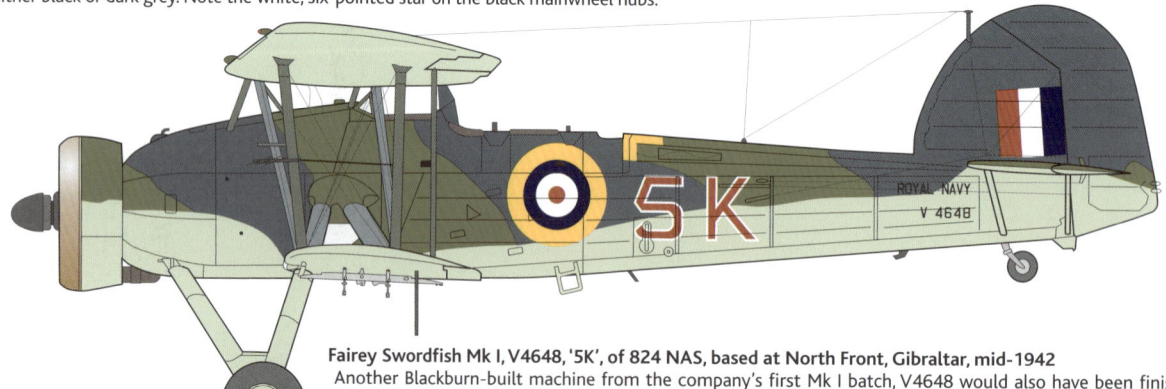

Fairey Swordfish Mk I, V4648, '5K', of 824 NAS, based at North Front, Gibraltar, mid-1942
Another Blackburn-built machine from the company's first Mk I batch, V4648 would also have been finished on the production line in the shadow-compensating S1E scheme, possibly originally with Sky Grey under surfaces, which were subsequently overpainted in Sky. Standard early wartime National Markings were carried – but note the wider than standard Yellow outline to the fuselage roundel – with no roundels below the lower mainplane, and the 'standardised' fin flash. The serial number was applied to the rear fuselage in approximately 4 inch high black characters, with the legend ROYAL NAVY above it. The Aircraft Class numeral '5' and the individual aircraft letter 'K' were positioned on the rear fuselage in red, thinly outlined in white. Spinner cap was either black or dark grey. Note the yellow (?) patch on the upper fuselage to the rear of the TAG's cockpit.

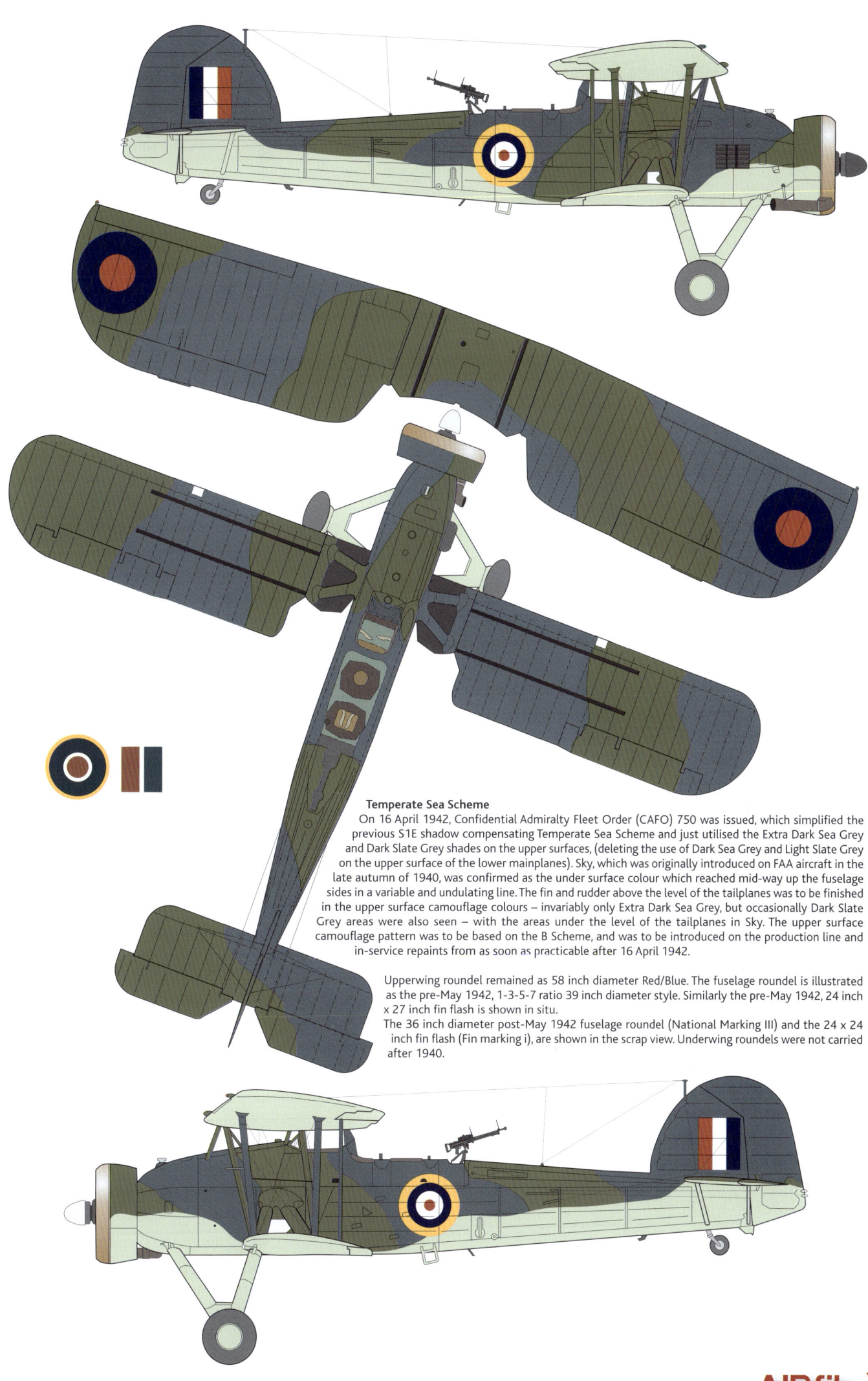

Temperate Sea Scheme

On 16 April 1942, Confidential Admiralty Fleet Order (CAFO) 750 was issued, which simplified the previous S1E shadow compensating Temperate Sea Scheme and just utilised the Extra Dark Sea Grey and Dark Slate Grey shades on the upper surfaces, (deleting the use of Dark Sea Grey and Light Slate Grey on the upper surface of the lower mainplanes). Sky, which was originally introduced on FAA aircraft in the late autumn of 1940, was confirmed as the under surface colour which reached mid-way up the fuselage sides in a variable and undulating line. The fin and rudder above the level of the tailplanes was to be finished in the upper surface camouflage colours – invariably only Extra Dark Sea Grey, but occasionally Dark Slate Grey areas were also seen – with the areas under the level of the tailplanes in Sky. The upper surface camouflage pattern was to be based on the B Scheme, and was to be introduced on the production line and in-service repaints from as soon as practicable after 16 April 1942.

Upperwing roundel remained as 58 inch diameter Red/Blue. The fuselage roundel is illustrated as the pre-May 1942, 1-3-5-7 ratio 39 inch diameter style. Similarly the pre-May 1942, 24 inch x 27 inch fin flash is shown in situ.

The 36 inch diameter post-May 1942 fuselage roundel (National Marking III) and the 24 x 24 inch fin flash (Fin marking i), are shown in the scrap view. Underwing roundels were not carried after 1940.

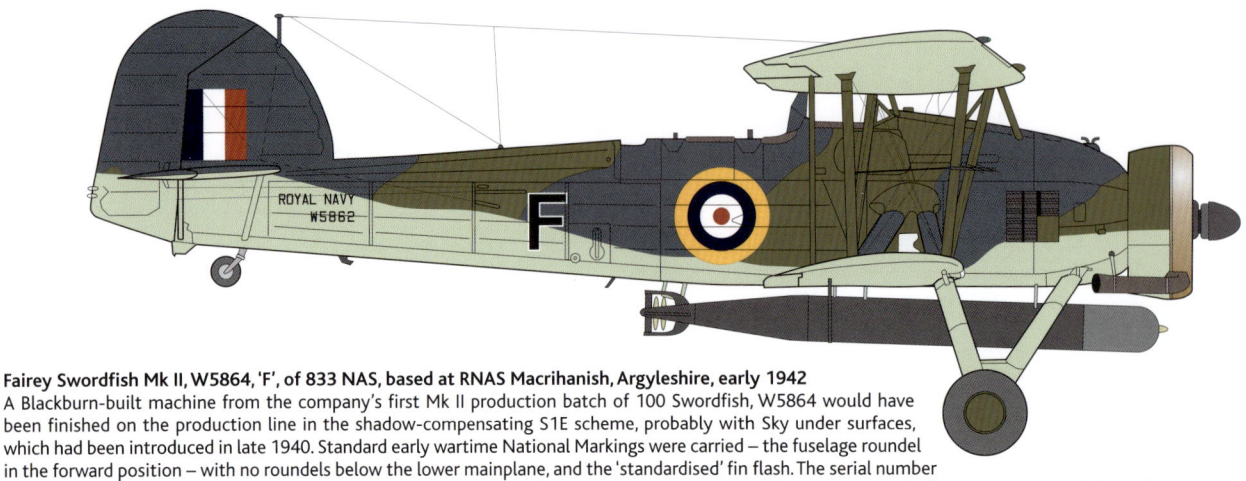

Fairey Swordfish Mk II, W5864, 'F', of 833 NAS, based at RNAS Macrihanish, Argyleshire, early 1942
A Blackburn-built machine from the company's first Mk II production batch of 100 Swordfish, W5864 would have been finished on the production line in the shadow-compensating S1E scheme, probably with Sky under surfaces, which had been introduced in late 1940. Standard early wartime National Markings were carried – the fuselage roundel in the forward position – with no roundels below the lower mainplane, and the 'standardised' fin flash. The serial number was applied to the rear fuselage in approximately 4 inch high black characters, with the legend ROYAL NAVY above it. The individual aircraft letter 'F' was positioned on the mid fuselage in black thinly outlined in white. Spinner cap was either black or dark grey. Note the Dark Slate Grey mainwheel hubs.

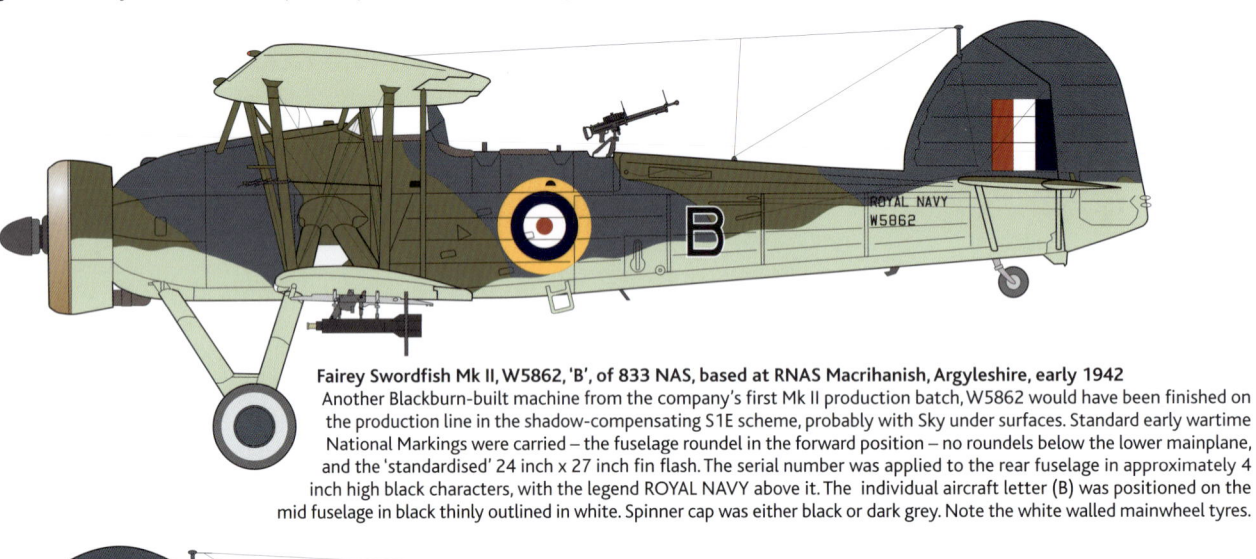

Fairey Swordfish Mk II, W5862, 'B', of 833 NAS, based at RNAS Macrihanish, Argyleshire, early 1942
Another Blackburn-built machine from the company's first Mk II production batch, W5862 would have been finished on the production line in the shadow-compensating S1E scheme, probably with Sky under surfaces. Standard early wartime National Markings were carried – the fuselage roundel in the forward position – no roundels below the lower mainplane, and the 'standardised' 24 inch x 27 inch fin flash. The serial number was applied to the rear fuselage in approximately 4 inch high black characters, with the legend ROYAL NAVY above it. The individual aircraft letter (B) was positioned on the mid fuselage in black thinly outlined in white. Spinner cap was either black or dark grey. Note the white walled mainwheel tyres.

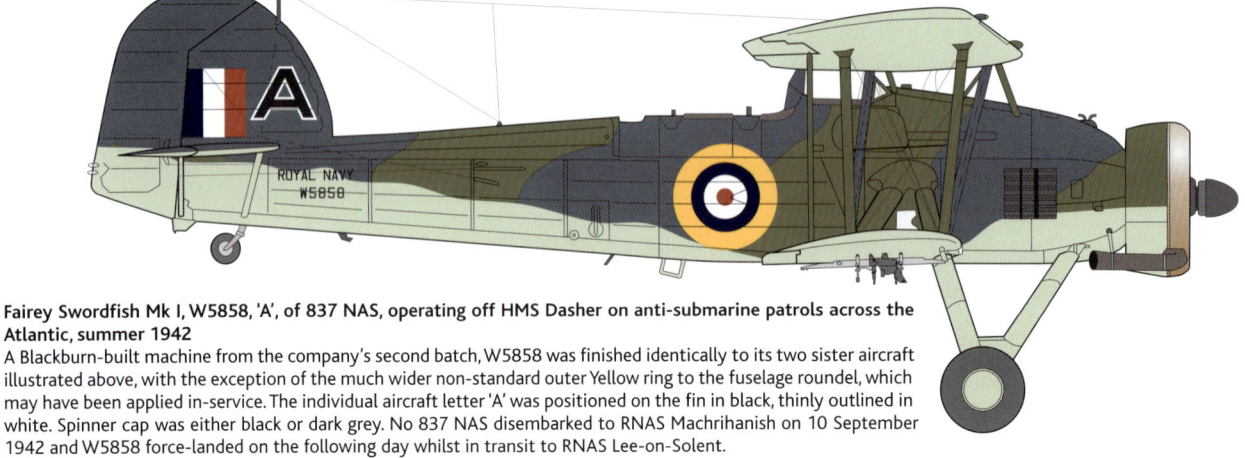

Fairey Swordfish Mk I, W5858, 'A', of 837 NAS, operating off HMS Dasher on anti-submarine patrols across the Atlantic, summer 1942
A Blackburn-built machine from the company's second batch, W5858 was finished identically to its two sister aircraft illustrated above, with the exception of the much wider non-standard outer Yellow ring to the fuselage roundel, which may have been applied in-service. The individual aircraft letter 'A' was positioned on the fin in black, thinly outlined in white. Spinner cap was either black or dark grey. No 837 NAS disembarked to RNAS Machrihanish on 10 September 1942 and W5858 force-landed on the following day whilst in transit to RNAS Lee-on-Solent.

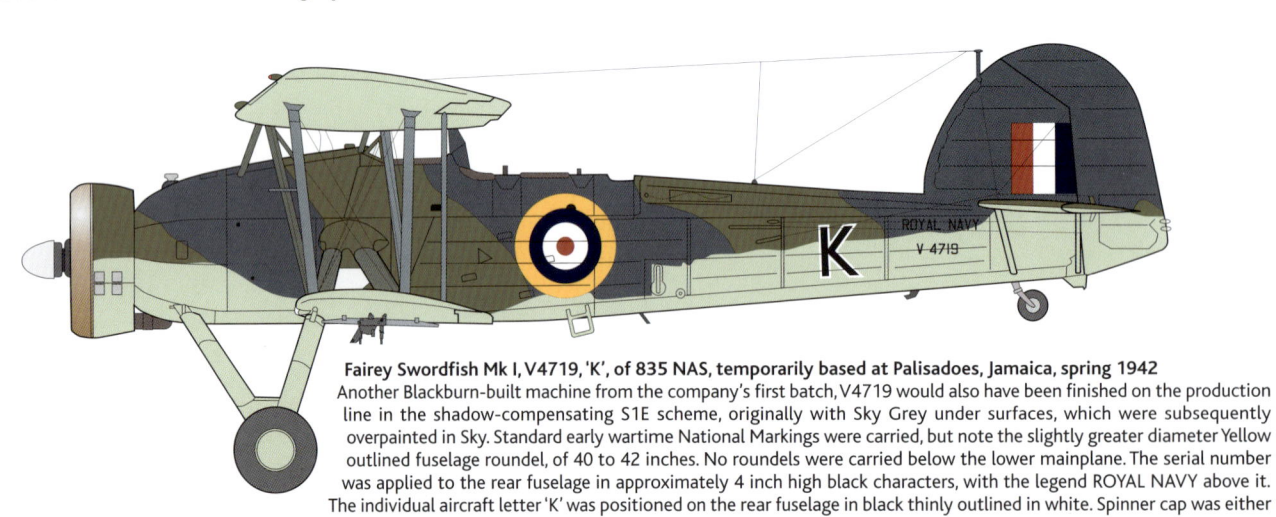

Fairey Swordfish Mk I, V4719, 'K', of 835 NAS, temporarily based at Palisadoes, Jamaica, spring 1942
Another Blackburn-built machine from the company's first batch, V4719 would also have been finished on the production line in the shadow-compensating S1E scheme, originally with Sky Grey under surfaces, which were subsequently overpainted in Sky. Standard early wartime National Markings were carried, but note the slightly greater diameter Yellow outlined fuselage roundel, of 40 to 42 inches. No roundels were carried below the lower mainplane. The serial number was applied to the rear fuselage in approximately 4 inch high black characters, with the legend ROYAL NAVY above it. The individual aircraft letter 'K' was positioned on the rear fuselage in black thinly outlined in white. Spinner cap was either natural metal or pale grey.

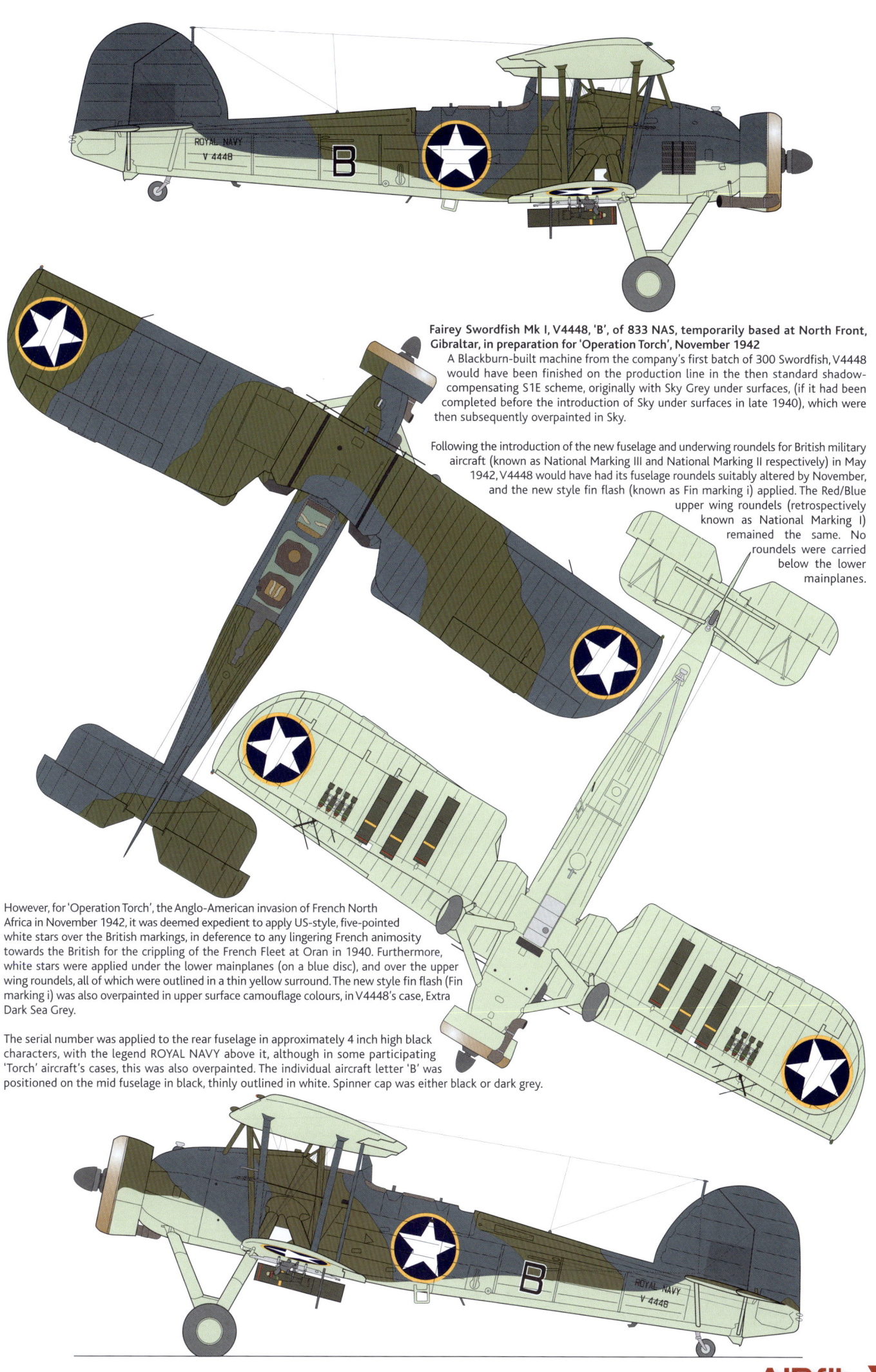

Fairey Swordfish Mk I, V4448, 'B', of 833 NAS, temporarily based at North Front, Gibraltar, in preparation for 'Operation Torch', November 1942

A Blackburn-built machine from the company's first batch of 300 Swordfish, V4448 would have been finished on the production line in the then standard shadow-compensating S1E scheme, originally with Sky Grey under surfaces, (if it had been completed before the introduction of Sky under surfaces in late 1940), which were then subsequently overpainted in Sky.

Following the introduction of the new fuselage and underwing roundels for British military aircraft (known as National Marking III and National Marking II respectively) in May 1942, V4448 would have had its fuselage roundels suitably altered by November, and the new style fin flash (known as Fin marking i) applied. The Red/Blue upper wing roundels (retrospectively known as National Marking I) remained the same. No roundels were carried below the lower mainplanes.

However, for 'Operation Torch', the Anglo-American invasion of French North Africa in November 1942, it was deemed expedient to apply US-style, five-pointed white stars over the British markings, in deference to any lingering French animosity towards the British for the crippling of the French Fleet at Oran in 1940. Furthermore, white stars were applied under the lower mainplanes (on a blue disc), and over the upper wing roundels, all of which were outlined in a thin yellow surround. The new style fin flash (Fin marking i) was also overpainted in upper surface camouflage colours, in V4448's case, Extra Dark Sea Grey.

The serial number was applied to the rear fuselage in approximately 4 inch high black characters, with the legend ROYAL NAVY above it, although in some participating 'Torch' aircraft's cases, this was also overpainted. The individual aircraft letter 'B' was positioned on the mid fuselage in black, thinly outlined in white. Spinner cap was either black or dark grey.

Fairey Swordfish Mk II, HS164, '2F', of 810 NAS, HMS Illustrious, mid -1942
A Blackburn-built machine, from the company's third batch of (400) Mk IIs, HS164 would have probably been finished on the production line in the then recently introduced 'simplified' Temperate Sea Scheme scheme, with Sky under surfaces. The new style National Markings, introduced in May 1942, would have been applied either on the production line or in-service. The serial number was applied to the rear fuselage in approximately 4 inch high black characters, with the legend ROYAL NAVY above it. The Aircraft Class numeral '2' and the individual aircraft letter 'F' were positioned on the mid fuselage in red. Spinner cap was either black or dark grey.

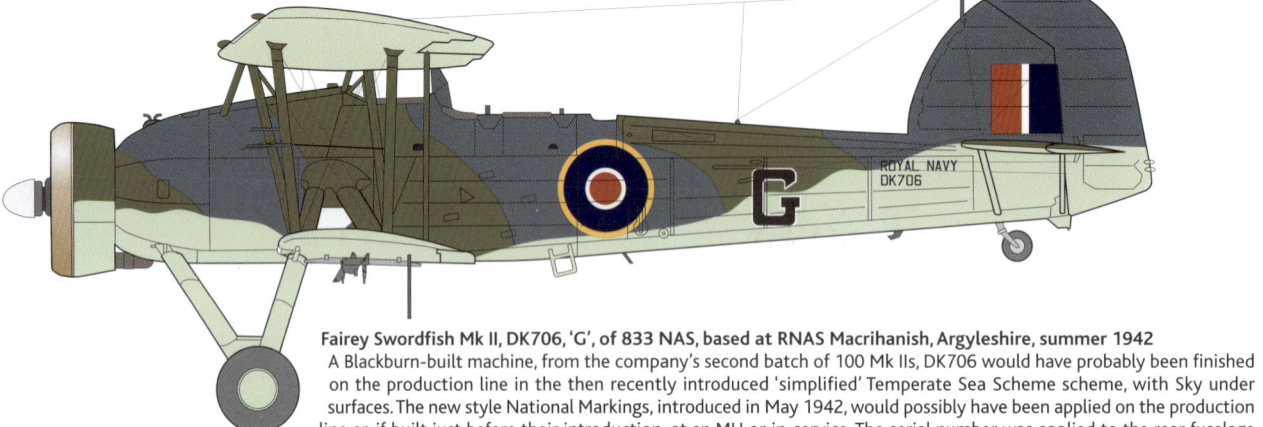

Fairey Swordfish Mk II, DK706, 'G', of 833 NAS, based at RNAS Macrihanish, Argyleshire, summer 1942
A Blackburn-built machine, from the company's second batch of 100 Mk IIs, DK706 would have probably been finished on the production line in the then recently introduced 'simplified' Temperate Sea Scheme scheme, with Sky under surfaces. The new style National Markings, introduced in May 1942, would possibly have been applied on the production line or, if built just before their introduction, at an MU or in-service. The serial number was applied to the rear fuselage in approximately 4 inch high black characters, with the legend ROYAL NAVY above it. The individual aircraft letter 'G' was positioned on the rear fuselage in black thinly outlined in white. Spinner cap was either natural metal or pale grey.

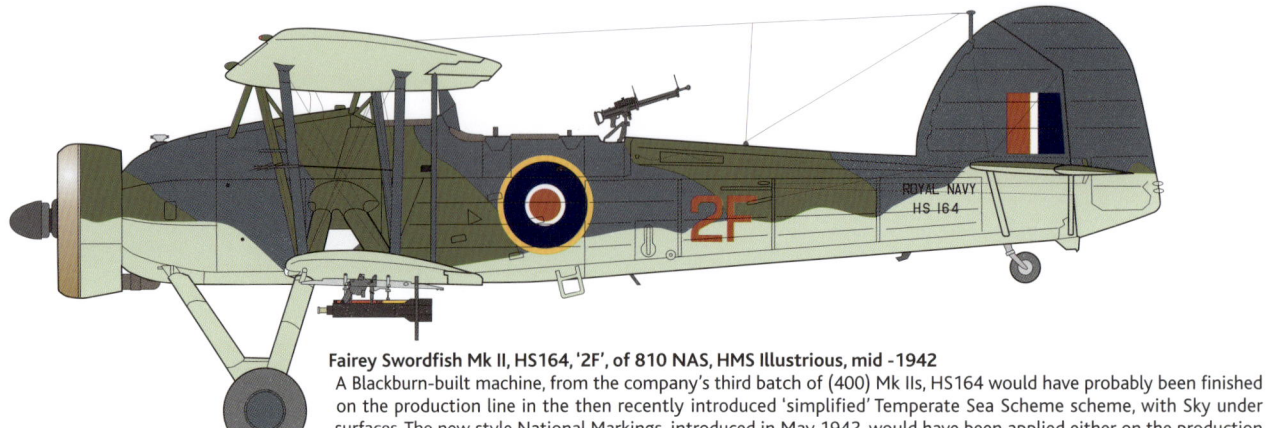

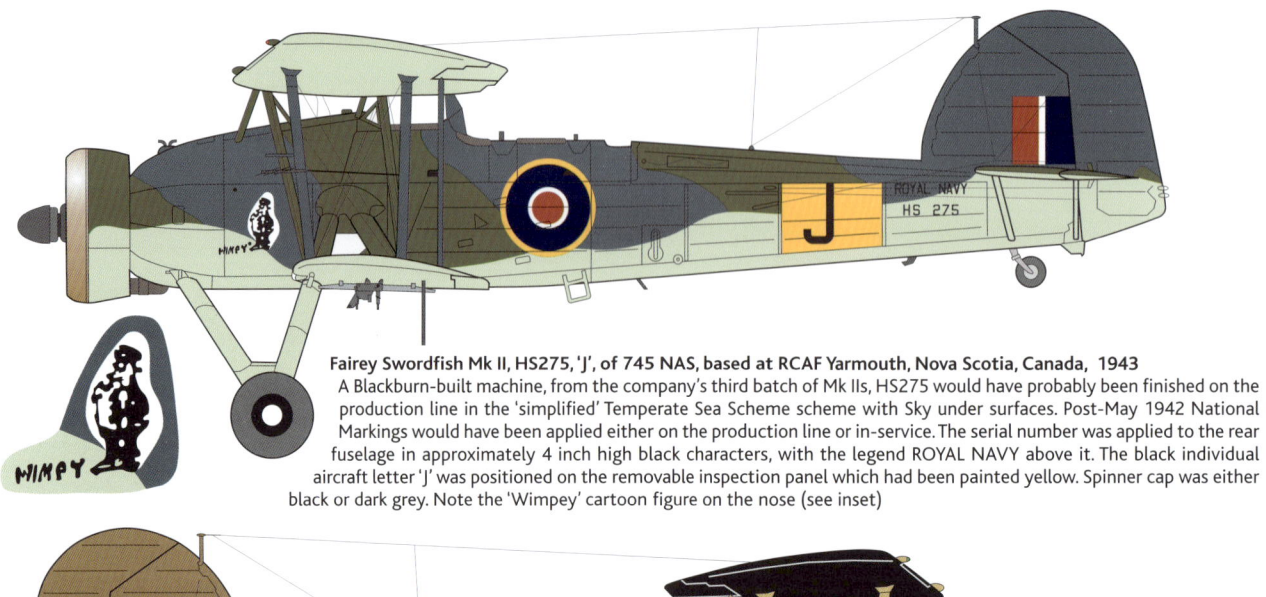

Fairey Swordfish Mk II, HS275, 'J', of 745 NAS, based at RCAF Yarmouth, Nova Scotia, Canada, 1943
A Blackburn-built machine, from the company's third batch of Mk IIs, HS275 would have probably been finished on the production line in the 'simplified' Temperate Sea Scheme scheme with Sky under surfaces. Post-May 1942 National Markings would have been applied either on the production line or in-service. The serial number was applied to the rear fuselage in approximately 4 inch high black characters, with the legend ROYAL NAVY above it. The black individual aircraft letter 'J' was positioned on the removable inspection panel which had been painted yellow. Spinner cap was either black or dark grey. Note the 'Wimpey' cartoon figure on the nose (see inset)

Fairey Swordfish Mk I, V4697, of 775 NAS, based at Fayid, Egypt, November 1942
A Blackburn-built machine from the company's first batch, comprising 300 Mk Is, V4697 would also have been finished on the production line in the shadow-compensating S1E scheme, originally with Sky Grey under surfaces, which were then subsequently overpainted in Sky. The standard early wartime National Markings would have been applied but would have been subsequently altered to the post-May 1942 style, which probably explains the slightly greater diameter of the fuselage roundel. This machine crashed on 25 June 1942, but was repaired and subsequently repainted in what appears to be Mid Stone and Dark Earth upper surfaces, with Night undersides. The serial number was applied to the rear fuselage with the legend ROYAL NAVY above it all in approximately 4 inch high white characters. Spinner cap was either black or dark grey. Note the Vokes tropical carburettor intake and the enlarged Mk II-style oil cooler on the starboard nose side.

Fairey Swordfish Mk II, DK757, '4H', of 813 NAS, based at Bone, Algeria, December 1942, crewed by Sub Lt P C Heath (pilot), Lt D A P Weatherall, (observer) and P/O(A) H T Goddard (TAG)

A Blackburn-built machine, from the company's second batch of 100 Mk IIs, DK757 would have probably been finished on the production line in the then recently introduced 'simplified' upper surface Temperate Sea Scheme of Extra Dark Sea Grey and Dark Slate Grey, with Sky under surfaces.

The new style National Markings, introduced in May 1942, would have been applied either on the production line, if the aircraft had been completed after mid-May, or if completed before, either at an MU or in-service. The serial number was applied to the rear fuselage in approximately 4 inch high black characters, with the legend ROYAL NAVY above it. The Aircraft Class numeral '4' and the individual aircraft letter 'H' were positioned on the rear fuselage in black, thinly outlined in white. Note the Dark Slate Grey mainwheel hubs and the spinner cap was either black or dark grey.

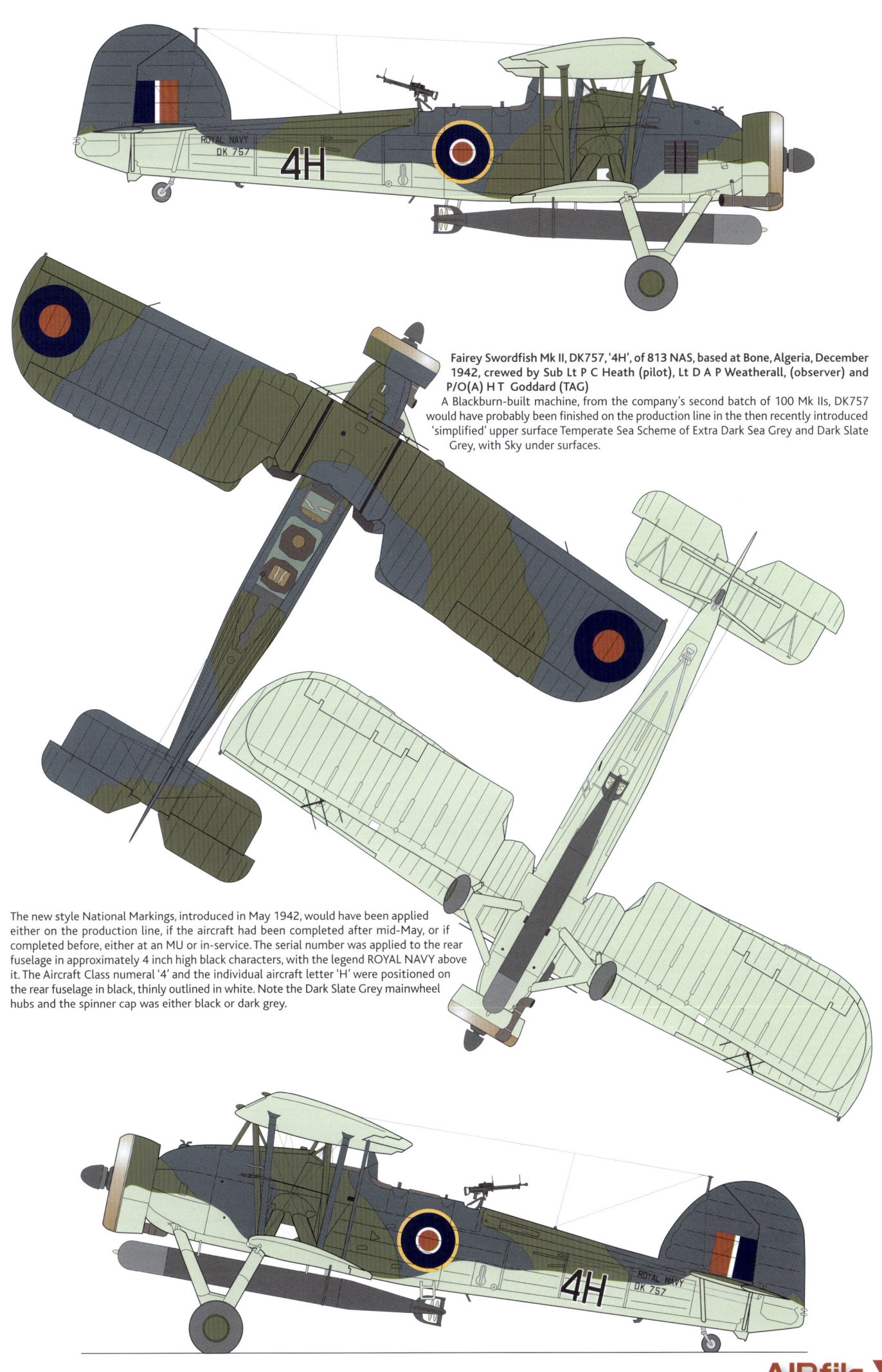

Chapter 6

Change of role
1943 to 1945

Swordfish Mk III, NS191, based at RNAS Macrihanish, Argyle in September 1944, fitted with Rocket Assisted Take Off Gear (RATOG), and used for testing the operational feasibility of taking-off from a floating airstrip anchored in Lamlash Harbour, Isle of Arran. A late production, Blackburn-built Mk III, NS191 was finished in the white 'anti-submarine' scheme, with Temperate Sea Scheme upper surfaces and the trials were flown by Lt Cdr C R Jeffs, RNVR. (see profile on p66)

Convoy escort and anti-submarine roles

With the development of new torpedo attack aircraft, the Swordfish was soon redeployed successfully in an anti-submarine role, armed with depth charges and/or eight 60lb Rocket Projectiles (RP) rockets and flying from the smaller escort carriers or even Merchant Aircraft Carriers (MAC) when equipped with Rocket-Assisted Take Off Gear (RATOG).

Its low stall speed and inherently robust design made it ideal for operation from the MAC carriers in the often severe mid-Atlantic weather. Indeed, its take-off and landing speeds were so low that it did not require the carrier to be steaming into the wind, unlike most carrier-based aircraft. On occasion, when the wind was right, Swordfish could even be flown from a carrier at anchor.

The Swordfish was meant to be replaced by the Fairey Albacore, also a biplane, but the type actually outlived its intended successor. It was, however, finally succeeded by the Fairey Barracuda monoplane torpedo bomber.

Swordfish Mk II, the most numerous variant built – 1,080 all by Blackburn Aircraft Ltd – was fitted with metal plated lower wing surfaces to enable the mounting of Rocket Projectiles, introduced in 1943.

The Swordfish Mk III added a Mark X centrimetric Air-to-Surface Vessel (ASV) radar pod between the landing gear, introduced in 1943, as well as fittings for rocket-assisted take-off gear (RATOG). The positioning of the large ASV pod meant the Mk III couldn't carry a torpedo or any other large centerline store. Some 320 were built, again all by Blackburn Aircraft Ltd.

The Swordfish Mk IV was the last serial-built version, (production ended in 1944), and were all converted from Mark IIs with an enclosed, heated, cockpit, built for operations in Canada with the Royal Canadian Air Force. 110 airframes were converted from existing Mk IIs.

The last Swordfish aircraft was delivered in August 1944 and operational sorties continued in to January 1945 with anti-shipping operations off Norway (by 835 and 813 NASs), where the Swordfish's manouvreability proved essential.

By the end of the war there were still thirteen operational squadrons flying the Swordfish – the last operational squadron was disbanded on 21 May 1945, after the fall of Germany, and the last training squadron was disbanded in the summer of 1946. The last operational squadron, 860 (Dutch) Naval Air Squadron, was established in June 1943 and was manned by Dutch naval personnel in exile. The largest Swordfish unit, 836 NAS, was equipped with some ninety-one aircraft at one time. Swordfish-equipped units accounted for fourteen U-boats sunk or destroyed during World War Two.

Opposite Top:
The Swordfish Mk II was the most numerous variant built – 1,080 all by Blackburn Aircraft Ltd – and was fitted with metal plated lower wing surfaces to enable the mounting of Rocket Projectiles, introduced in 1943. This particular unidentified example, coded Y8•C, probably served with 765 NAS, a training unit based at Lee-on-Solent, Hampshire, and was photographed armed with a full load of 60lb RPs.

Opposite Middle:
A Sherburn-in Elmet-built Mk II, from the fourth batch, comprising 250 airframes, produced by the company, LS268 would have been amongst the first Swordfish to be finished on the production line in the white 'anti-submarine' under surface scheme, which was introduced in September 1943. The upper surfaces remained in the Temperate Sea Scheme and post-May 1942 National Markings would also have been applied on the production line, with the ROYAL NAVY legend in 4 inch high characters and the serial number in 8 inch high characters.

Opposite Bottom:
An almost identical view to the photo above, this shows a Swordfish Mk III, NR951, also built by Blackburn Aircraft Ltd at Sherburn-in-Elmet, with the Mark X centrimetric Air-to-Surface Vessel (ASV) radar pod mounted between the landing gear legs, which was introduced in 1943. The positioning of the large ASV pod meant the Mk III couldn't carry a torpedo or any other large centerline store. Some 320 were built, all by Blackburn Aircraft Ltd.

AIRfile 55

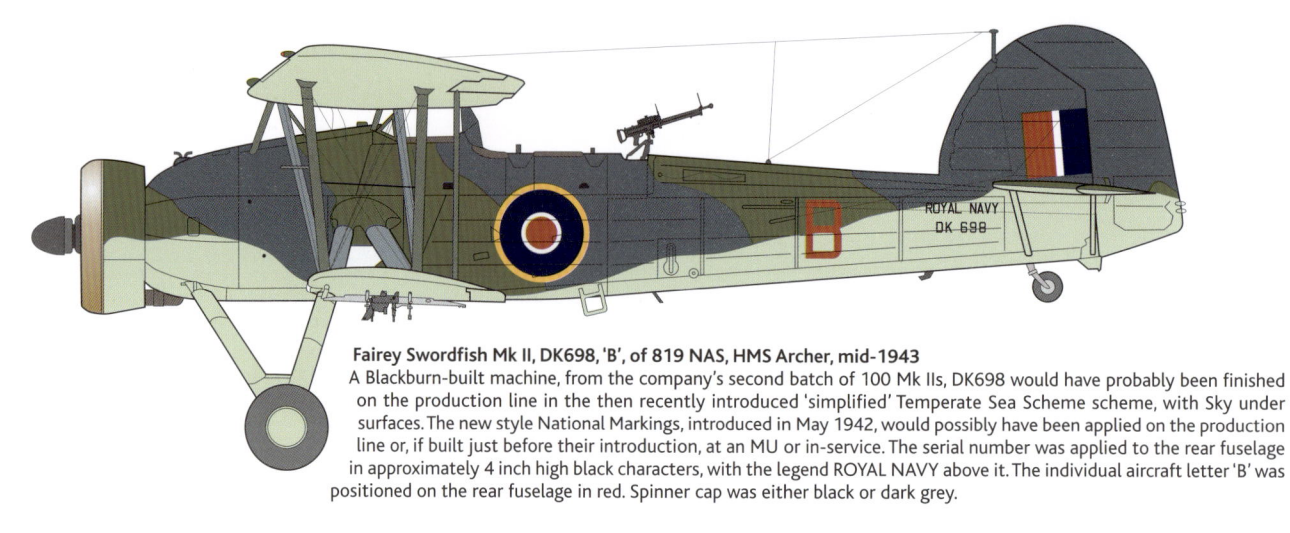

Fairey Swordfish Mk II, DK698, 'B', of 819 NAS, HMS Archer, mid-1943
A Blackburn-built machine, from the company's second batch of 100 Mk IIs, DK698 would have probably been finished on the production line in the then recently introduced 'simplified' Temperate Sea Scheme scheme, with Sky under surfaces. The new style National Markings, introduced in May 1942, would possibly have been applied on the production line or, if built just before their introduction, at an MU or in-service. The serial number was applied to the rear fuselage in approximately 4 inch high black characters, with the legend ROYAL NAVY above it. The individual aircraft letter 'B' was positioned on the rear fuselage in red. Spinner cap was either black or dark grey.

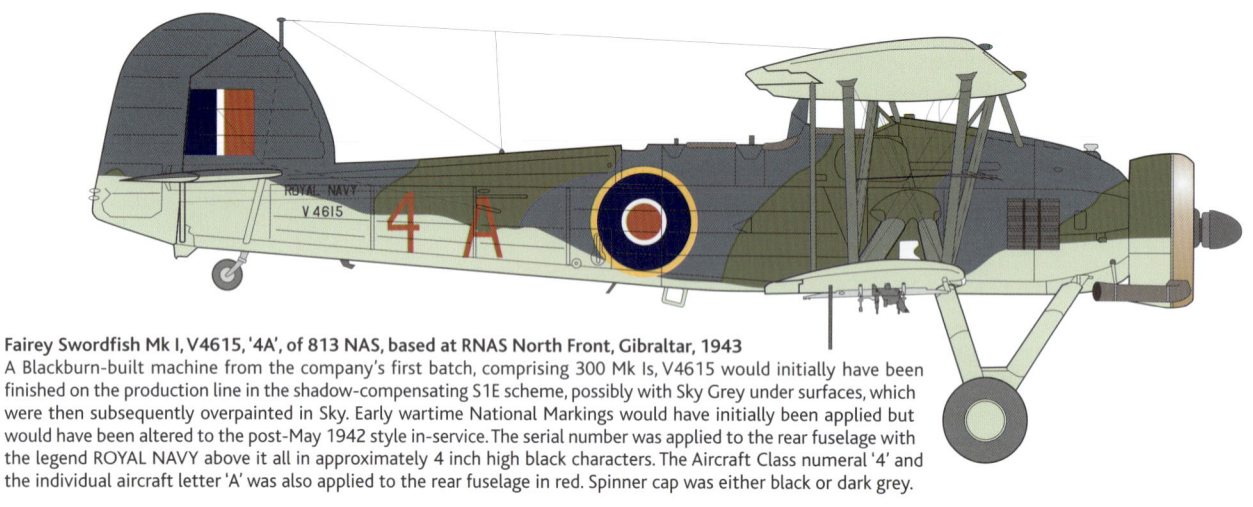

Fairey Swordfish Mk I, V4615, '4A', of 813 NAS, based at RNAS North Front, Gibraltar, 1943
A Blackburn-built machine from the company's first batch, comprising 300 Mk Is, V4615 would initially have been finished on the production line in the shadow-compensating S1E scheme, possibly with Sky Grey under surfaces, which were then subsequently overpainted in Sky. Early wartime National Markings would have initially been applied but would have been altered to the post-May 1942 style in-service. The serial number was applied to the rear fuselage with the legend ROYAL NAVY above it all in approximately 4 inch high black characters. The Aircraft Class numeral '4' and the individual aircraft letter 'A' was also applied to the rear fuselage in red. Spinner cap was either black or dark grey.

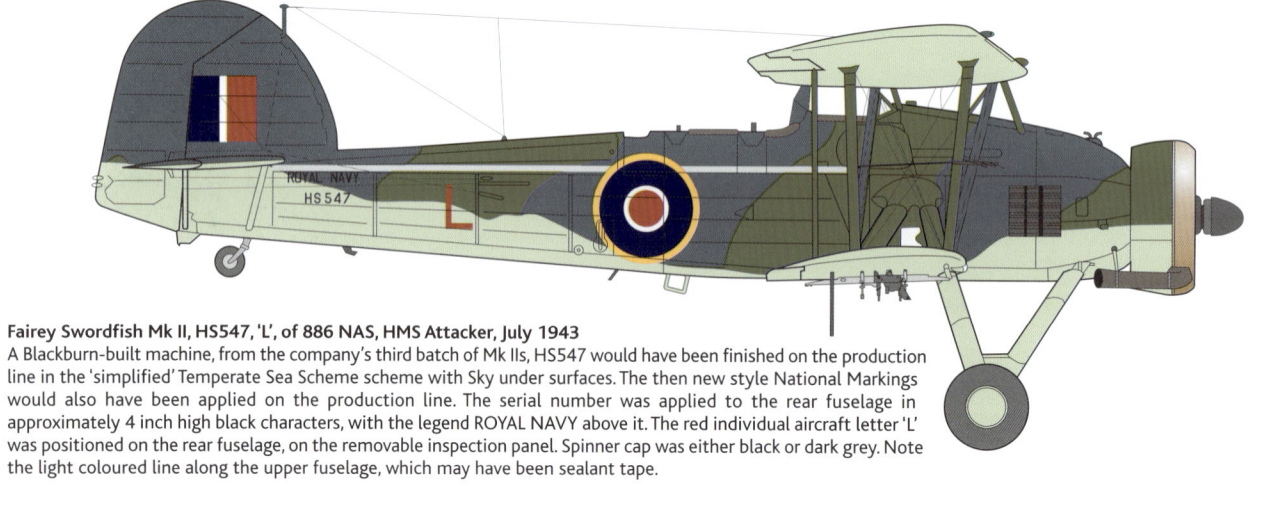

Fairey Swordfish Mk II, HS547, 'L', of 886 NAS, HMS Attacker, July 1943
A Blackburn-built machine, from the company's third batch of Mk IIs, HS547 would have been finished on the production line in the 'simplified' Temperate Sea Scheme scheme with Sky under surfaces. The then new style National Markings would also have been applied on the production line. The serial number was applied to the rear fuselage in approximately 4 inch high black characters, with the legend ROYAL NAVY above it. The red individual aircraft letter 'L' was positioned on the rear fuselage, on the removable inspection panel. Spinner cap was either black or dark grey. Note the light coloured line along the upper fuselage, which may have been sealant tape.

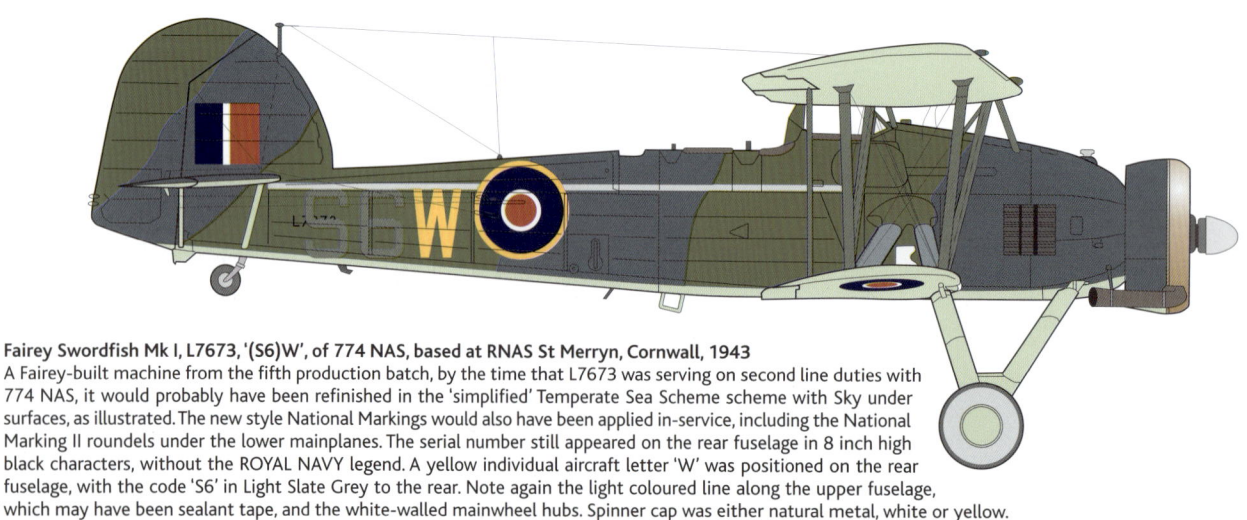

Fairey Swordfish Mk I, L7673, '(S6)W', of 774 NAS, based at RNAS St Merryn, Cornwall, 1943
A Fairey-built machine from the fifth production batch, by the time that L7673 was serving on second line duties with 774 NAS, it would probably have been refinished in the 'simplified' Temperate Sea Scheme scheme with Sky under surfaces, as illustrated. The new style National Markings would also have been applied in-service, including the National Marking II roundels under the lower mainplanes. The serial number still appeared on the rear fuselage in 8 inch high black characters, without the ROYAL NAVY legend. A yellow individual aircraft letter 'W' was positioned on the rear fuselage, with the code 'S6' in Light Slate Grey to the rear. Note again the light coloured line along the upper fuselage, which may have been sealant tape, and the white-walled mainwheel hubs. Spinner cap was either natural metal, white or yellow.

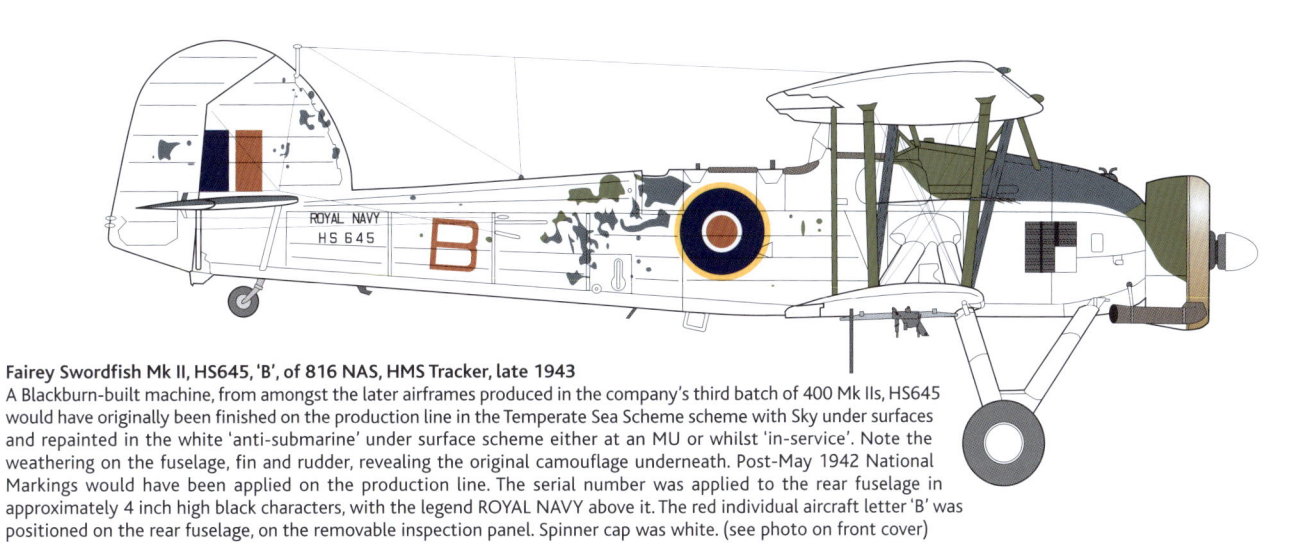

Fairey Swordfish Mk II, HS645, 'B', of 816 NAS, HMS Tracker, late 1943
A Blackburn-built machine, from amongst the later airframes produced in the company's third batch of 400 Mk IIs, HS645 would have originally been finished on the production line in the Temperate Sea Scheme scheme with Sky under surfaces and repainted in the white 'anti-submarine' under surface scheme either at an MU or whilst 'in-service'. Note the weathering on the fuselage, fin and rudder, revealing the original camouflage underneath. Post-May 1942 National Markings would have been applied on the production line. The serial number was applied to the rear fuselage in approximately 4 inch high black characters, with the legend ROYAL NAVY above it. The red individual aircraft letter 'B' was positioned on the rear fuselage, on the removable inspection panel. Spinner cap was white. (see photo on front cover)

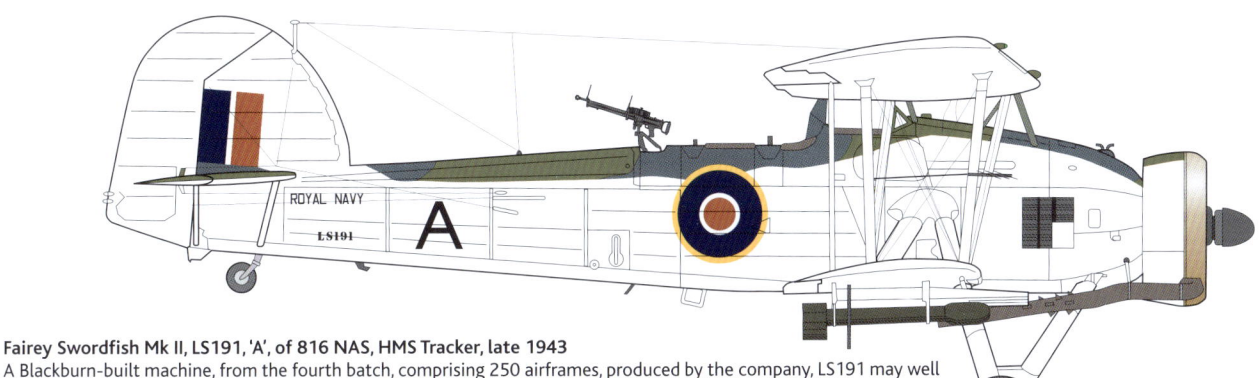

Fairey Swordfish Mk II, LS191, 'A', of 816 NAS, HMS Tracker, late 1943
A Blackburn-built machine, from the fourth batch, comprising 250 airframes, produced by the company, LS191 may well have been one of the first Swordfish to have been finished on the production line in the white 'anti-submarine' under surface scheme, which was introduced in September 1943. The upper surfaces remained in the Temperate Sea Scheme. The post-May 1942 National Markings would also have been applied on the production line, with the serial number and ROYAL NAVY legend in 4 inch high characters. The black individual aircraft letter 'A' was positioned on the rear fuselage, again on the removable inspection panel. Spinner cap was either black or dark grey. Note the non-standard variation of the fin flash. (see photo on p62)

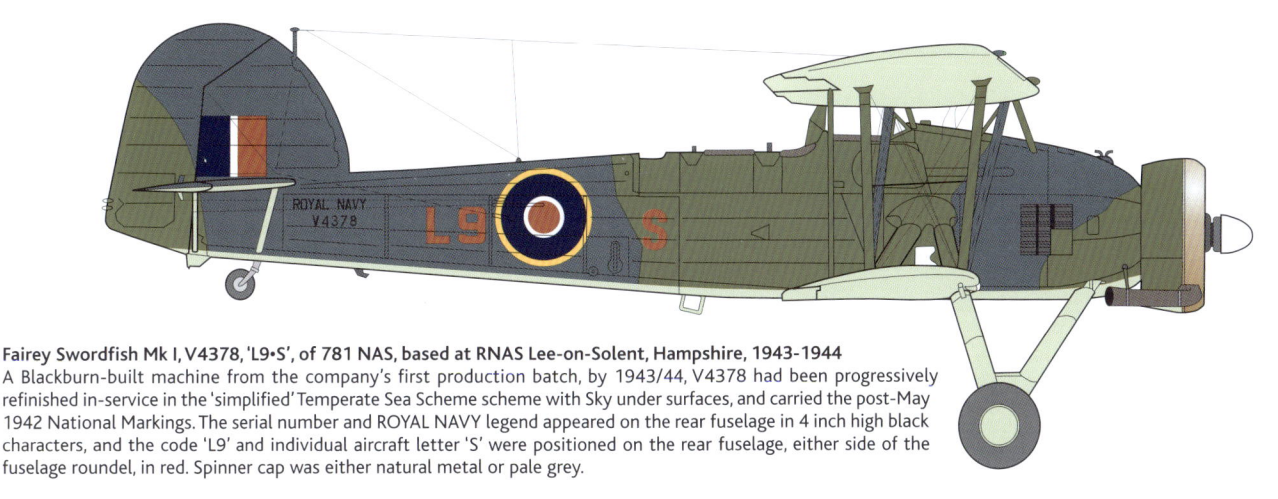

Fairey Swordfish Mk I, V4378, 'L9•S', of 781 NAS, based at RNAS Lee-on-Solent, Hampshire, 1943-1944
A Blackburn-built machine from the company's first production batch, by 1943/44, V4378 had been progressively refinished in-service in the 'simplified' Temperate Sea Scheme scheme with Sky under surfaces, and carried the post-May 1942 National Markings. The serial number and ROYAL NAVY legend appeared on the rear fuselage in 4 inch high black characters, and the code 'L9' and individual aircraft letter 'S' were positioned on the rear fuselage, either side of the fuselage roundel, in red. Spinner cap was either natural metal or pale grey.

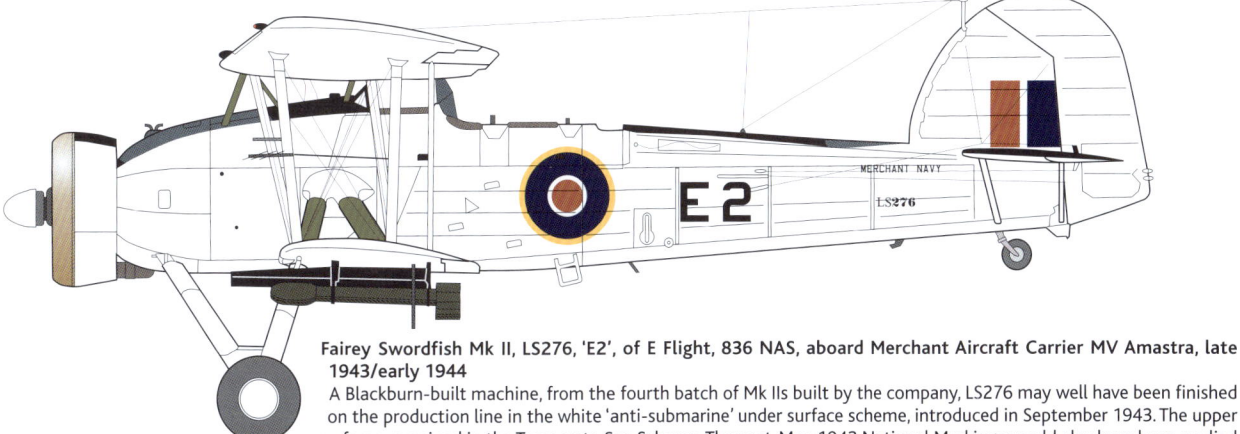

Fairey Swordfish Mk II, LS276, 'E2', of E Flight, 836 NAS, aboard Merchant Aircraft Carrier MV Amastra, late 1943/early 1944
A Blackburn-built machine, from the fourth batch of Mk IIs built by the company, LS276 may well have been finished on the production line in the white 'anti-submarine' under surface scheme, introduced in September 1943. The upper surfaces remained in the Temperate Sea Scheme. The post-May 1942 National Markings would also have been applied on the production line, with the serial number and ROYAL NAVY legend in 4 inch high characters on the rear fuselage, which was subsequently altered to read MERCHANT NAVY! The black code, 'E' (for E Flight) and individual aircraft numeral '2' were positioned on a mid-fuselage removable inspection panel. Note the way the rear edge of the fin flash follows the rudder hinge line angle. Spinner cap was white.

Fairey Swordfish Mk II, DK682, 'F', of 860 NAS, Royal Netherlands Navy, based at RNAS Maydown, County Londonderry, Northern Ireland, mid-1944

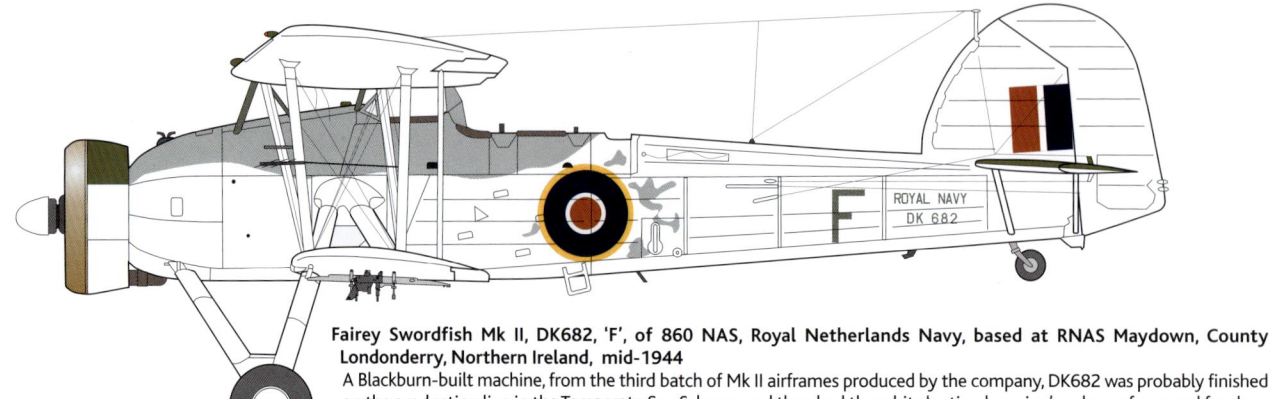

A Blackburn-built machine, from the third batch of Mk II airframes produced by the company, DK682 was probably finished on the production line in the Temperate Sea Scheme and then had the white 'anti-submarine' under surfaces and fuselage sides added whilst in service. The 'grey' colouring on the forward fuselage decking was probably faded and weathered Temperate Sea Scheme colours. Note the weathering on the fuselage sides too. The standard post-May 1942 National Markings would have been applied on the production line, together with the serial number and ROYAL NAVY legend in 4 inch high characters. The code letter 'F' was again positioned on the rear fuselage inspection panel, possibly in Slate Grey. Spinner cap was white. Note the way the fin flash is orientated to follow the rudder hinge line.

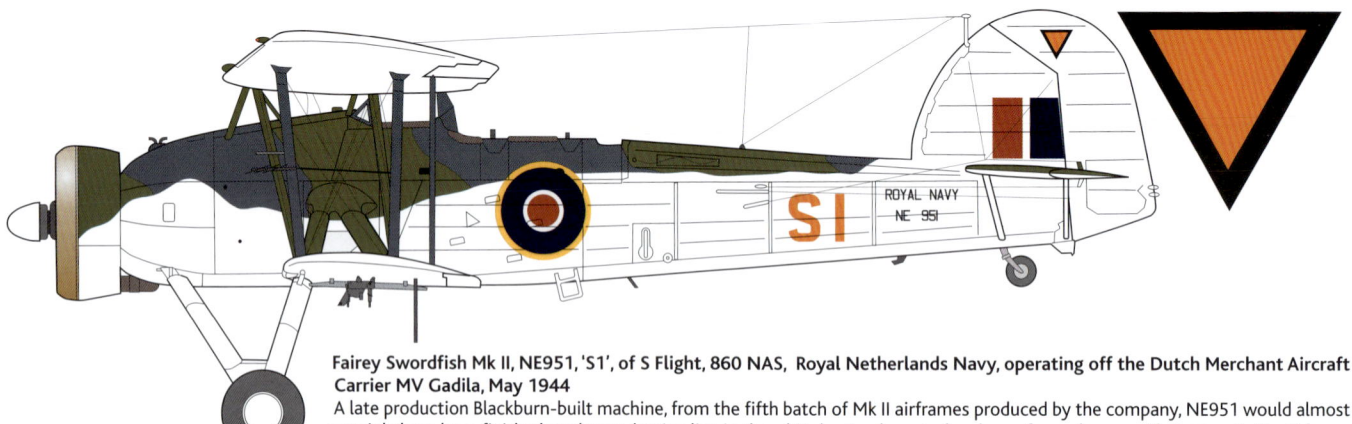

Fairey Swordfish Mk II, NE951, 'S1', of S Flight, 860 NAS, Royal Netherlands Navy, operating off the Dutch Merchant Aircraft Carrier MV Gadila, May 1944

A late production Blackburn-built machine, from the fifth batch of Mk II airframes produced by the company, NE951 would almost certainly have been finished on the production line in the white 'anti-submarine' under surface scheme, with Temperate Sea Scheme upper surfaces. Standard post-May 1942 National Markings would also have been applied on the production line, together with the serial number and ROYAL NAVY legend on the rear fuselage. The code 'S1' was positioned on the rear fuselage inspection panel, in orange, with the Netherlands wartime national orange triangle on the rudder (see inset). Spinner cap was white. Note again the way the rear edge of the fin flash follows the rudder hinge line angle.

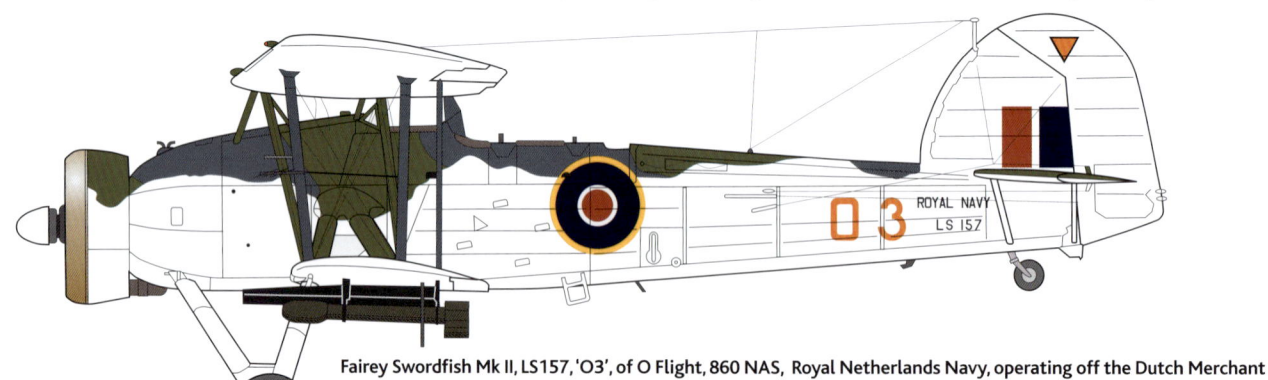

Fairey Swordfish Mk II, LS157, 'O3', of O Flight, 860 NAS, Royal Netherlands Navy, operating off the Dutch Merchant Aircraft Carrier MV Macoma, June 1944

A Blackburn-built machine, from the fourth batch of Mk II airframes produced by the company, LS157 may well have been finished on the production line in the white 'anti-submarine' under surface scheme, with Temperate Sea Scheme upper surfaces, introduced in September 1943. Standard post-May 1942 National Markings would also have been applied on the production line, together with the serial number and ROYAL NAVY legend in 4 inch high characters in black. The code 'O3' was positioned on the rear fuselage, in orange, with the Netherlands wartime national orange triangle on the rudder. Spinner cap was white. Again, note the way the rear edge of the fin flash follows the rudder hinge line angle.

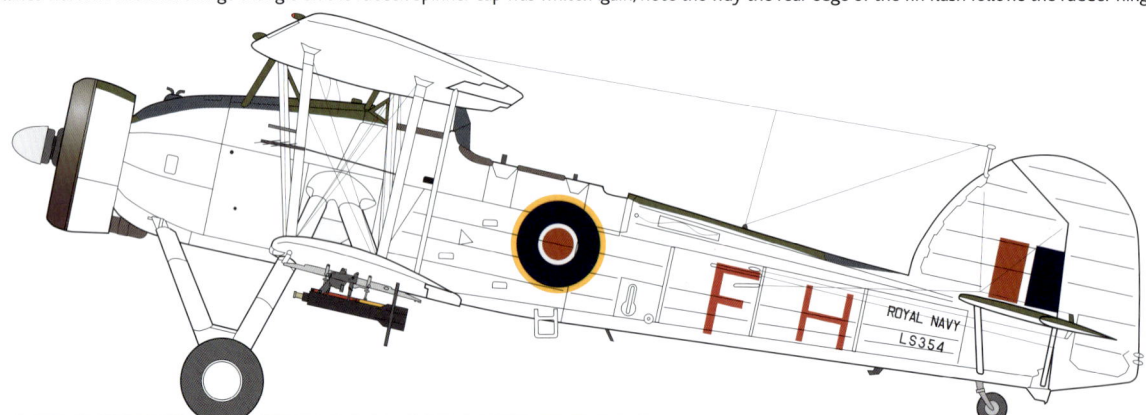

Fairey Swordfish Mk II, LS354, 'FH', of 842 NAS, HMS Fencer, 1944

A Blackburn-built machine, from the fourth batch of Mk II airframes produced by the company, LS354 may well have been finished on the production line in the white 'anti-submarine' under surface scheme, with Temperate Sea Scheme upper surfaces, introduced in September 1943. Standard post-May 1942 National Markings would have been applied on the production line, with the serial number and ROYAL NAVY legend in 4 inch high characters. The code 'FH' was positioned on the rear fuselage, in red – note the difference in height of the letters. Spinner cap was white. As with the previous profiles, the rear edge of the fin flash follows the rudder hinge line angle.

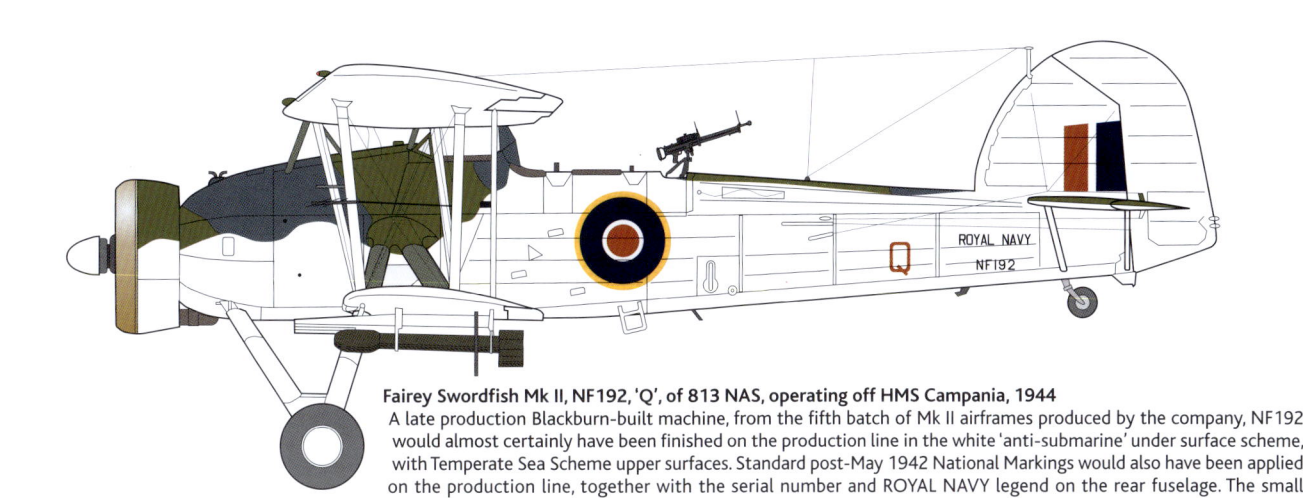

Fairey Swordfish Mk II, NF192, 'Q', of 813 NAS, operating off HMS Campania, 1944
A late production Blackburn-built machine, from the fifth batch of Mk II airframes produced by the company, NF192 would almost certainly have been finished on the production line in the white 'anti-submarine' under surface scheme, with Temperate Sea Scheme upper surfaces. Standard post-May 1942 National Markings would also have been applied on the production line, together with the serial number and ROYAL NAVY legend on the rear fuselage. The small individual aircraft letter 'Q' was positioned on the rear fuselage inspection panel, in red. Spinner cap was white. Note the way the rear edge of the fin flash follows the rudder hinge line angle.

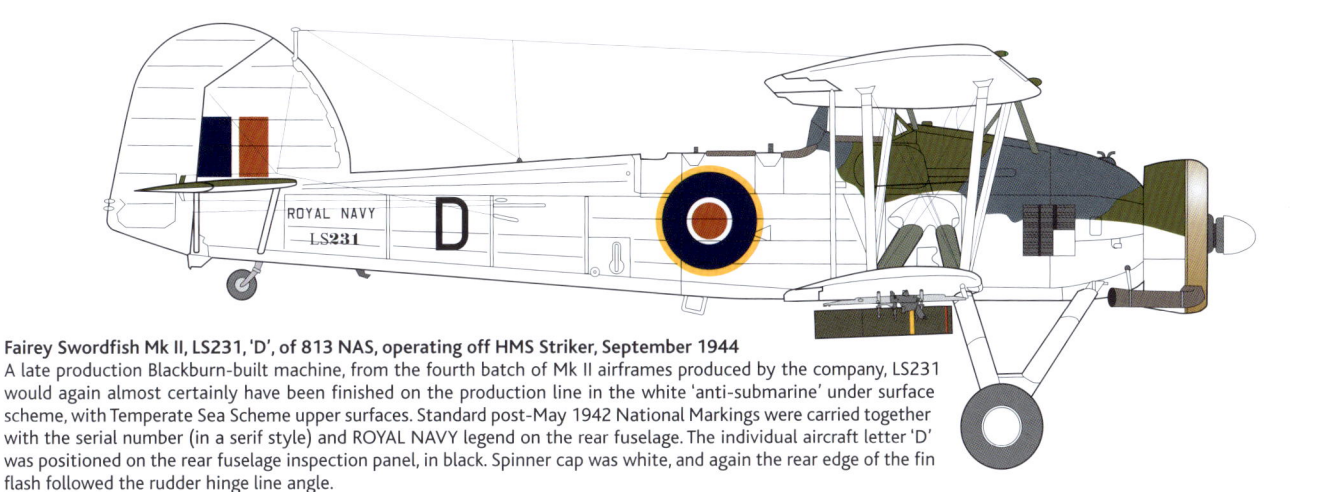

Fairey Swordfish Mk II, LS231, 'D', of 813 NAS, operating off HMS Striker, September 1944
A late production Blackburn-built machine, from the fourth batch of Mk II airframes produced by the company, LS231 would again almost certainly have been finished on the production line in the white 'anti-submarine' under surface scheme, with Temperate Sea Scheme upper surfaces. Standard post-May 1942 National Markings were carried together with the serial number (in a serif style) and ROYAL NAVY legend on the rear fuselage. The individual aircraft letter 'D' was positioned on the rear fuselage inspection panel, in black. Spinner cap was white, and again the rear edge of the fin flash followed the rudder hinge line angle.

Fairey Swordfish Mk II, NF190, 'F', of 811 NAS, operating off HMS Biter, 1944
A late production Blackburn-built machine, from the fifth batch of Mk II airframes produced by the company, NF190, like the other aircraft above, would almost certainly have been finished on the production line in the white 'anti-submarine' under surface scheme, with Temperate Sea Scheme upper surfaces. Standard post-May 1942 National Markings would also have been applied on the production line, together with the serial number and ROYAL NAVY legend on the rear fuselage. The individual aircraft letter 'F' was again positioned on the rear fuselage inspection panel, in red. Spinner cap was white, but this time the fin flash was non-standard, being taller with the whole marking orientated to follow the angle of the rudder hinge line.

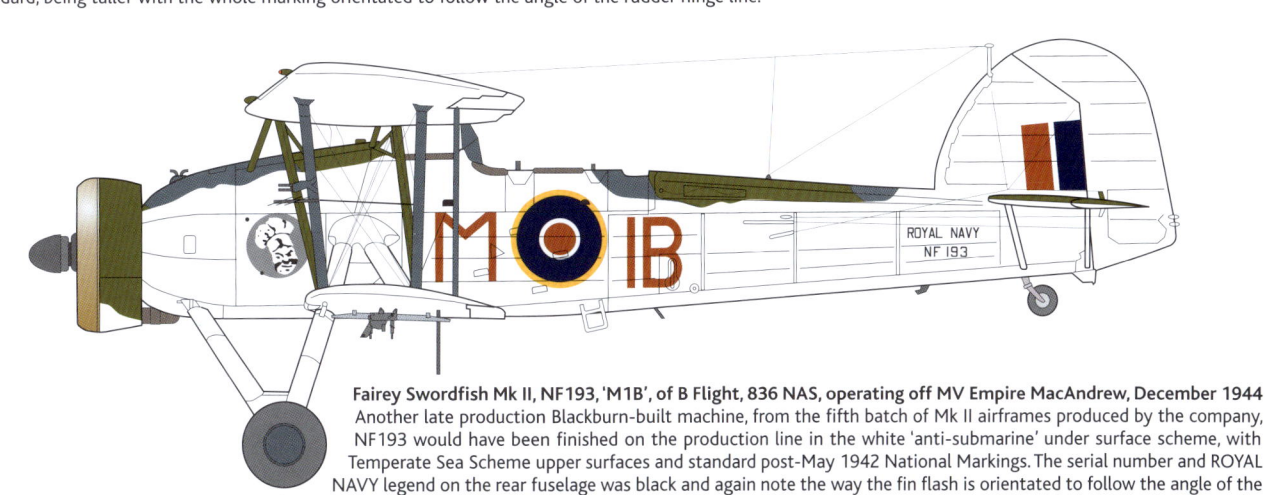

Fairey Swordfish Mk II, NF193, 'M1B', of B Flight, 836 NAS, operating off MV Empire MacAndrew, December 1944
Another late production Blackburn-built machine, from the fifth batch of Mk II airframes produced by the company, NF193 would have been finished on the production line in the white 'anti-submarine' under surface scheme, with Temperate Sea Scheme upper surfaces and standard post-May 1942 National Markings. The serial number and ROYAL NAVY legend on the rear fuselage was black and again note the way the fin flash is orientated to follow the angle of the rudder hinge line. The code letters 'M1B' straddled the fuselage roundel and were red. Note the 'Baker's Head' badge on the port side, possibly with the aircraft's code on the headband – see also 4-view on p61. The spinner cap was either black or dark grey.

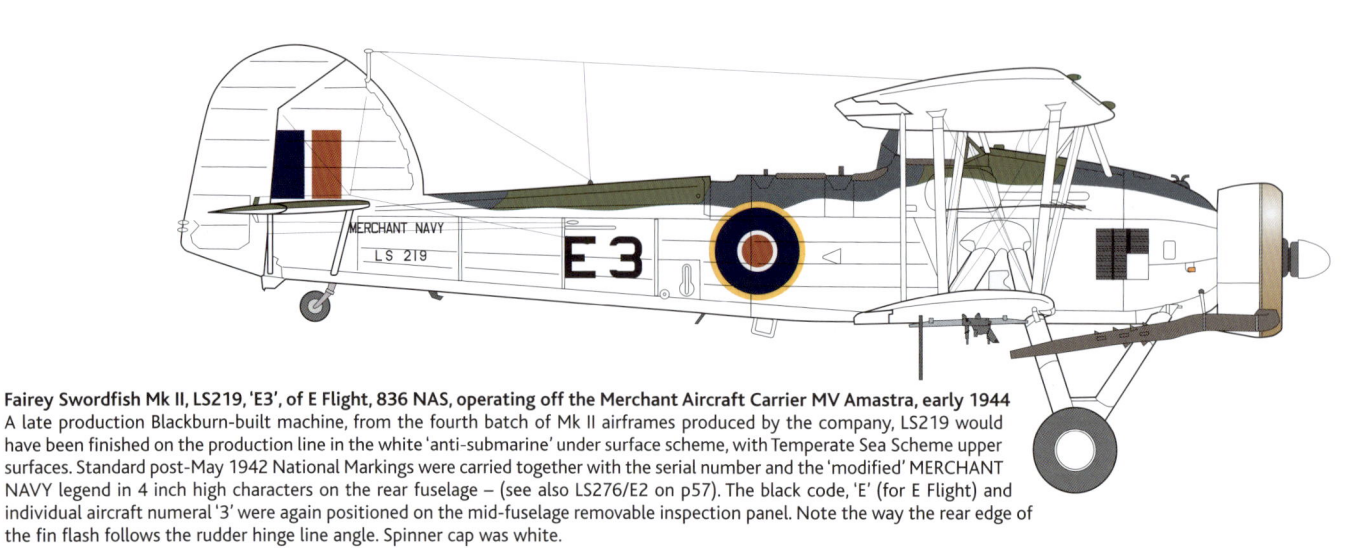

Fairey Swordfish Mk II, LS219, 'E3', of E Flight, 836 NAS, operating off the Merchant Aircraft Carrier MV Amastra, early 1944
A late production Blackburn-built machine, from the fourth batch of Mk II airframes produced by the company, LS219 would have been finished on the production line in the white 'anti-submarine' under surface scheme, with Temperate Sea Scheme upper surfaces. Standard post-May 1942 National Markings were carried together with the serial number and the 'modified' MERCHANT NAVY legend in 4 inch high characters on the rear fuselage – (see also LS276/E2 on p57). The black code, 'E' (for E Flight) and individual aircraft numeral '3' were again positioned on the mid-fuselage removable inspection panel. Note the way the rear edge of the fin flash follows the rudder hinge line angle. Spinner cap was white.

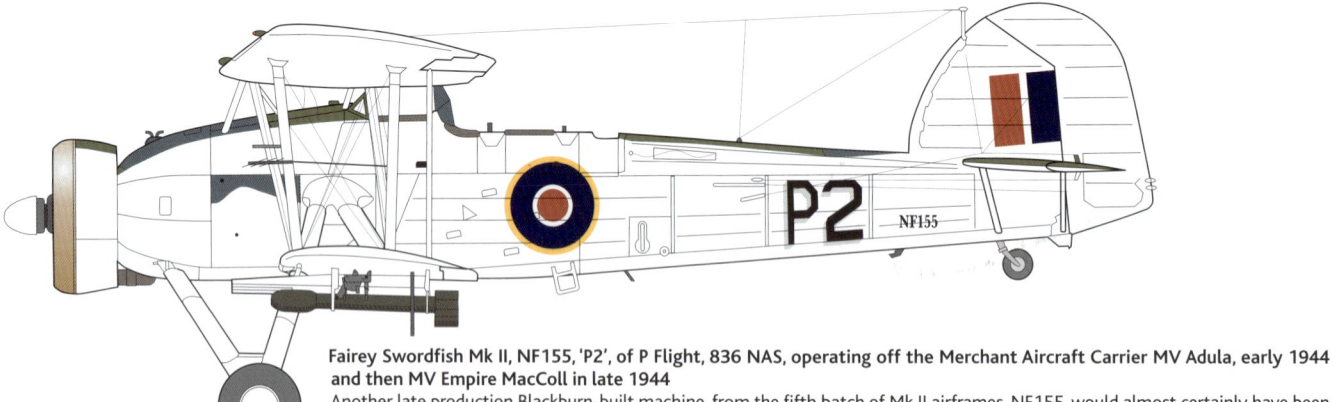

Fairey Swordfish Mk II, NF155, 'P2', of P Flight, 836 NAS, operating off the Merchant Aircraft Carrier MV Adula, early 1944 and then MV Empire MacColl in late 1944
Another late production Blackburn-built machine, from the fifth batch of Mk II airframes, NF155, would almost certainly have been finished on the production line in the white 'anti-submarine' under surface scheme, with Temperate Sea Scheme upper surfaces. Standard post-May 1942 National Markings would also have been applied on the production line, together with the serif style serial number, but strangely no ROYAL NAVY legend, which appears either to be missing or overpainted? The code, 'P' (for P Flight) and individual aircraft numeral '2', were black with what appears to be a grey 'drop shadow', positioned on the rear-fuselage removable inspection panel. Spinner cap was white. Note the fin flash, applied at an angle to follow the rudder hinge line and the area of camouflage(?) on the forward cowling side panel which may have been a replacement from another, slightly differently camouflaged, Swordfish.

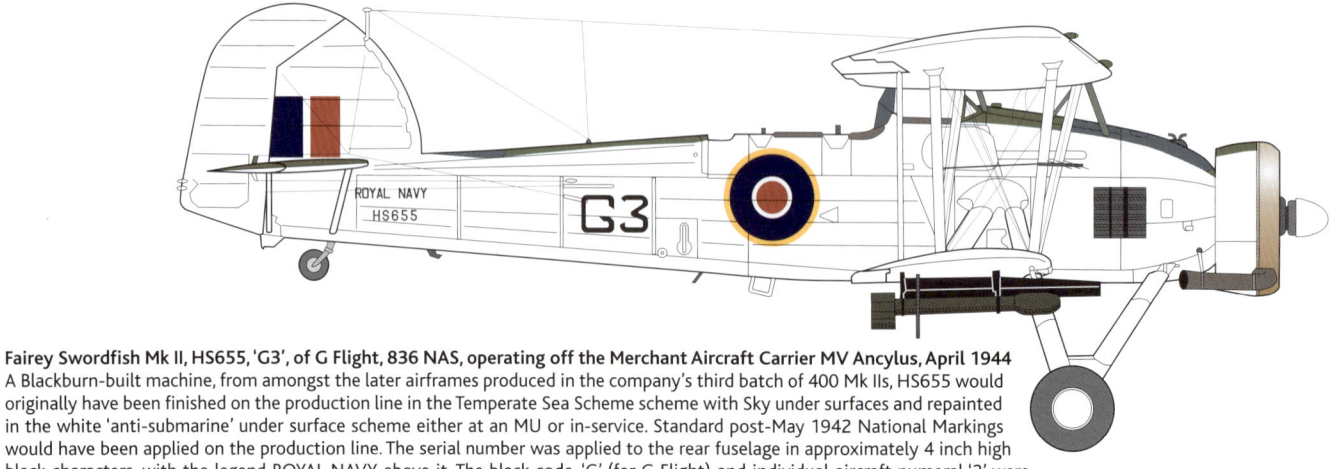

Fairey Swordfish Mk II, HS655, 'G3', of G Flight, 836 NAS, operating off the Merchant Aircraft Carrier MV Ancylus, April 1944
A Blackburn-built machine, from amongst the later airframes produced in the company's third batch of 400 Mk IIs, HS655 would originally have been finished on the production line in the Temperate Sea Scheme scheme with Sky under surfaces and repainted in the white 'anti-submarine' under surface scheme either at an MU or in-service. Standard post-May 1942 National Markings would have been applied on the production line. The serial number was applied to the rear fuselage in approximately 4 inch high black characters, with the legend ROYAL NAVY above it. The black code, 'G' (for G Flight) and individual aircraft numeral '3' were positioned on the mid-fuselage removable inspection panel. Note the way the rear edge of the fin flash follows the rudder hinge line angle. Spinner cap was white.

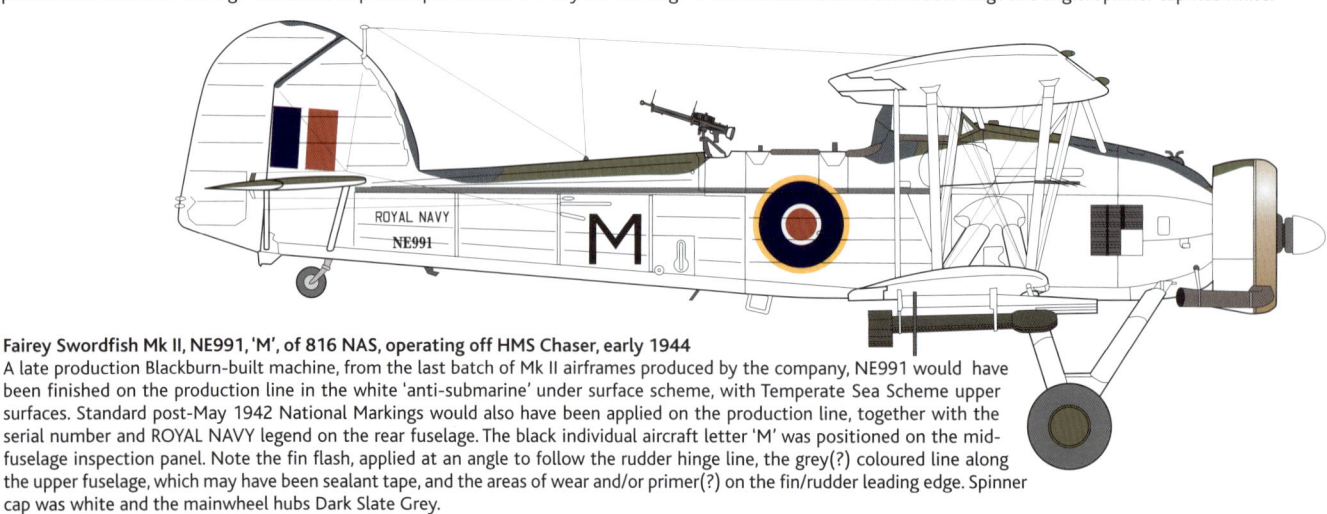

Fairey Swordfish Mk II, NE991, 'M', of 816 NAS, operating off HMS Chaser, early 1944
A late production Blackburn-built machine, from the last batch of Mk II airframes produced by the company, NE991 would have been finished on the production line in the white 'anti-submarine' under surface scheme, with Temperate Sea Scheme upper surfaces. Standard post-May 1942 National Markings would also have been applied on the production line, together with the serial number and ROYAL NAVY legend on the rear fuselage. The black individual aircraft letter 'M' was positioned on the mid-fuselage inspection panel. Note the fin flash, applied at an angle to follow the rudder hinge line, the grey(?) coloured line along the upper fuselage, which may have been sealant tape, and the areas of wear and/or primer(?) on the fin/rudder leading edge. Spinner cap was white and the mainwheel hubs Dark Slate Grey.

Fairey Swordfish Mk II, LS434, 'B3', of Baker Flight, 836 NAS, operating off the Aircraft Carrier MV Empire MacAndrew, 1943-1944

LS434 was a Blackburn-built machine, from the fourth batch of Mk II airframes produced by the company. On 16 September 1943, Confidential Admiralty Fleet Order (CAFO) 1951 was issued, which introduced the white 'anti-submarine' under surface scheme, with Temperate Sea Scheme upper surfaces, which was immediately implemented on Blackburn's Swordfish production line. Standard post-May 1942 National Markings were also applied on the production line, together with the serial number and ROYAL NAVY legend on the rear fuselage, in black 4 inch high characters.

The upperwing Red/Blue roundel was 58 inches in diameter, with the fuselage roundel of 36 inches diameter. The fin flash was basically 24 inches square, but note the way the rear edge follows the rudder hinge line angle, which seems to have been the normal presentation.

The code 'B3' was positioned on the mid fuselage inspection panel, in black. Note the 'Baker's Head' badge on the port side, with the aircraft's code on the headband, and the name 'Benvorlich' on both sides of the forward fuselage. The spinner cap was black or dark grey. The aircraft is illustrated armed with eight 60lb RPs, a typical offensive load for these aircraft, and is fitted with ASV aerials on the outer interplane struts.

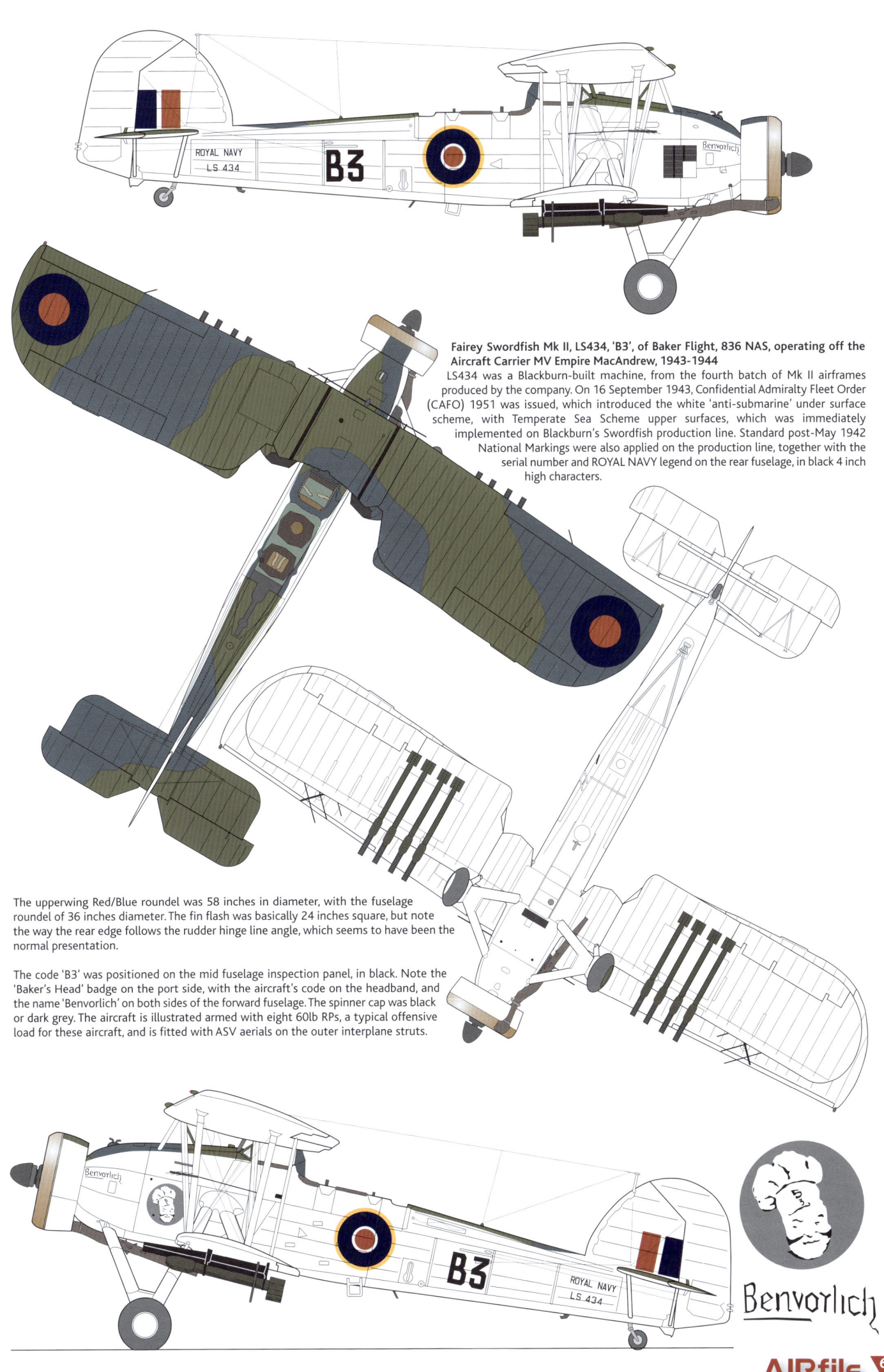

Swordfish Mk II, LS191, 'A', of 842 NAS, photographed just after it had stalled on HMS Fencer's pitching deck on 1 November 1943, knocking the undercarriage off. It was repaired and returned to service but was Struck Off Charge on 20 December 1943 after missing all the arrester wires and crashing in to the barrier. Note the serif style of the 4 inch high serial number. (see profile on p57)

Trio of Swordfish Mk IIs from 816 NAS, based at RNAS St Merryn, Cornwall, in June/July 1944 in full invasion stripes applied around both surfaces of the upper and lower mainplanes and around the fuselage, the outer white stripes on the fuselage and the under surfaces of both mainplanes, having a thin black 'border' to contrast against the white 'anti-submarine' scheme. Operating with Coastal Command, the squadron was engaged on attacks on enemy shipping approaching the invasion area in Normandy, and the aircraft were fitted with ASV aerials on the outer interplane struts and armed with 60lb RPs. (see 4-view opposite)

Fairey Swordfish Mk II, NF243, 'S', of 816 NAS, based at RNAS St Merryn, Cornwall, June/July 1944

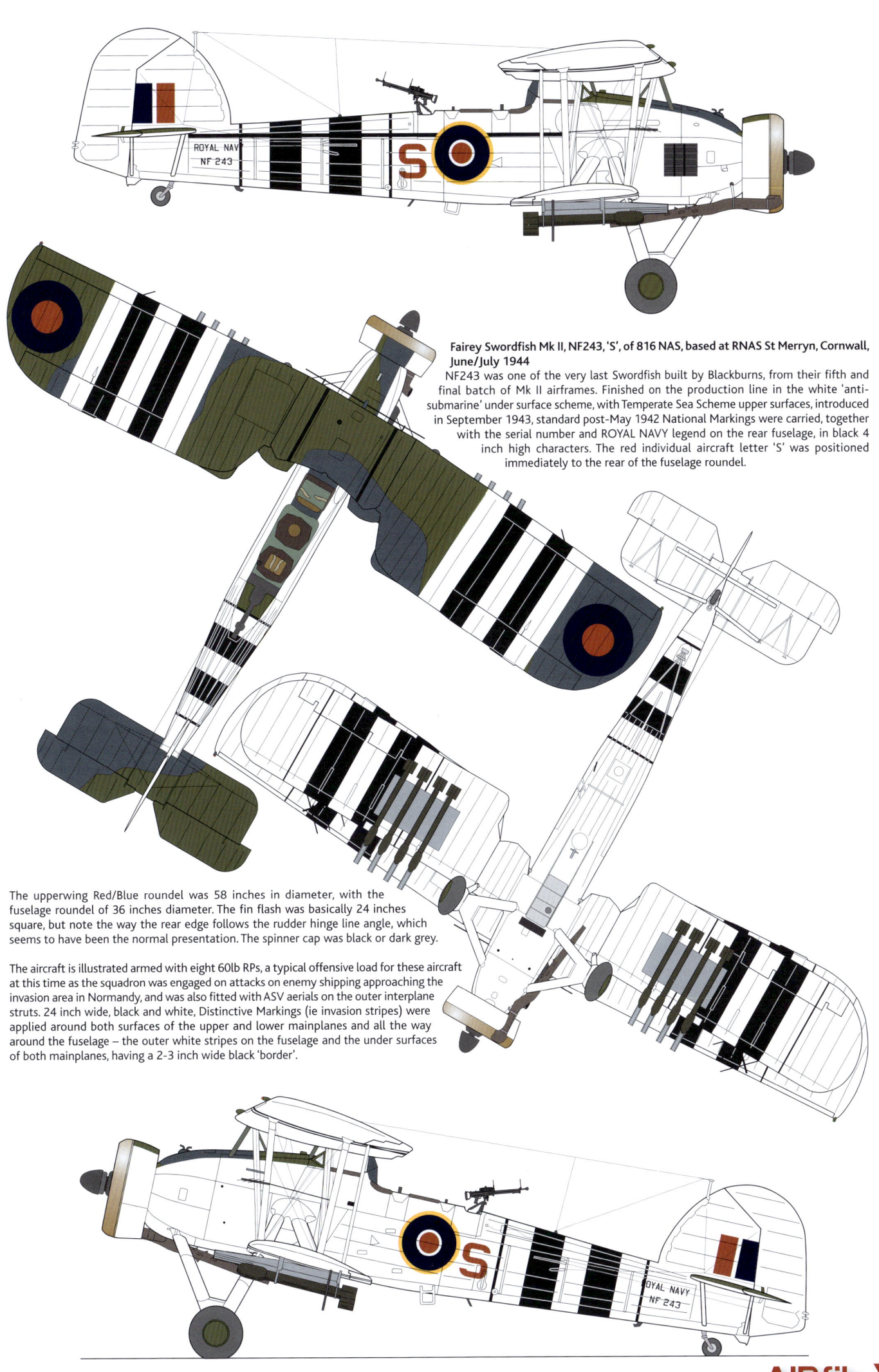

NF243 was one of the very last Swordfish built by Blackburns, from their fifth and final batch of Mk II airframes. Finished on the production line in the white 'anti-submarine' under surface scheme, with Temperate Sea Scheme upper surfaces, introduced in September 1943, standard post-May 1942 National Markings were carried, together with the serial number and ROYAL NAVY legend on the rear fuselage, in black 4 inch high characters. The red individual aircraft letter 'S' was positioned immediately to the rear of the fuselage roundel.

The upperwing Red/Blue roundel was 58 inches in diameter, with the fuselage roundel of 36 inches diameter. The fin flash was basically 24 inches square, but note the way the rear edge follows the rudder hinge line angle, which seems to have been the normal presentation. The spinner cap was black or dark grey.

The aircraft is illustrated armed with eight 60lb RPs, a typical offensive load for these aircraft at this time as the squadron was engaged on attacks on enemy shipping approaching the invasion area in Normandy, and was also fitted with ASV aerials on the outer interplane struts. 24 inch wide, black and white, Distinctive Markings (ie invasion stripes) were applied around both surfaces of the upper and lower mainplanes and all the way around the fuselage – the outer white stripes on the fuselage and the under surfaces of both mainplanes, having a 2-3 inch wide black 'border'.

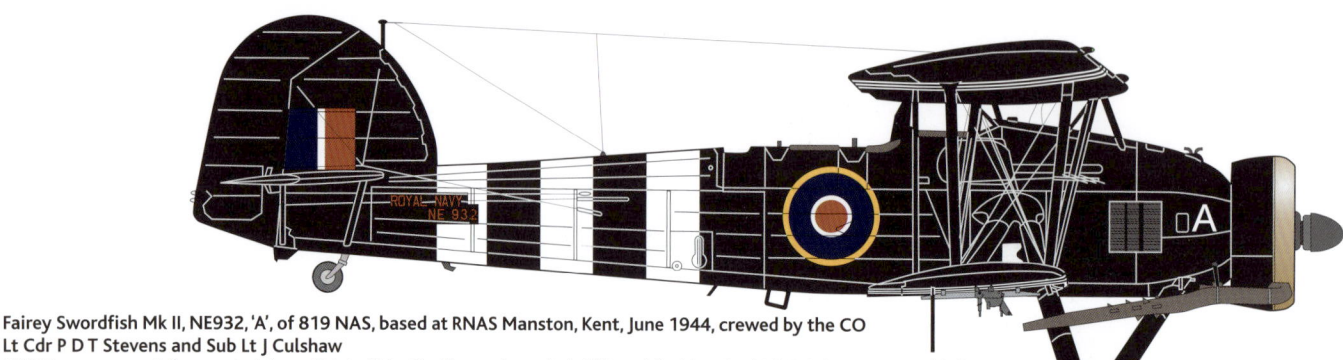

Fairey Swordfish Mk II, NE932, 'A', of 819 NAS, based at RNAS Manston, Kent, June 1944, crewed by the CO Lt Cdr P D T Stevens and Sub Lt J Culshaw
NE932 was amongst the very last Swordfish built by Blackburns, from their fifth and final batch of Mk II airframes. It would almost certainly have been finished on the production line in the white 'anti-submarine' scheme, and then repainted in-service in overall black, probably Special Night. The standard post-May 1942 National Markings were retained but the serial number and ROYAL NAVY legend on the rear fuselage, were repainted in red 4 inch high characters. A white individual aircraft letter 'A' was positioned on the nose immediately to the rear of the cowling. 24 inch wide, black and white, Distinctive Markings (invasion stripes) were applied around both surfaces of the upper and lower mainplanes and all the way around the fuselage. The spinner cap was black or dark grey. The aircraft were armed with eight 60lb RPs as the squadron was engaged on nocturnal attacks on enemy shipping in the Normandy invasion area.

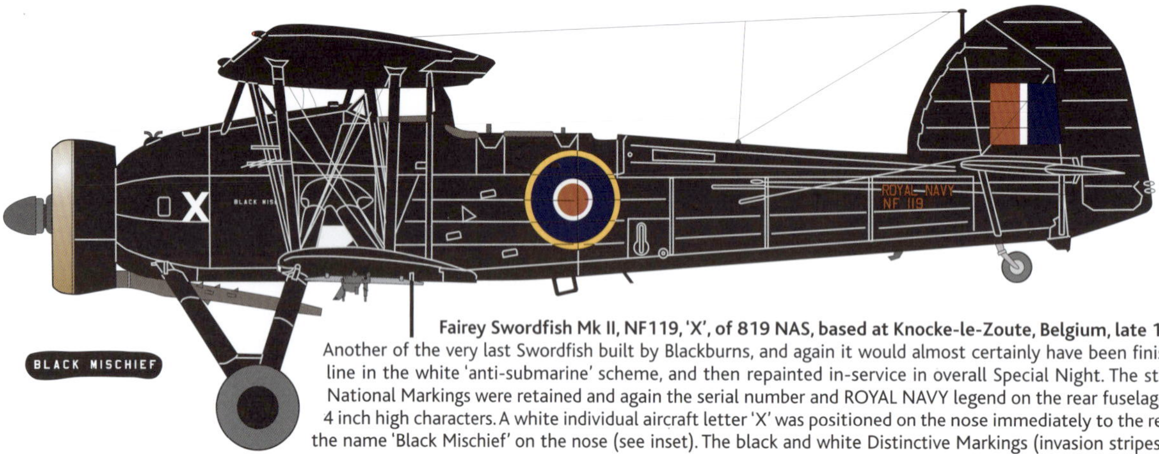

Fairey Swordfish Mk II, NF119, 'X', of 819 NAS, based at Knocke-le-Zoute, Belgium, late 1944
Another of the very last Swordfish built by Blackburns, and again it would almost certainly have been finished on the production line in the white 'anti-submarine' scheme, and then repainted in-service in overall Special Night. The standard post-May 1942 National Markings were retained and again the serial number and ROYAL NAVY legend on the rear fuselage, were repainted in red 4 inch high characters. A white individual aircraft letter 'X' was positioned on the nose immediately to the rear of the cowling. Note the name 'Black Mischief' on the nose (see inset). The black and white Distinctive Markings (invasion stripes) had been removed by this date. The spinner cap was black or dark grey. The squadron was operating from the continent at this stage, engaged in disrupting enemy coastal traffic in the Channel. This particular machine was severely damaged when it hit the perimeter fence during take-off on 3 February 1945.

Fairey Swordfish Mk III, NF325, NH•P, of No 119 Sqn, RAF based at Knocke-le-Zoute, Belgium, spring 1945
NF325 was one of some 320 Swordfish built by Blackburns to Mk III standard, fitted with the large Mark X centrimetric Air-to-Surface Vessel (ASV) radar pod between the landing gear. As with the late production Mk IIs, NF325 would almost certainly have been finished on the production line in the white 'anti-submarine' scheme, and then repainted in-service. In this instance, the aircraft was issued to No 119 Sqn RAF in September 1944 which was involved in coastal patrol duties, utilising the excellent Mark X ASV radar to search out German midget submarines, mainly at night. NF325 appears to have had Special Night applied to the wing undersides and fuselage side surfaces, whilst retaining the Temperate Sea Scheme upper surfaces, although some of the squadron's other Swordfish aircraft may have been black overall. The standard post-May 1942 National Markings were retained and the serial number was applied in red, 8 inch high, characters on the rear fuselage. The squadron codes, NH•P, were positioned either side of the fuselage roundel, also in red. The spinner cap was black or dark grey.

Fairey Swordfish Mk III, NF410, NH•F, of No 119 Sqn, RAF based at Knocke-le-Zoute, Belgium, spring 1945
Another of No 119 Squadron's ASV equipped Mk IIIs, NF410 was again repainted in-service with Special Night wing underside and fuselage side surfaces whilst retaining its Temperate Sea Scheme upper surfaces. The positioning of the ASV pod meant the Mk III couldn't carry a torpedo, or any other large centreline store, and so 500lb and 250lb bombs (and possibly depth charges) appear to have been the offensive weapons of choice. The standard post-May 1942 National Markings were retained and the serial number was applied in red, 8 inch high, characters on the rear fuselage. The squadron codes, NH•F, were positioned either side of the fuselage roundel, also in red. The spinner cap was black or dark grey. Many of No 119's aircraft carried cartoon characters on the forward fuselage, including NF410 which had 'Donald Duck' in yellow (see inset).

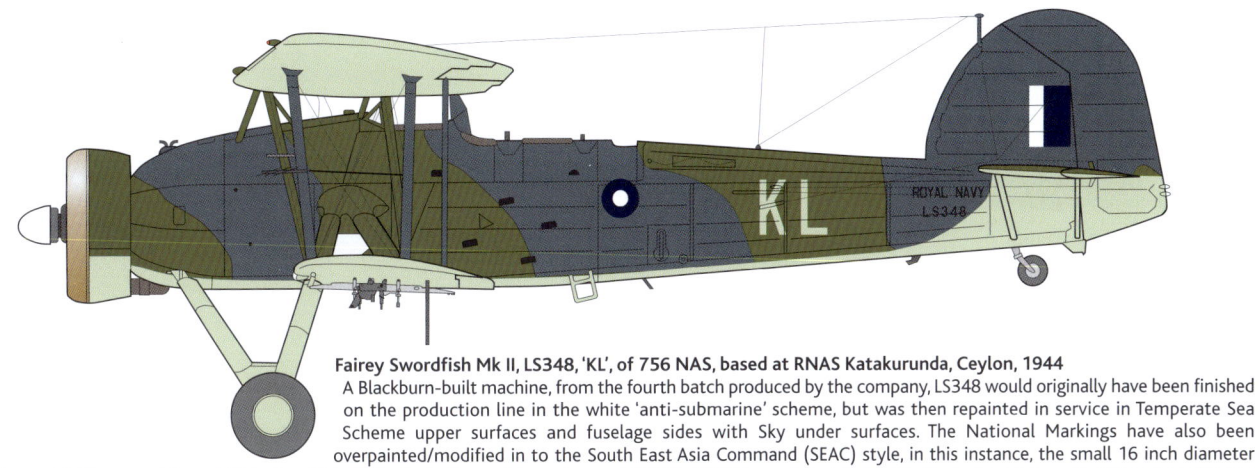

Fairey Swordfish Mk II, LS348, 'KL', of 756 NAS, based at RNAS Katakurunda, Ceylon, 1944
A Blackburn-built machine, from the fourth batch produced by the company, LS348 would originally have been finished on the production line in the white 'anti-submarine' scheme, but was then repainted in service in Temperate Sea Scheme upper surfaces and fuselage sides with Sky under surfaces. The National Markings have also been overpainted/modified in to the South East Asia Command (SEAC) style, in this instance, the small 16 inch diameter Roundel Blue and White roundels and 18 inch x 24 inch fin flash. The serial number and ROYAL NAVY legend, in 4 inch high black characters, was retained on the rear fuselage, with the codes 'KU' in Sky positioned near the removable inspection panel. Spinner cap was white.

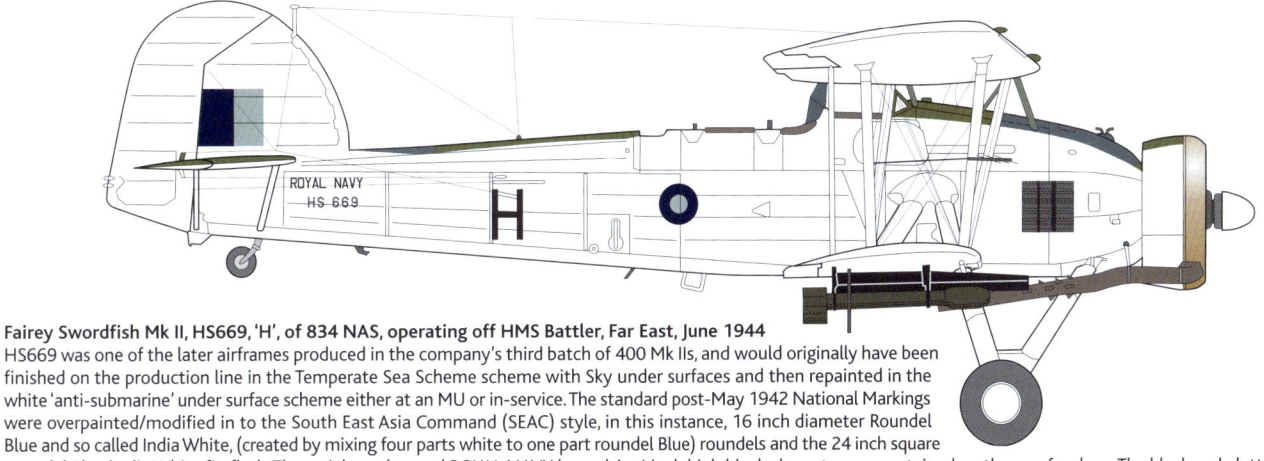

Fairey Swordfish Mk II, HS669, 'H', of 834 NAS, operating off HMS Battler, Far East, June 1944
HS669 was one of the later airframes produced in the company's third batch of 400 Mk IIs, and would originally have been finished on the production line in the Temperate Sea Scheme scheme with Sky under surfaces and then repainted in the white 'anti-submarine' under surface scheme either at an MU or in-service. The standard post-May 1942 National Markings were overpainted/modified in to the South East Asia Command (SEAC) style, in this instance, 16 inch diameter Roundel Blue and so called India White, (created by mixing four parts white to one part roundel Blue) roundels and the 24 inch square Roundel Blue/India White fin flash. The serial number and ROYAL NAVY legend, in 4 inch high black characters, was retained on the rear fuselage. The black code letter, 'H' was positioned on the mid-fuselage removable inspection panel. Note the way the rear edge of the fin flash follows the rudder hinge line angle. Spinner cap was white.

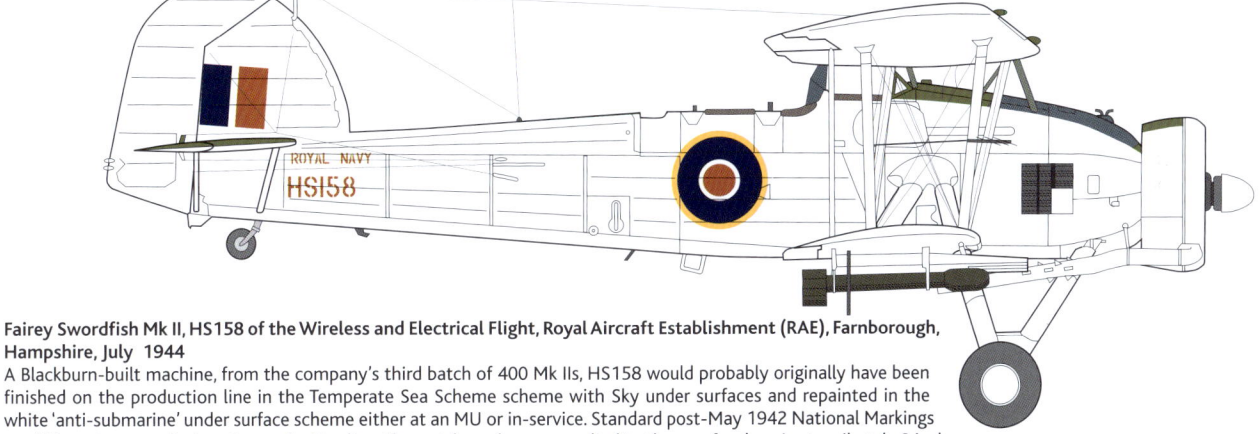

Fairey Swordfish Mk II, HS158 of the Wireless and Electrical Flight, Royal Aircraft Establishment (RAE), Farnborough, Hampshire, July 1944
A Blackburn-built machine, from the company's third batch of 400 Mk IIs, HS158 would probably originally have been finished on the production line in the Temperate Sea Scheme scheme with Sky under surfaces and repainted in the white 'anti-submarine' under surface scheme either at an MU or in-service. Standard post-May 1942 National Markings would have been applied on the production line. The serial number was applied to the rear fuselage in stencil-style 8 inch high characters, with the 4 inch high ROYAL NAVY above it, all in red. Note the fin flash, applied at an angle to follow the rudder hinge line and the white painted flame-damping exhaust manifold. Spinner cap was white. This particular aircraft was involved in 'Harvest Moon' trials at the RAE.

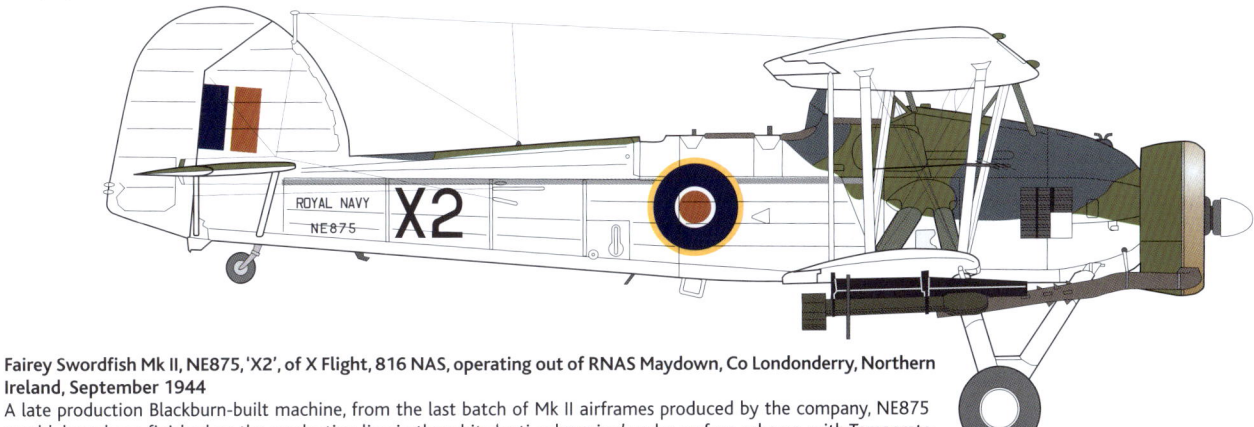

Fairey Swordfish Mk II, NE875, 'X2', of X Flight, 816 NAS, operating out of RNAS Maydown, Co Londonderry, Northern Ireland, September 1944
A late production Blackburn-built machine, from the last batch of Mk II airframes produced by the company, NE875 would have been finished on the production line in the white 'anti-submarine' under surface scheme, with Temperate Sea Scheme upper surfaces. Note how the upper surface camouflage sweeps down the forward fuselage towards the nose. Standard post-May 1942 National Markings were in the usual positions with the serial number and ROYAL NAVY legend on the rear fuselage. The black codes 'X2' were positioned on the rear fuselage inspection panel. Note the fin flash, applied at an angle to follow the rudder hinge line and the grey(?) coloured line along the upper fuselage, which may have been sealant tape. Spinner cap was white.

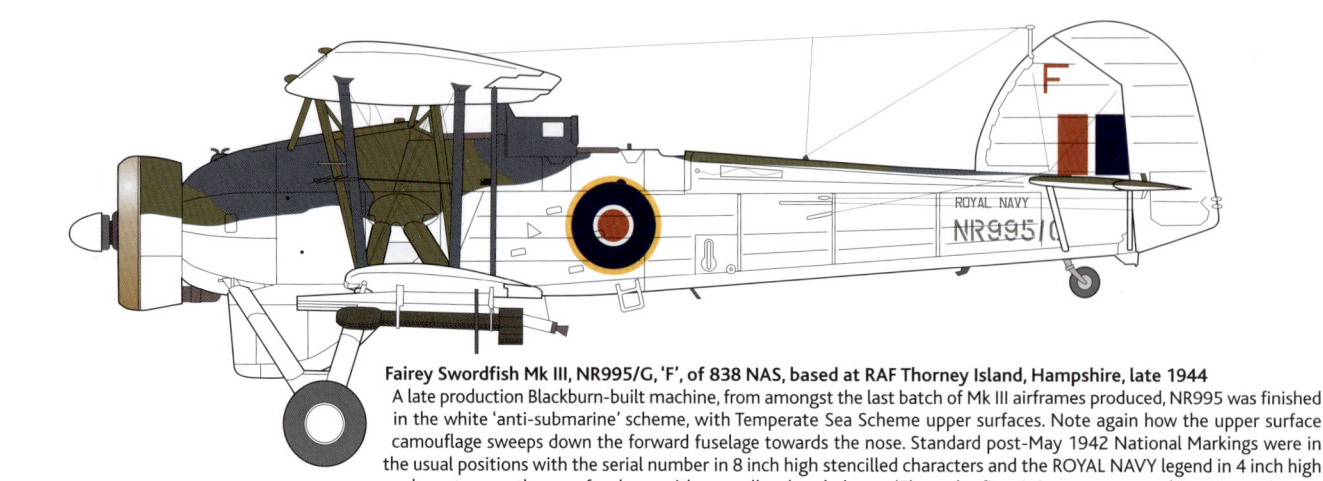

Fairey Swordfish Mk III, NR995/G, 'F', of 838 NAS, based at RAF Thorney Island, Hampshire, late 1944
A late production Blackburn-built machine, from amongst the last batch of Mk III airframes produced, NR995 was finished in the white 'anti-submarine' scheme, with Temperate Sea Scheme upper surfaces. Note again how the upper surface camouflage sweeps down the forward fuselage towards the nose. Standard post-May 1942 National Markings were in the usual positions with the serial number in 8 inch high stencilled characters and the ROYAL NAVY legend in 4 inch high grey characters on the rear fuselage, with a small red code letter, 'F', on the fin. Spinner cap was white. NR995/G was involved in Rocket Assisted Take Off Gear (RATOG) trials, hence the suffix 'G' after the serial to indicate that the aircraft was to be guarded at all times when on the ground as RATOG was still secret at this time.

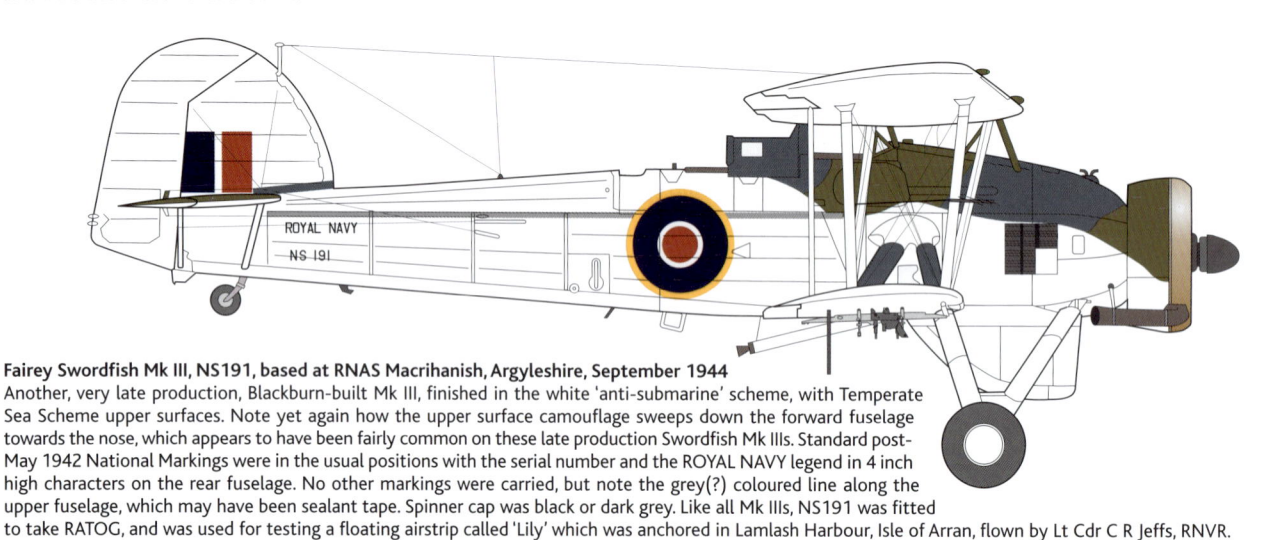

Fairey Swordfish Mk III, NS191, based at RNAS Macrihanish, Argyleshire, September 1944
Another, very late production, Blackburn-built Mk III, finished in the white 'anti-submarine' scheme, with Temperate Sea Scheme upper surfaces. Note yet again how the upper surface camouflage sweeps down the forward fuselage towards the nose, which appears to have been fairly common on these late production Swordfish Mk IIIs. Standard post-May 1942 National Markings were in the usual positions with the serial number and the ROYAL NAVY legend in 4 inch high characters on the rear fuselage. No other markings were carried, but note the grey(?) coloured line along the upper fuselage, which may have been sealant tape. Spinner cap was black or dark grey. Like all Mk IIIs, NS191 was fitted to take RATOG, and was used for testing a floating airstrip called 'Lily' which was anchored in Lamlash Harbour, Isle of Arran, flown by Lt Cdr C R Jeffs, RNVR.

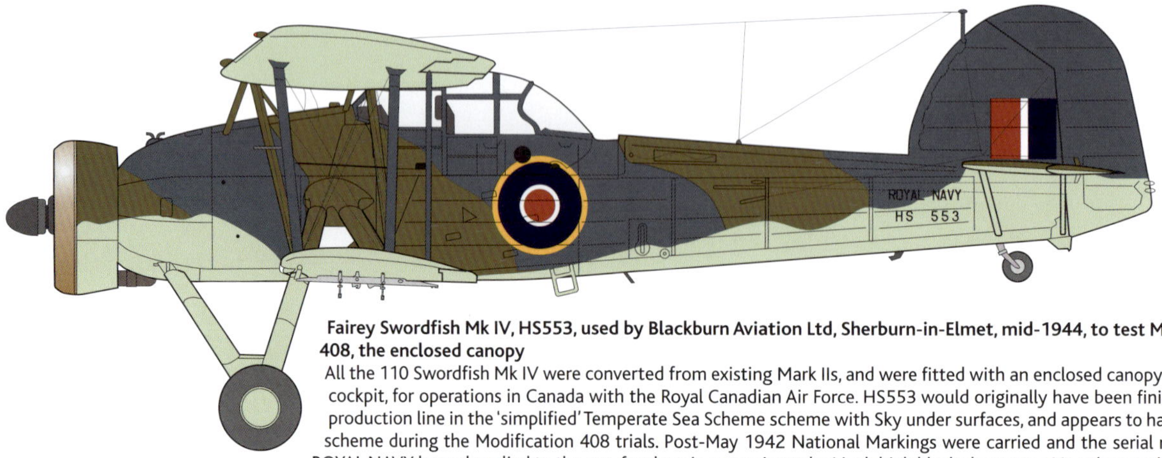

Fairey Swordfish Mk IV, HS553, used by Blackburn Aviation Ltd, Sherburn-in-Elmet, mid-1944, to test Modification 408, the enclosed canopy
All the 110 Swordfish Mk IV were converted from existing Mark IIs, and were fitted with an enclosed canopy and heated cockpit, for operations in Canada with the Royal Canadian Air Force. HS553 would originally have been finished on the production line in the 'simplified' Temperate Sea Scheme with Sky under surfaces, and appears to have kept this scheme during the Modification 408 trials. Post-May 1942 National Markings were carried and the serial number and ROYAL NAVY legend applied to the rear fuselage in approximately 4 inch high black characters. No other markings appear to have been carried. Spinner cap was either black or dark grey.

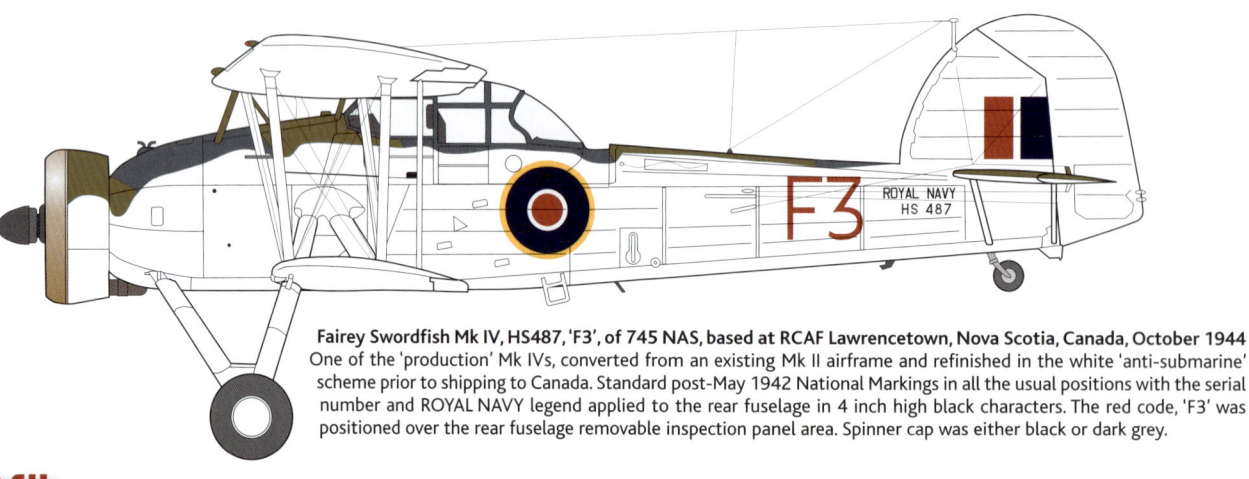

Fairey Swordfish Mk IV, HS487, 'F3', of 745 NAS, based at RCAF Lawrencetown, Nova Scotia, Canada, October 1944
One of the 'production' Mk IVs, converted from an existing Mk II airframe and refinished in the white 'anti-submarine' scheme prior to shipping to Canada. Standard post-May 1942 National Markings in all the usual positions with the serial number and ROYAL NAVY legend applied to the rear fuselage in 4 inch high black characters. The red code, 'F3' was positioned over the rear fuselage removable inspection panel area. Spinner cap was either black or dark grey.

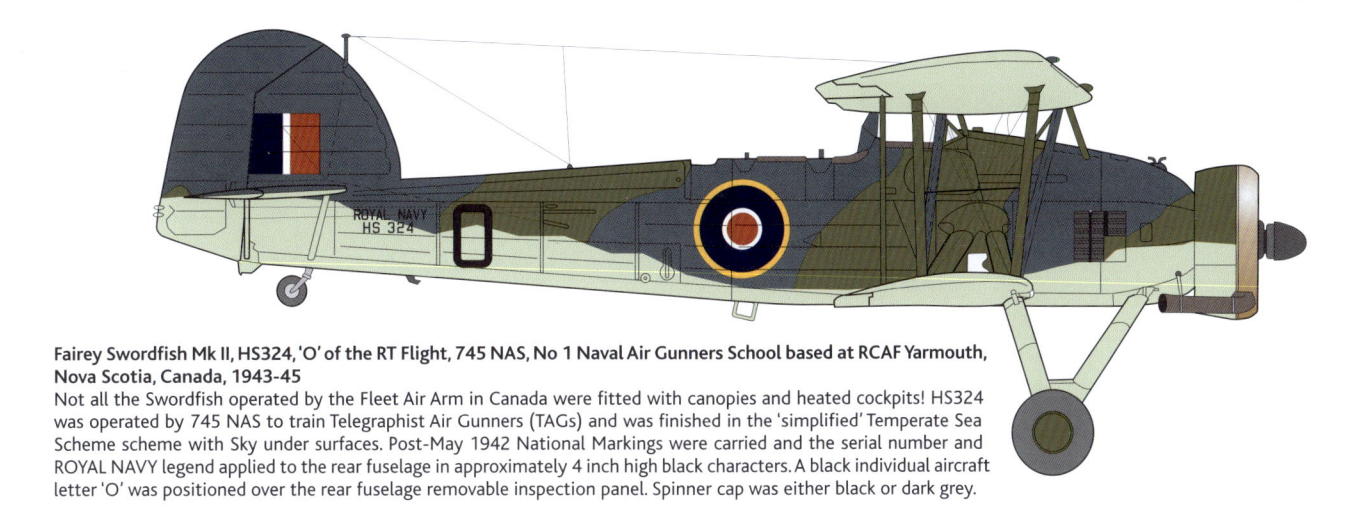

Fairey Swordfish Mk II, HS324, 'O' of the RT Flight, 745 NAS, No 1 Naval Air Gunners School based at RCAF Yarmouth, Nova Scotia, Canada, 1943-45
Not all the Swordfish operated by the Fleet Air Arm in Canada were fitted with canopies and heated cockpits! HS324 was operated by 745 NAS to train Telegraphist Air Gunners (TAGs) and was finished in the 'simplified' Temperate Sea Scheme scheme with Sky under surfaces. Post-May 1942 National Markings were carried and the serial number and ROYAL NAVY legend applied to the rear fuselage in approximately 4 inch high black characters. A black individual aircraft letter 'O' was positioned over the rear fuselage removable inspection panel. Spinner cap was either black or dark grey.

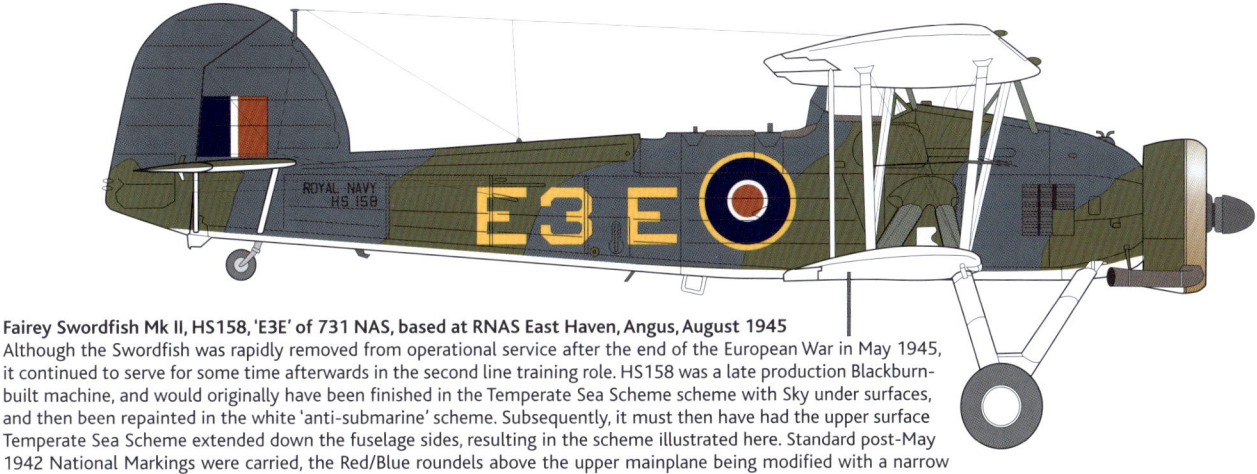

Fairey Swordfish Mk II, HS158, 'E3E' of 731 NAS, based at RNAS East Haven, Angus, August 1945
Although the Swordfish was rapidly removed from operational service after the end of the European War in May 1945, it continued to serve for some time afterwards in the second line training role. HS158 was a late production Blackburn-built machine, and would originally have been finished in the Temperate Sea Scheme scheme with Sky under surfaces, and then been repainted in the white 'anti-submarine' scheme. Subsequently, it must then have had the upper surface Temperate Sea Scheme extended down the fuselage sides, resulting in the scheme illustrated here. Standard post-May 1942 National Markings were carried, the Red/Blue roundels above the upper mainplane being modified with a narrow white ring to create the late-war/immediate post-war National Marking IA variation. The serial number and ROYAL NAVY legend were applied to the rear fuselage in approximately 4 inch high black characters. The yellow Training unit code, 'E3E', was positioned along the mid-fuselage. Spinner cap was either black or dark grey.

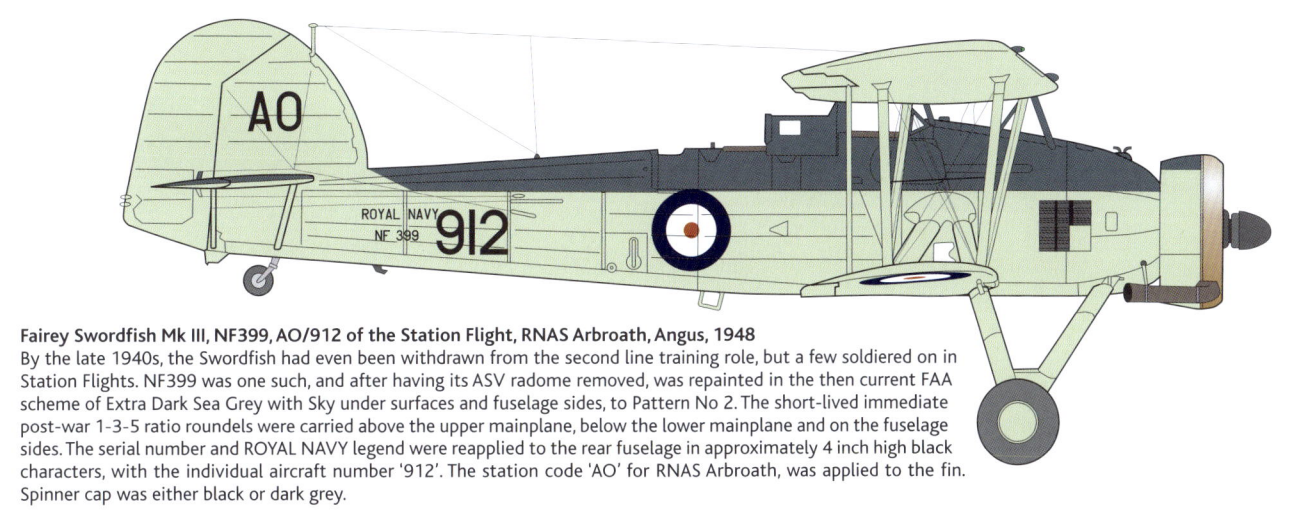

Fairey Swordfish Mk III, NF399, AO/912 of the Station Flight, RNAS Arbroath, Angus, 1948
By the late 1940s, the Swordfish had even been withdrawn from the second line training role, but a few soldiered on in Station Flights. NF399 was one such, and after having its ASV radome removed, was repainted in the then current FAA scheme of Extra Dark Sea Grey with Sky under surfaces and fuselage sides, to Pattern No 2. The short-lived immediate post-war 1-3-5 ratio roundels were carried above the upper mainplane, below the lower mainplane and on the fuselage sides. The serial number and ROYAL NAVY legend were reapplied to the rear fuselage in approximately 4 inch high black characters, with the individual aircraft number '912'. The station code 'AO' for RNAS Arbroath, was applied to the fin. Spinner cap was either black or dark grey.

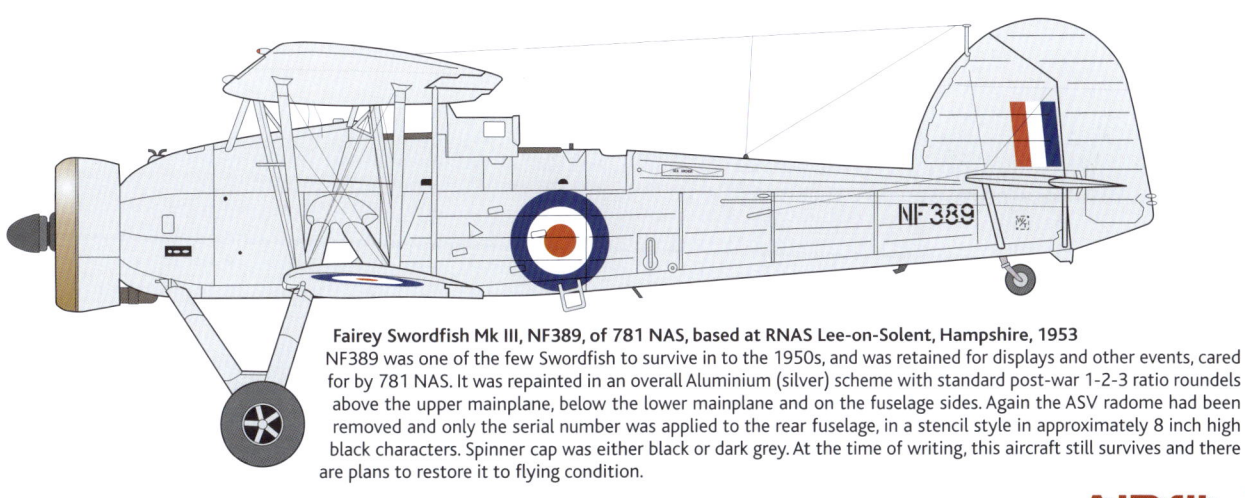

Fairey Swordfish Mk III, NF389, of 781 NAS, based at RNAS Lee-on-Solent, Hampshire, 1953
NF389 was one of the few Swordfish to survive in to the 1950s, and was retained for displays and other events, cared for by 781 NAS. It was repainted in an overall Aluminium (silver) scheme with standard post-war 1-2-3 ratio roundels above the upper mainplane, below the lower mainplane and on the fuselage sides. Again the ASV radome had been removed and only the serial number was applied to the rear fuselage, in a stencil style in approximately 8 inch high black characters. Spinner cap was either black or dark grey. At the time of writing, this aircraft still survives and there are plans to restore it to flying condition.

Operational Swordfish units

Royal Navy Fleet Air Arm
(prior to May 1939 part of RAF)

701 Naval Air Squadron (Ship's Flights)
702 Naval Air Squadron (Catapult Flights)
703 Naval Air Squadron (Catapult Flights)
705 Naval Air Squadron (float-equipped aircraft from the battle cruisers Repulse and Renown)
810 Naval Air Squadron
811 Naval Air Squadron
812 Naval Air Squadron
814 Naval Air Squadron
815 Naval Air Squadron
816 Naval Air Squadron
817 Naval Air Squadron – transferred to South Africa in 1945
818 Naval Air Squadron
819 Naval Air Squadron
820 Naval Air Squadron
821 Naval Air Squadron
822 Naval Air Squadron
823 Naval Air Squadron
824 Naval Air Squadron
825 Naval Air Squadron
826 Naval Air Squadron
828 Naval Air Squadron
829 Naval Air Squadron
830 Naval Air Squadron
833 Naval Air Squadron
834 Naval Air Squadron
835 Naval Air Squadron
836 Naval Air Squadron
837 Naval Air Squadron
838 Naval Air Squadron
840 Naval Air Squadron
841 Naval Air Squadron
842 Naval Air Squadron
860 (Dutch Naval Air Service) Squadron
886 Naval Air Squadron
826 Naval Air Squadron

Royal Air Force
No 8 Squadron RAF
No 119 Squadron RAF
No 202 Squadron RAF
No 209 Squadron RAF
No 73 Squadron RAF
No 613 Squadron RAF
No 3 Anti-Aircraft Co-operation Unit (3 AACU), Malta and Gibralter
No 4 Anti-Aircraft Co-operation Unit (4 AACU), Singapore
No 9 (Pilot) Advanced Flying Unit

References used

'The Squadrons of the Fleet Air Arm', by Ray Sturtivant, Air Britain 1984, ISBN 0-85130-120-7.

'Fleet Air Arm Aircraft 1939 to 1945', by Ray Sturtivant with Mick Burrow, Air Britain, ISBN 0-85130-232-7.

'Fleet Air Arm Camouflage & Markings 1937 - 1941' by Stuart Lloyd, Dalrymple & Verdun Publishing, 2008. 978-1-905414-08-6.

'Swordfish Special' by W A Harrison, Ian Allan Publishing Ltd 1977. ISBN 0-7110-0742-X.

'Swordfish at War' by W A Harrison, Ian Allan Publishing Ltd 1987. ISBN 0-7110-1676-3.

'The Swordfish Story' by Ray Sturtivant, Arms & Armour Press, 1993. ISBN 0-304-35711-1.

'Fairey Swordfish in Action' (No 75), by W A Harrison, Squadron/Signal Publications, 2001. ISBN 0-89747-421-X.

'Fairey Swordfish' Warpaint Series 12, by W A Harrison, Hall Park Books, 1998, ISSN 1361-0369

'The Fairey Swordfish Mks. I-IV' (Aircraft in Profile 212), by Ian G Scott, Profile Publications, 1971. No ISBN.

'British Naval Aircraft Since 1912' by Owen Thetford, Putnam & Company Ltd, Fourth edition, 1978. ISBN 0-370-30021-1.
 and
'British Naval Aircraft Since 1912' by Owen Thetford, Putnam Aeronautical Books, 1994. ISBN 0-85177-861-5.

'British Naval Aviation: Fleet Air Arm 1917-1990' by Ray Sturtivant, Arms & Armour Press, 1990. ISBN 0-85368-938-5.

'Fairey Swordfish and Albacore' by W A Harrison, Crowood Press, 2002. ISBN 1-86126-512-3.

'To War in a Stringbag' by Charles Lamb, Cassell & Co, 2001. ISBN 0-304-35841-X.

'The Attack on Taranto: Blueprint for Pearl Harbor' by Thomas P Lowry and John Wellham, Stackpole Books, 2000. ISBN 0-81172-661-4.

'Fairey Aircraft since 1915' by H A Taylor, Putnam & Company Ltd, 1974. ISBN 0-370-00065-X.

'The Escort Carrier in World War II' by David Wragg, Pen & Sword Books, 2005. ISBN 1-84415-220-0.

'Stringbag: The Fairey Swordfish at War' by David Wragg, David, Pen and Sword Books, 2005. ISBN 1-84415-130-1.

'The Story of the Taranto Raid' by David Wragg, Weidenfeld and Nicolson, 2003. ISBN 0-29784-667-1.

... and with special thanks to the late Barry Ketley for the use of photos from his private collection.

Left:
A 756 NAS Swordfish Mk II, coded 'KM' based at RNAS Katakurunda, Ceylon, 1944. Repainted in service in the Temperate Sea Scheme with Sky under surfaces, the National Markings have been modified in to the South East Asia Command (SEAC) style in small diameter blue and pale blue roundels and fin flash.

Below:
Ooops, up and over... two photographs in sequence, showing a Swordfish Mk II, coded 'T', of 834 NAS, operating off HMS Battler, in the Far East in July 1944, not quite managing to clear the Swordfish coded 'A' and ripping a hole in the starboard wing's fabric. HMS Battler had re-embarked the Swordfish element of 834 NAS on completion of her refit in June, the squadron's Seafires remaining ashore, and proceeded to Cape Town to join a north bound convoy, CM53. Her next operation, beginning on 11 July, was to escort the Indian Ocean convoy KR11 to Colombo which is probably when this event was photographed. Unfortunately the serial numbers of both aircraft are not known, but their camouflage schemes are interesting. Aircraft 'T' is finished in the Temperate Sea Scheme with Sky under surfaces, and the National Markings overpainted and small diameter South East Asia Command (SEAC) style blue and pale blue roundels and fin flashes. The aircraft coded 'A' appears to be in the process of being repainted. Individual aircraft code letters on both aircraft, positioned on the mid-fuselage removable inspection panel, are probably Sky or pale blue.

Opposite, Above and Below:
A selection of photographs taken of P4127, '4F', a Swordfish Mk I, of 820 NAS operating off HMS Ark Royal, which force-landed at Bacu Abis, Sardinia, on 2 August 1940, after receiving flak damage following an attack on Cagliari, Sardinia. Of the three crew, Lt G R Humphries and Lt D Williams were taken prisoner, but LA C Pendleton was killed. P4127 was taken to Caproni and repaired at Elmas, and fitted with an Alfa Romeo 125 engine and sent to the Stabilimento Costruzioni Aeronautiche, (Aircraft Construction Establishment), Guidonia, Italy, for flight testing in February 1941, and was still there in June 1942.

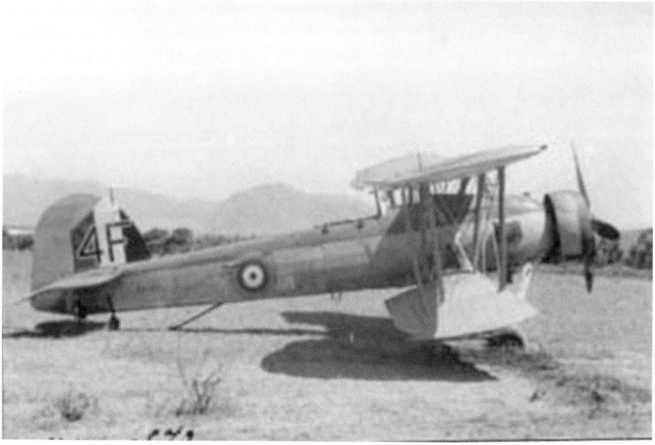

A Fairey-built machine from last parent company production batch, P4127 was probably finished on the production line in the S1E upper surface scheme with Sky Grey under surfaces, with a fairly high and straight fuselage camouflage demarcation. Red/Blue roundels were carried above the top mainplane with Red/White/Blue/Yellow roundels on the fuselage sides and Red/White/Blue roundels under the lower mainplanes all in the wartime darker shades, as were the Red/White/Blue stripes covering the whole of the fin area. The serial number was applied to the rear fuselage in 4 inch high black characters. The Aircraft Class numeral '4' and the individual aircraft letter 'F' were applied over the fin stripes in black, thinly outlined in white where they passed over the Red and Blue stripes. Spinner cap was either black or dark grey. (see profile on p30)